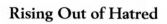

Rising Out of Hatred

ALSO BY ELI SASLOW

Ten Letters: The Stories Americans Tell Their President

Rising
Out of
Hatred

THE AWAKENING

OF A

FORMER

WHITE

NATIONALIST

Eli Saslow

 DOUBLEDAY *New York*

www.doubleday.com

DOUBLEDAY and the portrayal of an anchor with a dolphin are
registered trademarks of Penguin Random House LLC.

Book design by Maria Carella
Jacket design by John Fontana

Library of Congress Cataloging-in-Publication Data
Names: Saslow, Eli, author.
Title: Rising out of hatred : the awakening of a former white nationalist /
    Eli Saslow.
Other titles: Awakening of a former white nationalist
Description: First edition. | New York : Doubleday, a division of Penguin
    Random House LLC, 2018.
Identifiers: LCCN 2017061173| ISBN 9780385542869 (hardcover) |
    ISBN 9780385542876 (ebook)
Subjects: LCSH: Black, Derek. | White supremacy movements—United
    States—History—21st century. | White nationalism—United States—
    History—21st century. | Men, White—United States—Biography |
    New College of Florida (Sarasota, Fla.)—Students—Biography. |
    Attitude change. | Intercultural communication—United States—
    Case studies. | Hate groups—United States. | Whites—Race identity—
    United States. | United States—Race relations—21st century. |
    BISAC: POLITICAL SCIENCE / Political Ideologies / Nationalism. |
    SOCIAL SCIENCE / Discrimination & Race Relations.
Classification: LCC E184.A1 S245 2018 | DDC 320.54092 [B] —dc23
    LC record available at https://lccn.loc.gov/2017061173

MANUFACTURED IN THE UNITED STATES OF AMERICA

10 9 8 7 6 5 4 3 2 1

FIRST EDITION

For my parents

Contents

Introduction   1

1.   "The Great White Hope"   5

2.   "Have You Seen This Man?"   24

3.   "I'm Not Running Away"   46

4.   "Push the Rock"   74

5.   "Solid and Unshakable"   98

6.   "A Million Questions"   116

7.   "This Is Scary"   139

8.   "Another Debate, and Another Midnight"   161

9.   "I'm Torn"   187

10.   "I Have to Do This Now"   204

11.   "So Much Worse than I Ever Thought"   221

12.   "Primed for This Revolution"   236

13.   "All-Out Mayhem"   261

14.   "We Were Wrong"   276

Author's Note   285

Rising Out of Hatred

Introduction

When I first tried to contact Derek Black to write about his radical transformation, I couldn't find him anywhere. He had spent the first part of his life in the public spotlight as the future leader of white nationalism in the United States, and he left behind a daily record of his work on behalf of that ideology. It took only a few minutes of internet research to learn about his popular website for "proud white children," his daily radio show, and his successful campaign for political office in Florida. "The White Power Prodigy" was how one news article referred to him. But then, in Derek's last public interview in 2013, he disavowed his beliefs and apologized for everything he'd done, and that was it. In the public record, at least, he'd disappeared.

I finally located him a few years later, when he was living across the country and attending graduate school under a new legal name. I emailed to ask for an interview, hoping to write about Derek in my job as a reporter for *The Washington Post*, but his answer was unequivocal. "No, I am not interested," he told me, and then he asked that I respect his privacy and leave him alone. It was a reasonable request. Few people on his current college campus knew that Derek had once been the rightful heir to America's white nationalist movement— the son of Don Black, who founded the internet's largest hate site, Stormfront.org; and the godson of David Duke, a former KKK Grand Wizard. Few white nationalists knew exactly where Derek was living now, what he believed, or why he changed his mind. On the dark corners of the internet, neo-Nazis and skinheads were calling him a traitor and plotting revenge. Derek had separated his life into two parts, a before and an after, and he had no interest in connecting the two. His renunciation of white nationalism resulted in both traumatic familial consequences and nationwide speculation. What he wanted now was anonymity—to "keep the past in the past," he told me. I thanked him for writing back to me, and we didn't speak again for more than a year.

During those next months, the ideology he once helped spread continued to force its way into the political mainstream. Race was back at the epicenter of the country's most polarizing debates about Hispanic immigrants, Muslim refugees, and police shootings in the era of Black Lives Matter. Donald Trump rose toward the presidency thanks in part to white identity politics, and white nationalism rebranded itself into the alt-right and attached itself onto his campaign. Derek's godfather announced another run for U.S. Senate; his father purchased new web servers to accommodate a surge in Stormfront traffic. Each week on the campaign trail, Derek heard echoes of the language he helped popularize on his radio show—phrases like "white genocide," "reverse racism," and "racial realities."

His past was in fact present, and when we emailed again in the summer of 2016, Derek said he felt implicated by current events, sometimes even culpable. Maybe he had stopped planting the seeds of hate and division, but they were still growing all around him. "It's a critical time," he wrote to me, and by comparison his privacy seemed less important. "My relationship to the cultural moment is now more personal," he wrote. "I imagine I have some things to say about all of it. Let's find a time to meet."

Derek and I spent hundreds of hours together over the last few years, first so that I could report a story for *The Washington Post* and then for this book. I traveled to meet his friends and family members, and I am grateful to many of them for trusting me with not only their time but also copies of personal emails, Facebook conversations, and message board chats.

Of course, Derek took the greatest risk. Sometimes, when we spent time together, he wondered how it would feel to see his old white nationalist talking points printed out again on the page. But his commitment to this project never wavered. If parts of his story traced the country's path to this contentious racial moment, then maybe the details of his transformation can also point a way ahead.

1. "The Great White Hope"

The Klansmen and neo-Nazis arrived for their meeting in the fall of 2008 dressed in suits with aliases written on their name tags and began sneaking into the hotel just after dawn. They walked past the protesters waving rainbow flags on the sidewalk, past the extra state troopers stationed outside the hotel lobby, past the FBI informants hoping to infiltrate their way inside. For several days, the government of greater Memphis had been working to prevent this "white rights conference" from taking place. One suburb declared a state of emergency so it could hire additional police officers; another issued a temporary ban on all public gatherings. But by 7:00 on Saturday morning, about 150 of the world's preeminent white nationalists had gathered inside a nondescript hotel conference room where a small sign hung on the wall.

"The fight to restore White America begins now," it read.

The United States had elected its first black president just four days earlier, and already the Department of Homeland Security warned of a "significant spike in activity" on the white racist fringe. President-elect Obama was receiving an average of thirty death threats each day. Gun sales had skyrocketed to historic levels, and by some reports far-right militia groups had tripled their membership numbers during the last year. But the white uprising that concerned the Department of Homeland Security most of all was the one beginning now in Memphis, where acoustic guitar played through the speakers and sack lunches with turkey and swiss waited on a buffet table. "It's the polite face of the racist movement that now has a chance to recruit new members and broaden in scope," one DHS analyst said.

David Duke, the conference organizer, stepped behind a podium to welcome his guests. Duke, then fifty-eight, had spent his life working to push the white supremacist movement from the radical fringes ever closer to the far conservative Right, rebranding himself from an Imperial Wizard of the Klan into a self-described "racial realist" politician who nearly became governor of Louisiana in the early 1990s. He was two decades removed from the pinnacle of his international fame, and he'd tried to hold time in place by repackaging his old speeches into YouTube rants. He wore the tired look of a performer who'd stayed on tour too long, but he was still the public face of white nationalism. "The future of our movement is to become fully mainstream," Duke told the crowd, so he'd reserved one of the conference's keynote speeches for an up-and-coming white nationalist leader who represented that future.

"I'd like to introduce the leading light of our movement," Duke said. "I don't know anybody who has better gifts. He may have a much more extensive national and international career than I've had. Derek, can you come on up?"

Duke motioned to the corner of the room, where a nineteen-year-old community college student was hunched behind a laptop, running a live radio broadcast of the event for the online radio station he started himself.

"We are so privileged to be with you," Duke said, before turning back to the audience. "Ladies and gentlemen, here is Derek Black."

The crowd began to applaud, and Derek stood from

his computer with a slight wave and walked to the front of the room. Most of the white nationalists already knew him, because how could they not? He was at least a generation younger than almost everyone else, with shoulder-length red hair and a large black cowboy hat that he wore in an effort to make himself more memorable. He'd grown up within the insular world of white nationalism, attending dozens of conferences just like this one. Already he'd built his own website for "white children of the globe," visited more than half a million times. He'd launched a twenty-four-hour online radio network for white nationalists and won a local election as a Republican in Florida. He was not only a prodigy within the movement but also a product of it. His father, Don Black, led the Klan for nearly a decade and then created Stormfront, the internet's first and largest white pride website. His mother, Chloe, had once been married to David Duke, and Duke acted as Derek's mentor and godfather, sometimes referring to Derek as "the heir."

No family had done more to help white nationalism bully its way back into mainstream politics, and Derek was the next step in that evolution. He was precocious, thoughtful, and polite, sometimes delivering handwritten thank-you notes to conference volunteers. He never used racist slurs. He didn't advocate for outright violence or breaking the law. His core beliefs were the same as those of most white nationalists: that America would be better off as a whites-only country, and that all minorities should eventually be forced to leave. But instead of basing his public arguments on emotion or explicit prejudice, he spoke mostly about what he believed to be the facts of racial science, immigration, and a declining white middle class. Five evenings each week, he hosted an online radio show, often devoting the first half hour to innocuous stories about his favorite country musicians like Waylon Jennings, Alan Jackson, and Johnny Cash before turning the conversation to "the survival and continued dominance of the great white race," he said. His goal, he explained once on the radio, was to "normalize these white nationalist ideas that already fit so neatly within the divides of modern society."

"I've never lived in a country that I consider to be a white country," he told the audience in Memphis. "I've never enjoyed this good golden bag of advantage that white people are supposed to have."

He told the audience about his recent campaign to become a Republican committeeman in Palm Beach County, Florida, in which he had traveled door-to-door to meet with voters each afternoon after his community college German class. He seldom mentioned race in those conversations, and sometimes he barely spoke at all. Instead, he mostly listened as his white Republican neighbors told him about the reasons they felt their culture was under threat: the new highway signs in Spanish, urban crime, outsourced middle-class jobs, a collapsing economy, and a societal insistence on political correctness. For the first time in history, less than half of all babies born in the United States were white, and Derek believed whites would inevitably begin voting more explicitly for their interests like a typical minority bloc. "Most white people don't want to be called racists, but they do want to make sure their culture and their position in society isn't going to be undermined," Derek said on the radio. "People are just waiting for white candidates to come along who are brave enough to talk about these things, and when that happens, whites will go streaming to the polls." Even though he had campaigned as a teenager with no job history, no college diploma, and zero political experience, Derek beat out a Cuban American incumbent and won the election with more than 60 percent of the vote.

"The way white people have to respond is through politics," Derek told the crowd in Memphis. "Which way are the Republicans going to go? I'm kind of banking on them staking their claim as the White Party. We can infiltrate. We can take the country back."

A few people in the audience started to clap, and then a few more began to whistle, and before long the whole group was applauding. "Our moment," Derek said, because at least in this room everyone was in agreement. They believed the core tenets of white nationalism were about to drive a political revolution. They believed, at least for the moment, that Derek would help lead it.

"Years from now, we will look back on this," he said. "The great intellectual move to save white people started today."

The applause continued as Don Black, fifty-five, stood from the rows of folding chairs and moved slowly toward the lectern to join his son onstage for the next session of the conference, an audience Q&A with white nationalist leaders. Don had suffered a hemorrhagic stroke a few months earlier, and now he walked with a hunch and leaned against a cane to steady his debilitated left side. He had long prided himself on being the embodiment of physical and emotional toughness—what he called the "European ideal written into our genes." He stood over six feet tall, with thick gray hair, a hard jawline, and blue eyes. He had once been the strongest weight lifter in the rec yard of a federal prison, but now the short walk to the lectern required intermittent breaks, until Derek stepped out and offered his hand.

Don had been leaning on his only child more than ever lately, relying on him for rides to white nationalist meetings and help managing the growing business of Stormfront, which crashed under the weight of a record 120,000 users on the night of Obama's election to the presidency. Most of all, Don looked to Derek's recent political achievements to lift himself from stretches of depression and fatigue that he'd endured since his stroke. He had tried to heal himself with physical therapy, experimental electrotherapies, and a dozen nutritional supplements, but none of it was as efficacious as monitoring Derek's rising fame in the local newspaper and listening to him talk each night about "racial realities" on internet radio.

"I never thought it would feel so good to play second fiddle in my own house," Don joked in Memphis as he and Derek took their places on the stage.

Sometimes, standing eye to eye with Derek, Don marveled at the young adult his son was becoming. "So perceptive. So insightful and committed in his beliefs," Don said. At first those beliefs had come as a direct inheritance from Don. He sent six-year-old Derek out for Halloween dressed as a white Power Ranger, helped to decorate his childhood bedroom with a Confederate flag, and brought him to speeches where Don expressed doubt about the full severity of the Holocaust. Derek was socialized on Stormfront, and he began spending his nights in the private chat rooms as soon as he could type. After Derek finished third grade, Don and Chloe pulled him out of school, believing the public system in West Palm Beach was overwhelmed by an influx of

Haitians and Hispanics. "It's a shame how many white minds are wasted in that system," Derek wrote then, at age ten, on his own children's web page. "I am no longer attacked by gangs of non-whites. I am learning pride in myself, my family and my people."

"Unschooled," was the way Don and Chloe described Derek's education in the years after that. He stayed home during the day and worked on a curriculum largely of his own creation while Don monitored Stormfront at an adjacent desk. Don encouraged Derek to fill his days however he liked—riding his bike to the science museum, watching Discovery Channel, building a saltwater fish tank—and to Don's great delight many of Derek's interests continued to parallel his own. Derek taught himself basic coding and built the Stormfront children's website, where he shared white pride songs and inflammatory bedtime stories about "the liar and philanderer Martin Luther King." He learned to play guitar and sometimes sang about race at white nationalist conferences. As he grew into a teenager, Derek started to join Don in interviews with outlets like *USA Today*, Nickelodeon, and NBC, and more and more Don thought it was his son who made the more salient points. "He was already smarter than me," Don remembered thinking of Derek back then. "He could come up with ideas and see concepts that I hadn't been able to figure out in forty years. All of my weaknesses, he had overcome."

Don had spent his own life, he said, "trying to shock people awake on racial issues." In high school, he was shot in the chest while attempting to steal a mailing list on behalf of a white power organization. In college, he joined the KKK and rose to head of its Alabama chapter. In his late twenties, he and several other white supremacists were caught by the

FBI with dynamite, tear gas, and a van full of ammunition on their way to overthrow the tiny island nation of Dominica, which Don hoped to turn into a white utopia. Even after he settled into life as a young father and an IT consultant in the late 1990s, Don continued working to spark a revolution, launching Stormfront from his computer as a self-described "battle cry for the white race." Under his watch, Stormfront grew into a gigantic, international community of message boards and chat rooms that offered everything from academic research on racial differences, to daily Nazi news links, to dating profiles rife with racial slurs. A few of Stormfront's frequent users went on to bomb synagogues or murder minorities; the Southern Poverty Law Center, a hate-watch group, published a report connecting Stormfront to more than a hundred murders. Don discouraged violence in his own messages on the site, but he also managed the website with the language of a wartime commander, writing about "enemies" and "comrades," in the "fight for our future."

Derek, meanwhile, was studious, quieter, and more understated in his approach. As a teenager, he pored over world history in the family's 1914 *Encyclopaedia Britannica*— the version Don thought best reflected the family's beliefs about race because it still referred to the Klan only as a "fraternal organization." Derek bought an etymology dictionary and read a few entries each day, studying the origin of words, delighting in the evolution of language. In Stormfront chat rooms, he began to pick up German and some French. He decided white nationalism could only grow into a viable political movement if it adopted a new language of its own—a vocabulary that sanitized the ideology and distanced it from a history of violence. "We have to take back the moral high ground with how we talk about this," he said one day on the radio. As Derek explained it to his listeners, white nationalists were not fighting *against* minority rights but fighting *for* rights of their own. As the white population in the United States continued to drop, Derek and other activists were "simply trying to protect and preserve an endangered heritage and culture," he said. They were trying to save whites from an "inevitable genocide by mass immigration and forced assimilation." Theirs was the righteous cause. *They* were the social justice warriors. "What's happening right now is a genocide of our people, plain and simple," Derek said. "We are Europeans. We have a right to exist. We will not be replaced in our own country."

At first, Don thought it was strange to market white nationalism by connecting it to the idea of mass murder. Genocide? Really? But before long, Derek and others within the movement had managed to spread the concept across blogs and chat rooms in the insular world of white nationalism, and Don repeated the idea of an ongoing white genocide in an interview with *The New York Times*. A few months before Obama's election, Don decided to follow Derek's lead by imposing new rules on Stormfront in an attempt to clean up its image. He banned slurs, Nazi insignia, and threats of violence or lawbreaking. Many longtime members quit in protest, but the website began to grow by a few thousand registered users each month.

"One of the true titans who has shown us the way," Derek said of his father as they stood together at the podium in Memphis, but lately Don was feeling less sure about his own legacy. Increasingly, he believed it was Derek who was showing the way—and Derek who might one day carry out Don's lifework.

"The future is bright," Don said in Memphis. "We have

more potential now than we've ever had. I've never seen so many mad people. Their country is being taken away from them. They are looking for answers and we will provide those answers. I'm now convinced that any successful white revolution in this country will come largely from inside politics."

But sparking a political revolution came with challenges, too, and back in Palm Beach County, Florida, the Republican committee had learned about Derek's racial views from a local reporter and voted to ban him from taking his elected seat. The committee chairman, a sixty-two-year-old named Sid Dinerstein, ruled that Derek was ineligible because he had failed to submit a mandatory form during his campaign, a signed loyalty oath to the Republican Party. Derek countered in media interviews that the loyalty oath was a technicality and he was clearly being discriminated against as a "pro-white activist." The case proved once again, he said, that Jewish-controlled political elites would resort to manipulation whenever their power was threatened. "The people voted me in by popular vote," Derek said, during a small press conference at a local restaurant, and he promised to come to the first committee meeting to take his rightful seat.

"Of course they'll try to silence us. It won't ever be easy," Don wrote in a post to Stormfront members, and he also thought the moment might reveal something about his son. "Now we get to see who really has the stomach for all of this," Don said.

For several days in December 2008, Dinerstein and Derek jabbed at each other in a series of interviews as the controversy escalated into national news. A Florida columnist described Derek as a "real Hitler." The Anti-Defamation

League released a statement about his "abhorrent racist views." Duke flew in from Louisiana to offer his godson support, and together they met with media members at a local hamburger restaurant. "I am a white person who is concerned about discrimination against white people," was about all Derek would say during an interview with *The New York Times*, but the dialogue on Stormfront was much less diplomatic. Dozens of anonymous posters wrote that Dinerstein, a retiree who had moved to Florida and volunteered his way into politics, was "another vile Jew," "a filthy Jew," "a lying Jew," and "a stinking Jew rat."

On the morning of the committee meeting, a local disc jockey on FM radio took a break from playing classic rock and asked his listeners to phone in with their thoughts about Derek. "It's all anyone is talking about, and I'm not sure how anyone can defend this kid," the disc jockey said, but then the radio call-board lit up with listeners who wanted to do exactly that.

"He's saying what we've all been saying in our living rooms," one caller said.

"The white man is being played by all this racial equality and affirmative action," said the next.

"They have Black Entertainment TV. Why can't we have White Entertainment TV?"

"Why is it so wrong to stick with your own race?"

Don listened to the callers and began recording the show for his own records. For decades he had insisted that white nationalism was not just some fringe ideology held by a small number of extremists but in fact the "natural impulse" for a majority of whites in America. National polls by organizations like Reuters and the Associated Press often indicated that most whites considered America a white-European country.

Most whites said they wanted their heritage preserved. Most preferred living in neighborhoods that were predominantly white. Most held entrenched prejudices about immigrants and minorities, even if they didn't self-identify as racist. And now, for the first time, those same national polls also showed that a majority of whites felt "under attack."

Maybe this, finally, was the moment Don had been predicting for the last four decades, when the undercurrent of white dissatisfaction could no longer be quieted by political correctness. Maybe now, he thought, white people were finally beginning to realize that the United States was slipping from their grip. The white population in West Palm Beach had dropped from 39 percent to 29 percent in the last decade. Don's neighbors were predominantly Guatemalan and Haitian, and Jewish retirees from New York were buying up units in the new condo building across the street. "Usurpers," Don called these minority immigrants, and he thought that now other whites were beginning to see it that way, too.

"Derek's drawing enthusiastic supporters out of the woodwork," Don wrote on Stormfront, after listening to the radio calls. "He's really sparked something."

But there were also other phone calls that day before the meeting—coming from an unknown number that rang directly to Don and Derek's house. The first call came early in the evening. "Hey, Don," the caller said, leaving a message in a raspy voice. "I just wanted to let you know that we are going to have a scope trained on your son at the meeting come Wednesday night. We've had one on him now for days. We're not going to let the plague spread to the next generation. Have a good day."

Don replayed the message a few times, saved the recording, and then decided not to worry about it. His family had gotten threats a few dozen times before; it was inevitable, Don said, when you "lived in a place surrounded by the enemy." He despised West Palm Beach, but his wife, Chloe, had grown up there, and she didn't want to leave her aging mother or her steady job as an executive assistant at a sugar company. So for twenty-five years, their family had hunkered down in the home where Chloe was raised. They'd bought a German shepherd and let the vegetation grow thick and unruly around the house, forming a dense canopy of sea grapes, mangoes, and umbrella trees that hid their single-story bungalow from the street, setting it off in a world all its own. No visitors were allowed inside except for family members and a few white nationalist friends. Don had rarely left the house since his stroke. Most nights, he worked late at the computer before locking the doors and turning on the security cameras. Then he joined Chloe in bed, even though lately he rarely slept through the night. Instead there was usually the glow of his laptop on the bedside table, opened to Stormfront. There was the hum of the TV turned to cable news, keeping him company through the overnight hours. And there, on this night, was the sound again of the phone and that same raspy voice on the message machine, calling again and again.

At 12:11 a.m.: "Hey, Don, we are sitting outside the house. You crackers want to come play? Come on, Don. Get Chloe out. We've got the scope trained on your house right now."

At 12:27 a.m.: "Don, we're out here, waiting for you."

At 12:31 a.m.: "Don, I'm standing in your living room. Get Derek down here."

Don got up and checked around the house, but he found only darkness and shadows. For a few moments, he considered his options. He had never called the police to ask for help or to file a report. Much more often, the police had been called on *him*. But this wasn't just a threat against Don's life. This was Derek who was suddenly at risk, so Don decided to call the police in the middle of the night. A few officers arrived with their guns drawn and searched the property. Don walked them into the house and played the voice mail recordings, and then the officers began asking questions for their investigation. Exactly when was this Republican committee meeting the caller had spoken about? Where? Did Derek have any enemies the police should know about? And something about the impossibility of that last question made Don wonder if maybe Derek would be better off staying home from the meeting after all. Why chance disaster? Why risk so much for a dinky little committee seat? Don had given over his own life to the white nationalist movement—had traded away his reputation and his career—but now there was at least one thing that didn't seem worth sacrificing. "A part of me wanted Derek to back away from it and just stay home," Don remembered thinking.

But by then Derek was already burning with his own ambition. He wanted to rise up through local politics. He wanted to build a Stormfront headquarters in the mountains of Tennessee. He wanted to start an influential media company and somehow pack the Supreme Court with justices who would overturn the Fourteenth Amendment, which promised birthright citizenship, and instead reinstate a limited, European-only immigration system. "My life's goals were essentially to overturn our social order and replace it," Derek remembered of that time, and on some nights he would stay at his computer until 4:00 a.m., his eyes burning from the glow of the screen as he plotted out a white nationalist takeover while listening to Pink Floyd on his bulky headphones. He wasn't worried about unpopularity, political correctness, or even death threats. "The only thing that scared me was the idea of failing, or falling short of this plan for my life, and then having the white race collapse because of it," he said.

So early that next evening, Derek rode with his family to the committee meeting in a rented black sedan that nobody would recognize. He hurried through the side entrance of a government building and took the elevator to the sixth floor. Almost three hundred people had come to the event, mostly to watch what would happen with Derek. He wore his long-brimmed hat and walked up to Dinerstein in the hallway before the meeting began. "Very nice to finally be meeting you," Derek said as a dozen television cameras closed in. Dinerstein reiterated that Derek would not be allowed to take his seat, and then he excused himself as the meeting was called to order. Derek interrupted the meeting and walked up to the podium to speak, but the committee members shouted him down. He returned to the podium a few minutes later, but this time security officers asked him to leave.

On his way out the door, Derek told the press that he planned to file a lawsuit. He said the fight over his seat was only beginning. But to at least one person who watched the meeting unfold, Derek had already proven his resolve.

"These Republican Jews are particularly vile," Don later wrote on Stormfront. "They'd kill us without a second thought, like they've been threatening to do, if they thought they could get away with it."

Then, later, he added, "But Derek is just getting started. He plans on coming back."

•

Welcome to the *Derek Black Show*," Derek was saying many months later, broadcasting live from a station in Lake Worth, Florida. He'd failed to take back his seat on the Republican committee, but he parlayed his newfound notoriety into a regular show on AM radio. It was one of the first explicitly white nationalist broadcasts over mainstream airwaves in more than two decades, and Florida law enforcement promised to monitor it daily. Early in 2010, listeners tuned in to the first broadcast to hear a twenty-year-old introduce himself in a slow, folksy southern accent. "What do I believe?" Derek asked as his intro music, from Merle Haggard's song "I'm a White Boy," faded out behind him. "I believe that white people have a real interest in this country. This is a racially diverse place, and there are a lot of problems for it. We have gangs. We have conflict. I'm not a hateful person, but I will talk in public about what other people won't say."

Don and other Stormfront users agreed to pay the radio station several hundred dollars each week to broadcast the show. Don's budget was tight; he raised about seventy-five hundred dollars a month from eight hundred "sustaining" Stormfront members, which barely covered the site's expenses while the family lived on Chloe's salary. But Don thought paying for the radio show was "a bargain," considering that Derek could use the airtime to promote both himself and a litany of other white nationalists. Derek recommended the writings of Ernst Zündel, a German publisher known for promoting Holocaust denial. He talked about the "emotional power" of attending a KKK cross-lighting ceremony in Harrison, Arkansas. He interviewed a series of white nationalist icons like Jared Taylor, Gordon Baum, and Duke. And he did it all while continuing to reframe the language of the movement, insisting that white people were the victims—not the perpetrators—of structural racism.

"We are the reasonable people here because we are the ones who are really in favor of the common man," Derek said one day on the show during a conversation with Duke. "The people who are opposed to us are these arrogant, terrible liberals and multi-culturists who say that the basic white American is inherently a bad person and the only way they will be redeemed is by bringing in these people from third-world countries to take their jobs or fill their neighborhoods. It is an ideology based on hatred of us, of white people, who are living in a country that's being destroyed by a population brought in from the third world. We are the ones who have the best interests of America at heart."

"That's right," Duke said. "I learned a long time ago that whatever they call us, that's exactly what they're guilty of."

"They call us haters, discriminators, racists," Derek said.

"Government policy today is genocidal," Duke said. "Why isn't it a crime to wipe white people out of the United States?"

Derek's show quickly became the most downloaded on the station, and his time slot expanded from two days each week to three and then eventually to five. It was too much airtime for one person to fill. Derek needed a partner, and there was only one logical choice. "Welcome to the *Don and Derek Black Show*," Derek announced one morning, midway through 2010.

It was the way Derek's upbringing had always gone: Whatever he chose to pursue, Don and Chloe quickly invested their full support. As a child, Derek fell in love with the local science museum, so Don and Chloe started spending time there with him. He took up medieval reenactment, so his parents purchased their own costumes and joined the reenactment society. They helped pay for some of his ten-thousand-mile cross-country road trip to see America's national parks and for his flights to visit Europe. When Derek started playing guitar at open-mic nights in his late teens, his parents built their social lives around his schedule, arriving at South Florida bars a few hours early to reserve a table with the best view of Derek's twelve-minute set.

"Almost forcibly encouraging and supportive," Derek said of his parents, because when he was ambivalent about going to college, his mother insisted he enroll in the local community college, and when his parents saw his transcripts of straight As, they pushed him to transfer to a four-year school. He applied to only one, the school that seemed like the most logical choice—New College of Florida, the state's honors college, ranked as both the most affordable and the top liberal arts school in the state. He was accepted in the summer of 2010.

The campus was located across the state in Sarasota on the sprawling former estate of circus magnate Charles Ringling. The circus's elephant barn had become a student-run restaurant. The lion-grazing area was now a central quad. New College advertised itself as a "quirky" and "eccentric" home for "the non-traditional," and it catered specifically to homeschooled students like Derek who were used to little formal structure in their education. The school had only eight hundred students, with tiny class sizes and with professors who gave narrative evaluations instead of traditional grades. All students were required to write and then defend a senior thesis, and more than half continued on to graduate schools. Don and Chloe told Derek they would pay his full tuition. They considered it a good investment not only in Derek but also in their cause, because he could advance further as a white nationalist with the credibility of a mainstream degree. Derek told his parents he planned to double major in German and medieval history, which he had always associated with the glorious dominance of white Europeans. His parents reminded him that, ultimately, they hoped he would make history and not just study it.

New College was more than 80 percent white, but it was also listed in college guides as the most liberal school in Florida, the best school for hippies, the most gay-friendly, the most pot-friendly, the most likely to "transform your life and your worldview." One day on their radio show, as Derek readied to leave for a four-year college, a caller asked Don if he was worried about his son moving away from home to live "among the enemy in a hotbed of multiculturalism." Don started to laugh.

"Derek's the original nonconformist," he said. "It's not like any of these little commies are going to impact his thinking. If anyone is going to be influenced here, it will be them."

2. "Have You Seen This Man?"

Derek packed everything he could fit into his used PT Cruiser in the summer of 2010 and drove across the state alone. His parents had purchased the car for his move and offered to drive him to college, but he liked the idea of traveling by himself. He'd always enjoyed road trips; earlier in the summer he'd driven ten thousand miles coast-to-coast without an itinerary, sometimes staying with strangers he met online through chat rooms on Stormfront. Now he let his mind wander as he listened to country music and drove by Lake Okeechobee, passing through the farming towns of central Florida that were ripe with sugarcane fields and orange groves, until suddenly he realized he was lost. He'd made a wrong turn somewhere near New College and ended up a few blocks away from the scheduled orientation. He was already more than an hour late. The driving directions on his GPS kept leading him to the wrong building. And now there was another car pulling over alongside Derek's, with a student in the front seat who looked just as confused.

Juan Elias, twenty, rolled down his window and explained that he was also looking for the New College orientation. He spoke with a Peruvian accent, and he had long sideburns and a wispy beard. Like Derek, he was a community college transfer student from across the state. They were strangers in this place, so they agreed to find the orientation together.

Juan had driven to New College from Miami, the city

Derek once referred to on the radio as the "front lines of the third-world invasion." Juan had graduated from a high school of thirty-five hundred students—94 percent of them Hispanic, 4 percent black, and 2 percent "other." Nearly half of the school's students were immigrants, including Juan, who had moved to Miami from Peru just after he turned ten. At his small house in Little Havana, Juan had lived out what Derek had once described to other white nationalists as the "nightmare for America"—"a day when we will walk out of our houses and see barely a single white person, a whole country of outsiders."

To Juan, it was Derek who looked like the outsider on that first day, with his long hair, his country accent, and his heavy black hat shading him from the Florida afternoon sun. Derek said he was from West Palm Beach and that he'd first heard about New College from a community college German professor. He mentioned nothing else about his background. Even if he thought people who looked like Juan were ruining the country, he also believed that in one-on-one interactions it was always best to be polite and kind. "Just a down-to-earth, eccentric kind of guy," Juan remembered thinking. Derek had rarely spent time with anyone Hispanic; Juan had seldom befriended someone white. But they navigated together to orientation, where by coincidence they were assigned to the same small group for transfer students. They compared class schedules and discovered they shared two. They went to the dorms and found their rooms located in the same building, separated only by a small courtyard. Derek took out his guitar and played country songs. Juan sat with him, listening to Derek play while other students unpacked and moved into their rooms.

During the last few months, Juan had been thinking back

to the other major move in his life, a decade earlier, when he left Peru for the United States. He was born in the midst of a communist uprising in the late 1980s, in a country besieged from within by public executions, shootings, and car bombs. His mother went into labor just as a terrorist group sabotaged dozens of electrical towers across Lima. Doctors performed an emergency cesarean, and Juan arrived in the blackout of a terrorist revolution. A few years later, some of those terrorists murdered his uncle as punishment for working as a community organizer, and Juan's mother decided right then that she wouldn't raise her son in Peru. She left him with his grandmother when he was seven and traveled to the United States on a legal visa. She found a job waiting tables and a small house in the cheapest part of Miami. After three years, she finally saved enough money to send for Juan, but by then he didn't want to go. He spoke only a few words of English. All he knew was his life in Peru. He loved his grandmother and refused to leave her. So instead his mother told him that he was coming for a short vacation to Disney World. He flew in with a tourist visa and enough clothes to last a week. Only once he arrived at the airport did she tell him the truth: that he wasn't going back to Peru; that he was starting school in Miami; that, because of visa travel restrictions, he couldn't legally visit his grandmother in Peru for at least five years.

Juan experienced the move less as a transition than as a trauma. Somehow, he managed to survive middle school—to learn English in a year, Americanize his wardrobe, memorize most of the NBA basketball teams, move into honors classes, and eventually earn his green card—but he still felt cut off from one country and isolated in another. He traveled back to Lima in high school, but by then Peru felt foreign, too. So instead he began filling out the paperwork to apply for his U.S. citizenship. He finished community college and decided to move again, this time to New College, which he hoped would become the place that felt his own. "For me, the whole point of going to college was letting go of all my hang-ups and assumptions and just meeting people who were different," Juan said.

The sun dipped down over the bay that first night, and Juan and Derek went with other students from their dorm to explore more of the campus. They walked alongside Sarasota Bay, past the pink Gothic College Hall, where Charles Ringling once lived, and down a promenade of palm trees toward the center of campus. Some upper-year students ran by them, streaking naked on their way to the outdoor swimming pool, and several of the new students began to follow behind. The pool was officially closed for the night, but the air was still humid, and a few of the first-year students began jumping over the gate toward the pool to go skinny-dipping. They stripped off their clothes and leaped into the water—first just a handful of students and then several dozen; men and women, straight and gay, white and brown; all of them shedding inhibition and self-doubt until the pool was crowded with naked strangers from across Florida.

Craziness, Juan thought, as he stood next to Derek and watched the chaos unfolding in front of them. But maybe the only way to feel at home in a community was to let go and to trust. Juan took off his shirt and jumped into the pool. Derek walked away in his clothes and went back toward his dorm.

Even in the rare moments when Derek closed his door and walled himself off in his room, there was no avoiding the culture of New College. It came directly into his email in-box, several dozen messages arriving each day from the all-student email group known as the forum. It was the social epicenter of New College, a place where one student could broadcast whatever he or she liked to the other eight hundred and where everyone else could speak back. Each message included the sender's name, which kept the conversation civil; professors couldn't easily access the board, which kept the conversation honest and intimate. Each day brought dozens of new messages. On many of those days, the emphasis remained on social justice.

"How can we fight white-male domination?" one student wrote.

"It is way beyond time for us to talk about white privilege."

"Not all people of color are trespassing just because they're on campus. Some of us actually go here."

Like almost every other first-year student, Derek devoured the forum during those first weeks, paying particular attention as always to vocabulary. For him, New College was an introduction to another new language, in which upper classmen tried to educate new students on social issues. On the forum, micro-aggressions were never tolerated, and trigger warnings were used to protect peers from potentially upsetting content. Here was a place that strived for the ideals of universal equality and human respect. Students used the forum to plan a conference on civil disobedience and a protest in support of immigrant tomato pickers. They wrote that race was a social construct but that white privilege was structured into every part of American society. On the forum, identity was fluid, the right to self-expression was paramount, and a straight man was, in fact, a person whose chosen gender identity happened to match the sex he was assigned at birth—or, for short, a cis hetero male, a position of inherent privilege in the American patriarchy.

At New College, political correctness could sometimes become a contest of one-upmanship, and there was social cachet to be won by pointing out prejudice in its smallest manifestations. One student admitted that he liked to wear glasses despite having twenty-twenty vision, and then another student said that was "ableist," because he was appropriating the legitimate struggle of disabled people. "Maybe so," countered another student, but in fact there was no such thing as "disabled people," and that phrase was a micro-aggression against "people with disabilities."

And then there was Derek, the white nationalist prodigy living anonymously in his dorm room, helping to moderate the world's largest white pride website and calling in to his own political radio show five mornings each week. On the air, he repeatedly theorized about "the criminal nature of blacks" and the "inferior natural intelligence of blacks and Hispanics." He said President Obama was "anti–white culture," "a radical black activist," and "inherently un-American." There was nothing micro about Derek's aggressions. He knew that if his views were discovered at New College, he would be vilified on the forum and ostracized on campus. So he decided that semester to be a white activist on the radio and an anonymous college student in Sarasota. In the mornings while his classmates slept, he walked alone to a patch of grass outside the dorm and called in to his show to join his father on the air, and together they railed against the minority takeover. Whenever his classmates asked, Derek explained his morning ritual as a daily catch-up call with his unusually close family. Then he hung up the phone, returned to the center of campus, and befriended whoever walked by.

I. M. Pei had designed the student housing at New College in the 1960s as a series of small dormitories connected by covered bridges and redbrick courtyards, and Derek spent much of his time outside. He sat in the courtyard and did homework with Juan. He played acoustic Willie Nelson songs on his guitar, and one day a student wearing a yarmulke sat down to listen. His name was Matthew Stevenson, and he was the only Orthodox Jew on campus. "Jews are NOT white," Derek had written once on Stormfront, a few years earlier. But Matthew knew the lyrics to most of the country songs Derek liked to play, and he started joining Derek every few evenings to sing along with enthusiasm if not with pitch. Derek thought Matthew was funny and bright, with a sarcastic sense of humor and an interest in early world history that rivaled Derek's own, and they agreed to share a study guide for a medieval history class they were taking together. One night, Derek invited Matthew and Juan over to his dorm to watch a zombie movie, and they crowded together to sit on his bed. Maybe they were usurpers, as his father often said, but Derek also liked them, and gradually he went from keeping his political convictions quiet on campus to actively disguising them. Once, during lunch in the student center, another classmate mentioned to Derek that he had been reading about the racial implications of *The Lord of the Rings* on a website called Stormfront. Derek had created that section of the website a few years earlier, hoping to convert fans of the popular fantasy novels into avowed white nationalists, but now he pretended he'd never heard of it. "What's Stormfront?" he asked.

He was beginning to feel at home in this place, where he could blend in with his black-brimmed hat because there were a few more eccentric students who wore kilts, or capes, or no shoes. His German professor wrote that he was impressed by Derek's "graduate level work." The student body president offered to take Derek and some of his friends sailing on Sarasota Bay. Derek filmed a medieval reenactment with his classmates, forged his own armor, and dressed as a knight for Halloween. A young woman who lived in the dorm room upstairs began coming down to the courtyard more often to hear Derek play guitar, until one day he asked if there were any songs he could play for her.

Her name was Rose, and they had met for the first time at the New College orientation party during their first weekend on campus. As a homeschooled student, Derek had never been to a dance party, and he was sitting awkwardly against the wall when Rose came over to ask what was wrong. Derek said that he didn't know how to dance. Rose said neither did anyone else, and then she sat down next to him. She said she had known someone named Derek Black at her high school in northwestern Arkansas, and Derek misunderstood her and thought she knew something about him or his beliefs. Rose's hometown was not far from the private compound where Derek had once spent several weeks staying with Thomas Robb and his Knights of the Ku Klux Klan. He had attended Robb's conference, dated his granddaughter, and broadcast a live radio show from one of the group's weekly cross-lighting ceremonies. Maybe Rose had somehow seen him there, he thought, or maybe she was discreetly trying to signal to him that she shared some of his beliefs. They talked for awhile at the party and then danced to a song by Depeche Mode. Derek thought Rose was smart, thoughtful, and kind. He liked her, and after several weeks he told her as much. She appreciated his directness and how he always seemed eager to ask about her life, even as he revealed little of his own. They started circling around the possibility of dating, their talks stretching late into the night, and then in one of those talks she mentioned something offhand about a synagogue and how the High Holidays were coming up.

The conversation continued even as Derek's mind stayed locked in place: She was Jewish.

He had spent dozens of hours debating what people on Stormfront referred to as "the Jewish Question," a litmus test among white nationalists. Should Jews be considered whites or outsiders? Did they have a place in a European ethno-state that white nationalists hoped to build, or would they be forcibly deported from the United States along with all other minorities? The white nationalist movement had a long history of anti-Semitism—of synagogue bombings and "Sieg Heil!" salutes—but lately a rift had begun to develop as influential white nationalists like *American Renaissance* publisher Jared Taylor wrote admiring pieces about Israel and courted Jews as conference speakers.

Derek made his own conclusions public while still in his teens. "Jews are the cause of all the world's strife and misery," he wrote on Stormfront in 2008. "Their motivation comes from the destabilization of the White race."

It was the kind of thinking Derek's father and godfather had helped popularize on Stormfront: that Jews were not just another minority but an insidious enemy—the one race capable of undermining white Europeans. David Duke wrote a book called *Jewish Supremacism*, and Don and Derek helped promote it on Stormfront radio. In the chat rooms of Stormfront, blacks and most other minorities were typically considered both morally and intellectually inferior to whites, too addled by their "third-world nature" to pose any real threat to white superiority if left on their own. But Derek wrote that Jews were smart, calculating, and "possibly evil," and he thought they had orchestrated a brilliant plot to weaken the white race by promoting multiculturalism. Even though Jews already had their own ethno-state in Israel, they had pushed for greater control in the United States by supporting more lenient immigration policies and more wars to protect Israel's interests in the Middle East. Their singular purpose was a "constant effort to undermine homogeneous white nationhood and culture" through "media monopolization and government control," Derek wrote. He had directed other white nationalists to the website Jewhoo, a roll call of prominent American Jews, where the enemy was listed in plain sight. "Their every action in America and the western world has been as outsiders constantly trying to hurt us," he wrote.

And then there was Rose: sweet and unassuming, returning downstairs to Derek's room in the Pei dorm so they could study together for their money and banking class. Derek disliked math, and he'd often been able to avoid it in his homeschooled curriculum, so Rose patiently walked him through formulas and taught him how to efficiently read a math textbook. He'd never spent so much time with someone Jewish—or with anyone whom white nationalists considered an outsider. And because there was so much Derek wasn't yet ready to reveal about his own life, he began asking more and more about hers.

She had lived in Texas, Minneapolis, and Mexico before spending most of her childhood in northwestern Arkansas, in the Baptist Bible Belt. The University of Arkansas had offered her father a tenured position as a professor, and their family joined the only synagogue in town. It was a Reform congregation, liberal and inclusive, where a few dozen families could meet each Friday night in a rented house to hear a rotating guest rabbi welcome in Shabbat. The services were explicitly interfaith. The potlucks leaned heavily on barbecue. The mission of the congregation was not to plot some great, multicultural takeover of the white race but simply to "serve as a focal point of Jewish life in our small corner of the world," and that was challenge enough. The Jewish population in Arkansas had dropped dramatically over the last decades to only about seventeen hundred people—or 0.056 percent of the population—which meant that Judaism had become Rose's primary identity, whether she wanted that or not. In a high school where the board meetings began with a Baptist prayer and the official calendar celebrated "Christmas Break," her nickname had become "The Jew." She needed a note from a rabbi to clarify for her principal that, yes, Yom Kippur was a real holiday. She was teased for killing Jesus, for choosing to go to hell, and for attending a "strange church." She had written one of her college essays about that experience—about what it felt like to be a Jew in Arkansas, where even if she had never felt explicitly threatened, she had often been made to feel exotic, alien, and weird.

Derek made her feel none of those things. He listened. He asked insightful follow-up questions about her family. He pointed out stereotypes about men being good in math, and how that was sexist. He wrote her longhand letters about oceanic science, medieval religion, and fossil beds. He made mix CDs with songs she liked, and he used the correct "they" pronoun when asking about one of Rose's transgender friends. Most of her other first-year classmates at New College were eighteen years old, like Rose, and they were largely interested in drinking and going to parties, which Rose liked, too. But Derek was twenty-one, a transfer student who had already spent two years in community college, and Rose thought he was confident and mature. He rarely drank aside from the occasional beer, and he preferred intimate conversations to loud parties. "He was intense and respectful in an almost formal way," she remembered. "He had a sense of care that he put into everything. He wasn't just doing random stuff the way it felt like a lot of us were doing. He wanted to know about people's experiences and how they differed from his own. I was intrigued, and I wanted more. But he could be hot and then cold. Some days it was like he was pursuing me. Other times he seemed to be really indifferent."

What Rose didn't know was that Derek was constantly trying to quiet his own feelings and telling himself to back away. His two most serious former girlfriends had both been committed white nationalists, a daughter and a granddaughter of major leaders within the movement, people whose beliefs mirrored his own. It was one thing to befriend an outsider; his father and David Duke had both done plenty of that, and sometimes it could even be useful. But dating a Jew felt to Derek like a double betrayal—first and foremost of his own beliefs, and then also of Rose, who had no idea about his history or his racial convictions. He had publicly written that "Jews are NOT White." He had said race mixing was not only a bad idea but also a traitorous act. White Europeans needed to date white Europeans; anything else risked polluting the gene pool and accelerating the ongoing white genocide, he often said. Just one year earlier, on Stormfront, another white nationalist had come to the message board asking for advice about a new relationship. "I've started dating a woman who's really smart, pretty, funny, and cool. All is well . . . except she mentioned that some great, great relative was Native American. Her whole family looks textbook white. Am I being overly critical?"

Like most others on the message board, Derek's advice had been unequivocal. "Yes, this does make you a bastard," he had written. "You need to be decisive. It does you good, and her too."

It was easy to be certain and firm when the enemy remained impersonal and the issue was purely abstract, but now the issue was Rose. She was the only classmate who went off campus to hear Derek perform at an open-mic night. Once, sensing that Derek was feeling homesick on a weekend night, she left a party and went with him to a diner at 2:00 a.m. He liked her. He trusted her. He wanted to date her. She seemed nothing like the outsiders Derek had so often warned about on his radio show. As fall semester neared its end, Derek came up with an idea for a solution and then proposed it to Rose. He was leaving New College in the winter to study abroad for a semester in Ireland and Germany before returning to New College the following fall. What if his departure acted as an enforced end date to their relationship? They could date for two weeks without chancing anything serious, a harmless experiment before going their separate ways.

It was the first of many tortured bargains Derek would make with his convictions, and Rose thought it sounded strange. Why did their courtship need to have an enforced end date? But he had always been mysterious to her, and that was part of his appeal. She told him that she'd think about it, and then a few days later she agreed.

•

During the next month, Derek began to feel as if he were occupying two lives: breakfast at New College with Rose and one of her transgender friends and then Thanksgiving dinner with Don, Chloe, and a few former skinheads in West Palm Beach; overnight talks edging toward dawn with his Jewish girlfriend and then early mornings spent by himself in the courtyard outside, calling in to his white nationalist radio show as Rose continued to sleep, laughing along as his co-host mimicked a Jew by whining about Israel in a nasal, high-pitched voice. Once, Rose asked him for a ride to her early morning doctor's visit, and the appointment ran long. They were just beginning to drive back to New College at 9:00 a.m., when the cue-in music from "I'm a White Boy" began playing on the radio in West Palm Beach. Derek's co-hosts and his audience were depending on him. He couldn't miss the show. He lied to Rose and told her that he needed to make a phone call home, but instead he dialed into his radio show. He spent the next ten minutes broadcasting live on the air, making innocuous small talk to his white nationalist audience about the Florida weather while Rose sat oblivious in the passenger seat. She could only hear his side of the conversation, and she believed he was on a routine call with his parents.

Derek had been cultivating separate identities ever since he was about ten, when he built two websites in the same week. On one, DerekBlack.com, he shared photos of Spider-Man, Alan Jackson, and his baby niece, "A.K.A. The Cutest Baby in the World!!!" The other, kids.stormfront.org, was aimed at "white people across the globe," and it had links to racist songs and Duke's website. Children could play a white pride version of the video game *Doom*, shooting watermelons at villains who had black faces, talked in gangster slang, and wore big golden chains. Or visitors could cast a ballot in the fake presidential campaign Derek created, listing Don Black and Robert E. Lee as candidates for president and Adolf Hitler as a possible running mate. "Now is the time for white people to take back our freedom and win so all can see our heritage in its greatest glory," he had written.

Derek's personal web page generated a few thousand hits; his Stormfront page surpassed 400,000 visits within a few years. For almost a decade, Derek updated both pages, maintaining both a public and a private life, and there was always room for both. But now at New College it felt to him as if both identities were eating up ever more space—his fame expanding within the movement, his private relationships deepening—and a conflict between them seemed inevitable. Every day he waited to be unmasked, the tension exploding within him in waves of anxiety and guilt. Either his New College friends would learn about his political activism and shun him, or, much worse, white nationalists would discover that he had befriended a Peruvian immigrant and begun dating a Jewish woman, and he would become an embarrassment to his family and a discredit to the cause.

If ever he needed a reminder of his core beliefs, it was waiting for him on his bookshelf in the biography of Thomas Jefferson that he'd brought with him to school. Derek hated the suggestion that he'd simply been indoctrinated with his family's racial convictions; no idea was more insulting to him. His father had never forced him to participate in anything. As a child, whenever Derek did media interviews, Don made sure to walk out of the room so Derek felt free to say whatever he liked. Instead of just regurgitating family talking points, Derek sought out facts and information and followed the leads to what he called the "absolute, hidden truth about race," and one of those leads began with Thomas Jefferson.

In elementary school, Derek learned the version of Jefferson commonly taught in American history: his great egalitarianism, his famous phrasing in the Declaration of Independence that "all men are created equal." In his school textbook, Derek and his classmates read perhaps Jefferson's most famous quote about black slaves, one that had been chiseled onto his monument in Washington, helping to inspire the civil rights movement. "Nothing is more certainly written in the book of fate than that these people are to be free," Jefferson famously said. But Don encouraged Derek to do a bit more digging about that statement, and eventually Derek found the rest of Jefferson's quotation buried in an old white nationalist newsletter: "Nor is it less certain that the two races, equally free, cannot live in the same government. Nature, habit, opinion has drawn indelible lines of distinction between them. It is still in our power to direct the process of emancipation and deportation peaceably."

In later years, white nationalists would sometimes describe racial awareness as a choice between swallowing a blue pill or a red pill, an analogy that came from the movie *The Matrix*. The blue pill offered blissful ignorance, a make-believe story about racial equality fed to the masses. The red pill was the revelation of a thorny, hidden truth buried within America's founding, and the more Derek dug into American history, the more red pills he found. There was the popular effort to repatriate slaves back to Liberia in the early nineteenth century. There was Monrovia, the capital city of Liberia, which had been named after U.S. president and proud white nationalist James Monroe. There was Abraham Lincoln, the great abolitionist, debating in public with Senator Stephen Douglas in 1858. "There is a physical difference between the white and black races which I believe will forever forbid the two races from living together on terms of social and political equality," Lincoln said. "And I as much as any other man am in favor of having the superior position assigned to the white race."

It felt to Derek as if he were being let in on a secret. White nationalism wasn't just a fringe racist movement but something much more forceful and dangerous: a foundational concept embedded in the American DNA. So of course the cause must somehow be noble, even patriotic. Of course the movement would rise again once white people felt threatened. It was easy for whites to be generous and egalitarian so long as it wasn't costing them anything—so long as the American economy kept booming and whites continued to enjoy a vastly disproportionate share of the country's rising power and wealth. But what would happen when Spanish began to overtake English? Or when America's culture and identity started to fundamentally change? Derek believed the answer was written into the country's history: America had always defined itself as white, and when pressed, it would do so again. That knowledge had been Derek's secret, a certainty that motivated him, until he arrived at New College and welcomed in so many other secrets, too many to bear.

He couldn't stand the anxiety of waiting to be exposed on campus. Every day that went by, he felt as if he were building relationships that would inevitably implode once classmates discovered what he believed. He wanted it to be done already. He wanted to tell someone, but whom? Juan? Matthew, with his yarmulke, singing along to Willie Nelson? Rose? No, he would never have the courage to do it, so instead Derek decided he would set up an anonymous email account and send a tip to the student forum about his identity. But there was so much he liked about his happy life, and he kept putting the task off for another day. He was always starting an email in his mind that he could never bring himself to finish.

So instead, as his first semester at New College ended in December 2010, he grabbed a copy of a magazine from his room and carried it to the school gymnasium. Juan was already on his way home to Miami to spend Christmas with his mother and his grandmother, who had just moved to the United States from Peru. Rose was headed back to Arkansas after a tearful good-bye with Derek. In a few days, Derek would leave to visit Duke at his home in the European Alps before continuing on to work at an organic farm in Ireland and then attend an immersive language school in Germany. But first he went into the gymnasium with a 2009 issue of *Details* magazine, with Bradley Cooper's blue eyes staring out from the cover. Inside the magazine there was a gigantic picture of Derek spread across two glossy pages under the headline "Derek Black: The Great White Hope." In the photo, he wore his usual black-brimmed hat, which the author had described as "the sort of gear one might wear on horseback while herding minorities out of the country." It wasn't a perfect profile story, Derek thought, but it accurately reflected his views and his rising status in the white nationalist movement. It would expose him on campus. It would force him to fuse his two identities and live out his white nationalist beliefs.

He placed it at the front of the magazine rack, hiding in plain sight near the treadmills and elliptical machines, and then walked out of the gym.

Nothing in December. Nothing in January or February, and after a while Derek began to think a custodian had thrown out the *Details* magazine while the students were away during winter break. Maybe that was the end of it, he thought, and gradually during his time in Europe he returned to the familiar patterns of his double life. He called in to his radio show each day, delighting in the spread of the white genocide concept onto conservative radio. He helped publicize new polling data that showed more than 40 percent of whites believed they experienced more racism than minorities. "People are finally waking up!" Derek said one day, and meanwhile he was also logging in to his New College email account to read the student forum and writing to Rose, with one foot still planted in each world.

"I read the forum so much more than I did when I was there in person," he wrote to Rose that winter. "I actually checked it from a Starbucks in Leicester Square in London while I was laid over. It's my anchor so I don't lose touch."

Rose was still his anchor, too, even if they were no longer dating, and he continued to mail her CDs and write to her every few days. He had turned his semester abroad into a series of adventures—farming in Ireland, studying German, hiking in the Alps, surfing a man-made wave in a river, ride sharing with strangers across Europe, playing as a street musician in southwestern Germany. Rose read his updates and marveled at how he could be so independent and adventurous. "Keep telling me about your life," she wrote to him, so he began emailing her a regular series of travelogues:

> Ireland is all the best things you can imagine about it. The Irish are welcoming and the landscape is rugged and beautiful. I walked down to the ocean yesterday and old ladies walked their dogs on the beach while waves crashed high against the rocks on the outer edges of the bay.

> I'm studying German at the Goethe Institute in Göttingen, where I'm maybe the youngest of 50 students and only the second American. It has the pleasant air of a home for people whose German brains have collapsed. Classes go about five hours a day. The city is small, ancient, and entirely walkable, and there's an awesome forest across the street with miles of trails. My room is near the top of the stone tower. Everything's super comfortable here in the manor.

> I felt very nervous about playing music on the street on Saturday for the first time. It took me hours to get up the nerve. Then I did it and I got people who stopped and clapped, got to see hundreds of people walk by, and I made 30 Euros in two hours.

Derek always included a favorite song lyric at the end of each note, in keeping with a tradition he and Rose had started the previous semester. They both found meaning in music, so even though Derek's letters tended to be happy and light, Rose began focusing on his lyrics, which were often tormented, searching, and mysterious. The lyrics read to her like the clues to a puzzle. He was still such an enigma to her. If she could just make sense of the lyrics, maybe she could figure him out:

"This of life I know is true.
It's all a falling through
And so I reach for you."

"Born to be a soldier boy. Born to be a soldier boy."

"He said, 'Will you defeat them,
Your demons, and all the non-believers,
The plans that they have made?'"

"Beneath the sheets of paper lies my truth.
I have to go."

"Don't it make you feel bad?
When you're trying to find your way home
You don't know which way to go?"

If he was trying to tell her something, she wasn't getting it. So Derek kept writing her travelogues from his room in a place called "student city." It was a giant tower filled with foreign exchange students, and he had a tiny room on the first of the building's twenty floors. Every room was identical: A cot. A window. A bathroom. A desk. A bike. Most of the other college students were often out drinking and speaking in English, but Derek rarely drank and he was serious about perfecting his German. He went out with a classmate for bratwursts and German conversation, and then he came back alone to his room, which he sometimes referred to with fondness as "the cell." He watched German movies, emailed Rose, listened to American folk music on his computer, and regularly checked in on the New College forum, where one night in April he noticed a flurry of new messages. He scrolled to the top of the message thread and opened the first email, from a senior whose name he didn't recognize. The message had been sent to all New College students at 1:56 a.m.

"Have you seen this man?" it read, and beneath those words was a picture that was unmistakable. That black cowboy hat. That long red hair.

"Derek Black," the email read. "White supremacist, radio host . . . New College student???"

3. "I'm Not Running Away"

Tom McKay was in his final month at New College and nearly finished with the last assignment of his academic career, a senior thesis on domestic extremism. He had chosen to focus his 150-page thesis on U.S. paramilitary groups, a topic that required hours of research on Stormfront and also on the website of the Southern Poverty Law Center, one of the country's largest civil rights groups. During that spring of 2011, the SPLC was focused on what it called "explosive growth on the radical right." For the first time, the SPLC counted more than 1,000 designated hate groups in the United States, and it described Stormfront as being at "the head of the monster." The conspiracy-minded "Patriot movement" had doubled in size during the last year, and the number of domestic paramilitary groups had exploded from 78 before President Obama's election to at least 330 active militias training for a potential war against their own federal government. Much of that same insurgent anger had also come to define mainstream politics. U.S. representative Gabby Giffords and nineteen of her constituents had been shot in January during a casual meet and greet by a government conspiracy theorist, and, according to one *Washington Post* poll, 49 percent of Americans continued to believe the country's political tone "encouraged" violence. The far-right Tea Party movement, consisting mostly of disenfranchised whites, had helped to elect dozens of antiestablishment congressmen in 2010, and now some of those new legislators were proposing laws in Congress to end affirmative action and birthright citizenship.

As Tom finished his thesis research in April, the SPLC had also begun to write about another person whom it considered a radical conspiracy theorist: Donald Trump, the New York business mogul, who was making a spectacle out of his search for President Obama's long-form birth certificate. "I'm starting to wonder myself whether or not he was born in this country," Trump told Fox News, and in a series of news-making interviews he parroted white nationalist talking points by insinuating that Obama was inherently "un-American." Trump's charade made him a hero in the Tea Party movement and earned him 7 percent of the American news cycle that April of 2011, according to the Pew Research Center. "A shameless opportunist perfectly willing to exploit racism for personal benefit," the SPLC said of Trump and others in the so-called birther movement.

Tom spent most of his time on the SPLC website in a section called the "Extremist Files," a compilation of profiles detailing lone-wolf terrorists, synagogue bombers, border vigilantes, and political demagogues. Tom had become familiar with most of those names, a roll call of the most infamous bigots in America, but now as he scanned again through the list he noticed a picture of an extremist who looked different from the rest. The photo showed a smiling teenager with long red hair who was typing at a computer in a room adorned with a Confederate flag and a statue of Confederate general Nathan Bedford Forrest. Tom thought the boy's face looked vaguely familiar, so he clicked open the SPLC's file and started to read. "Derek Black's white nationalist pedigree is impeccable," the file began.

Derek Black. Tom knew that name. He had heard it

before on campus. He checked the New College directory just to make sure and found Derek listed as a first-year student from West Palm Beach. Tom thought he remembered seeing him at a party, but he wanted to confirm he had the right Derek Black, so he sent a note on Facebook to some New College classmates. "Help me divulge the truth," Tom wrote, and within a few minutes someone had responded that, yes, he had seen Derek on campus. "I've actually had a class with him," one student replied.

It was long after midnight on a Tuesday, with his thesis deadline closing in, but now Tom was consumed by something that felt more urgent. He had to act on this information about Derek, but how? Did Derek deserve to be treated as a private college student or as an infamous public figure? Tom considered writing an email to the New College admissions department, or notifying campus police, or writing Derek a private email, or going to the one place at New College that was always the most democratic and impactful of all.

"So tempted to email the forum," Tom wrote to a friend that night. "I'm kinda torn. On one hand why not . . ."

"There is no other hand," his friend wrote back.

Tom had spent four years amassing credibility on the forum, where the conversation was typically dominated by upperclassmen who were the most socially conscious. Tom had come to New College as an apolitical freshman from an overwhelmingly white part of Pittsburgh, and once during his first year in Florida he had made a joke to a few other New College classmates about how he thought the *Ms. Pac-Man* arcade game was "gay." He'd been called out as homophobic and chauvinistic, an experience that scarred him but also made him more socially aware, and now as a senior he considered it part of his responsibility to call out others when their behavior demanded it. He was on his way to becoming an investigative journalist, and his posts on the forum were usually factual, precise, and well researched. Now he began another email, attaching links to Derek's daily radio show, his archive of 4,257 Stormfront posts, his profile story in *Details* magazine, and his SPLC extremist file. "How do we as a community respond to this?" Tom wrote, and then, at 1:56 a.m., he sent his message to the entire school.

Within hours it had become the biggest forum thread in the college's history, totaling hundreds of responses before the end of the day. "Will I still be safe here?" one student wrote on the forum, expressing a fear that quickly became pervasive. The Hillel Jewish Association stopped hosting its weekly campus meeting to safeguard against a possible attack by Derek or by the Stormfront community that followed him. The student government called for an emergency town hall meeting. "Does all this stuff about Derek Black have you angry/frustrated/ready to yell?" the invitation read. A college administrator sent an email to faculty with the subject line "Important Matter," hoping to confirm that the Derek Black of Stormfront was indeed the same Derek Black at New College. "There's so much electronically-driven misinformation flying around these days that it's a good time to find a horse's mouth," the email read.

But what became most evident at New College during those first overnight hours was the beginnings of an ideological rift, a divide that would widen over the next few years on campus. Ultimately, similar debates at campuses all over the country would convulse, splitting America's liberal Left. What was the appropriate response to the most intolerant kinds of free speech? Exclusion or inclusion? Was it better to shame and demonize Derek? Or was it more effective to somehow reach out to him?

Even if most people rightly think his opinion is despicable, he does have the right to whatever opinion he wants. I don't think New College students should flip their shit and ostracize the crap out of him.

I disagree. We are talking about a kid who grew up surrounded by white power enthusiasts—social rejection might be exactly what he needs to realize how fucked up his ideas are. Which is to say I'm not gonna be nice to a racist.

One kid's private views are not really our business.

He's a public figure! What are you waiting for, a cross burning on Z Green?

This is just standing up and screaming, "She's a witch!"

It isn't witch hunting. It's a real, actual witch.

By rejecting him, we are only perpetuating the model he currently prescribes to, that those who are different are unworthy of our respect and acceptance. I believe the best way to handle this is to move past the discomfort and reach out to him as a friend and a peer with kindness. This could allow him to reassess his professed beliefs.

As a person of color, I am not comfortable having a one-on-one talk with the guy. Have you considered that maybe that's the case with other people here too? That maybe we worry about our safety? That maybe we'd rather be as far away from this guy as we can be?

We should get him kicked out.

I want him to experience three more years at New College. I want him to become a vegan, "identifying male." I think you're underestimating the effect New College culture has on a person.

It is kind of silly to think we can change him. I plan on actively ignoring him. You're just defending a Nazi under the guise of some misguided, liberal inclusiveness.

Who's clever enough to actually think of something we can do to change this guy's mind about things? It would be a victory for New College and civil rights. Seriously, it would be.

Now it was 4:11 a.m., still hours before dawn, and more than one hundred students had responded to Tom's post. But one voice was still absent.

I'd sure like to see Derek Black's response to all of this . . .

•

Derek had been receiving a deluge of hate mail for more than a decade, and so much practice had made him impervious to feedback from strangers. Sometimes, when he envisioned his army of critics, he thought back to an interview he had given just before his eleventh birthday, when he and Don were invited to appear on an episode of the Jenny Jones talk show titled "How to Confront a Racist." Don was ambivalent about bringing his son on daytime TV, but he also believed all media exposure introduced more disenfranchised whites to Stormfront. The show's producer sealed the deal by offering free airfare to Chicago and two tickets for Don and Derek to visit Disney Quest. As a safety precaution, Derek did his interview backstage under the cover of a fog machine while the Jenny Jones crowd watched it on a projection screen in the main theater. The crowd booed and shouted during the interview as security guards patrolled the aisles. "Bring him out!" the crowd chanted, and that was how Derek had come to depersonalize the enemy. His critics were nothing more to him than an anonymous chorus on the other side of a curtain—a circus of "usurpers" and "Neanderthals," he said. If he didn't respect them, then why would he care about their opinions? In the years after his appearance on *Jenny Jones*, Derek had gotten into the habit of deleting his abundant hate email without bothering to read it.

But now the forum messages flooding into his email in-box came from names he recognized, peers at a Florida honors college whom he knew and respected. "Ignorant and misinformed," wrote one of his economics classmates. "Despicable," wrote another. A few of Derek's friends wrote him personal emails away from the all-student forum, and in his one-on-one responses he worked to maintain his practiced indifference. "It's good that I'm abroad while the mob sorts out its problems," he wrote. Or: "Honestly, if people must riot anyway, it's best that I be abroad." Or: "I'm fine. I've got thick skin." But in truth Derek spent three days holed up alone in his room in Munich while he read every forum post. He had expected to feel some relief at being freed from his double identity, but instead he found himself mourning all of the relationships he'd lost. On the forum, the fallout was even worse than he'd feared. These were smart people whom he respected, and now they were calling him an "idiot," "a hatemonger," a "Hitler," and a "fraud." He sat for hours in a straight-backed chair at a Spartan desk in a country where he knew almost nobody and watched as each new classmate joined in on the thread, his relationships disappearing one message at a time as he waited for the response he worried about most.

From Rose. She emailed him late that next morning. "Oh whoa dude, you're famous on the forum now," she wrote. "Well, that was an early morning surprise. This is, um, weird."

She didn't know what else to say, so they set up a time to Skype later that night. When Derek called, he could see a few of Rose's friends seated behind her, and Rose explained that they had come to offer her emotional support. She had spent the day in her room, fighting off anxiety and hiding on a campus where she was now the object of speculation and derision. A neo-Nazi with a *Jewish* girlfriend? Had he been using her for cover? Rose had clicked through the forum thread and then read through many of Derek's Stormfront posts and interviews, trying to reconcile the quirky guy who made her feel so comfortable with the famous racial ideologue on the internet, but no amount of evidence could make it add up in her head. She wanted Derek to clarify it for her on Skype. Was there a colossal misunderstanding? Had his views dramatically changed in the months between writing these awful posts on Stormfront and meeting her at New College? "Just knowing him, I thought there had to be an explanation where he didn't actually believe this stuff," she said.

But instead Derek fumbled through apologies and then tried for one of the first times in his life to explain his ideology to an outsider. He wasn't a white supremacist, he said, but in fact a white nationalist—or, better yet, a racial egalitarian. He told her that he believed all races were in fact equal but that whites were better served living apart from other races. He told her words like "racist" had been invented to demonize well-meaning white people. He said races had inherent biological differences, and for evidence he cited discredited studies based on flawed data that showed a small average differential in IQ scores between whites and blacks. He said the cornerstone of his belief was fear of a white genocide, and for proof he showed her recent census data that indicated the rising minority population in the United States. For the better part of an hour, Rose sat on the computer with a pit in her stomach as he tried to make his prejudices sound sanitary and impersonal. None of it made any sense to her. Her confusion hardened into impatience and then eventually into anger. She ended the call in tears.

"Before I finally fall asleep, I apologize for keeping this from you," Derek wrote to her that night. "When we first met, I didn't mention it, because that would have been foolish. When we became friends, I just wanted things to stay the way they were. There's a time from last semester that I could live over again happily."

She didn't write back, and for the next few days Derek

sat in his room, watched movies, and thought about Rose as he listened to the same six mournful songs by one of his favorite folk bands, the Avett Brothers, replaying those tracks more than a dozen times over the course of a weekend. In the past, the victims of his rhetoric had always been out of sight on the other side of the curtain, imaginary enemies nursing imaginary wounds, but now he had seen the injuries firsthand. It was Rose who was offended; Rose who felt oppressed by his worldview; Rose whose reputation on campus had now been damaged. And because Derek was also reeling and Rose was the person he confided in, he decided to try again. Maybe he could speak to her in song lyrics, their own personal language.

"*Dear Sir or Madam, will you read my book? It took me years to write, will you take a look?*"

"*I sorta met Dakota introduced by Minnesota. I just smiled.*"

"No," she wrote. "You don't move me anymore. I can't talk to you right now. It's all too much."

"*I don't know what to say about it when all your ears are turned away.*"

Rose didn't respond. A while later, Derek sent one final message.

"*And the days went by like paper in the wind. Everything changed, then changed again. It's hard to find a friend.*"

A few days later, David Duke came to visit.

Duke was living three hours from Munich in the scenic ski town of Zell am See, located at the base of the Alps in Austria, one of the few European countries still willing to tolerate him. Duke had spent much of the last decade moving across Europe after being awarded a PhD from a Ukrainian university and then devoting himself to growing white nationalism in what he called "our ancestral homeland." At various times in his life, he had been banned from London after posing for photographs in his KKK robe at Scotland Yard; from Italy for being "socially dangerous"; from Switzerland for promoting white supremacist activities; and from the Czech Republic for denying the Holocaust. In Germany he was officially considered persona non grata, and traveling across the border meant risking arrest. But he wanted to see Derek and a few other friends who were visiting Munich, so Duke drove into town for a day trip with his girlfriend. Derek rode his bike from his apartment and met them at an outdoor bar in the Englischer Garten, the city's largest park.

Over the years Duke had referred to himself as Derek's "mentor," his "godfather," or "like his second dad," because the exact truth of their relationship was more complicated to explain. In the late 1960s, Duke and Don Black had met as teenagers in the white supremacy movement and become close friends. Don went to the University of Alabama, and Duke went to Louisiana State, where he fell in love with a blond classmate from Florida named Chloe Hardin, who shared his racial convictions. They'd married and had two daughters before getting divorced, and then several years later Chloe reconnected with Duke's best friend. She and Don began to date, eventually securing Duke's support, and they were married in the late 1980s with Duke serving as best man. Derek was born a year later, and ever since he could remember they had operated as a blended family: Don and Duke working together on behalf of white nationalism; Duke often joining the Blacks for Thanksgiving and Christmas in West Palm Beach; Don helping to raise Duke's two daughters and Duke promising to guide Don's son, Derek, just as he was doing now.

They ate pretzels, drank a beer, and then began touring the city. They talked about their usual favorite subjects, history and ideology, as they walked through Marienplatz, the city's central marketplace during the Middle Ages, and stopped to see Odeonsplatz, the town square where Hitler began organizing marches in 1923 for his new Nazi Party. They boarded a tourist bus, and Derek told Duke about the forum thread and the ensuing uproar, leaving out details about Rose.

Like many conversations, this one made Duke think about his own experiences. And as usual, he felt compelled to offer a bit of advice. He had been through a similar transformation in college, and it had launched his political career.

Forty years earlier, Duke had also arrived at college mostly content to blend in, moving into a dorm room in the LSU football stadium and befriending a diverse group of classmates. By then he was already a sworn member of the Klan who planned to devote his life to "the cause of our racial survival," he said, but he was also introverted and shy, more comfortable wandering through the library or hiking alone in the nearby swamps than he was arguing about politics with strangers. Each Wednesday afternoon, Duke and a few of his friends would listen to classmates give speeches on a grassy lawn outside the student union, an area known as Free Speech Alley. Any student could step onto a soapbox and talk to the crowd, but for almost two years Duke just watched as classmates spoke about the Vietnam War, civil rights, and black power, until one day Duke decided his social life was not worth the price of silence. "I said, 'To hell with this,'" he later told a biographer, Tyler Bridges, who wrote *The Rise of David Duke*. "I've got to do something sometime with my life. I'm just going to say everything I know and just spout it all."

And so one afternoon he stepped up in front of the small crowd, and within a few minutes he'd traded away his anonymity for a lifetime of infamy. He talked about how whites were "the master race." He said Nazi Germany was the ideal country, and "you can call me a Nazi if you want to." He said only ten thousand Jews had died in the Holocaust, not six million. And after about half an hour, the usual smattering of fifty or so students in Free Speech Alley had grown into a frenzied crowd of more than three hundred, according to news reports at the time. One black student stretched out his hand toward Duke's hand, noting their similarities, and asked Duke to explain the difference. "Yours is black," Duke said. Then the student took out a knife and cut into his own skin, and a white student in the crowd did the same. They joined their hands together and held them defiantly in the air. Both bleeding. Both red. Duke laughed and shouted back at them, "I could go across the street to the scientific laboratory and get the biggest, hairiest, dirty rat that you could find and slit that and it's going to bleed."

He had come back to speak every Wednesday in Free Speech Alley, returning each time with a little more confidence, a bit more clarity, until his audience sometimes swelled to more than a thousand. A Jewish woman attacked him onstage during one speech, slamming him in the chest until police came to his rescue. He tried to hand out white supremacy newspapers, and a black student lit a match and burned every one. Classmates slipped death threats under his door. His residence hall was evacuated for bomb scares.

The school newspaper proposed changing the rules of Free Speech Alley in an attempt to silence Duke or, failing that, shutting down the alley altogether.

His speeches unearthed a few hundred supporters on campus, but most of his classmates *hated* him, and that made Duke feel surprisingly liberated. For the first time, he wasn't worried about being liked. For once he didn't care about whose feelings he was hurting or whether his ideas were politically correct. He was free to become his true self, and that meant putting a photograph of Hitler above his desk, hanging a poster of a Nazi soldier on his wall, and draping a swastika flag over the dorm room window. That meant handing out copies of *Mein Kampf* at the student center and starting the White Youth Alliance, with more than two hundred people. That meant buying a cake each year to celebrate Hitler's birthday. That meant hiring a fifty-year-old security guard whom Duke once referred to as a "storm trooper" to follow him around campus and protect him from hostile classmates. That meant leaving LSU after his junior year, rejuvenating the Klan, remaking himself into a state-elected politician, winning a majority of white voters in a failed bid to become governor of Louisiana, running for president of the United States, and spending four decades as one of the world's most notorious racial zealots, until the only place left where he was free to be his true self was a little corner of Austria, where he could broadcast his views on the internet while running a bird-watching business and selling his photographs of local wildlife.

This was the person Duke had become in college. Maybe this would be Derek's path, too.

They went out to dinner at a nice restaurant in Munich. Then Duke and his girlfriend drove home to Austria, and

Derek went back to the quiet of his room. It was true that a part of him wanted to somehow prove his indifference to the hysteria at New College by redoubling his commitment to white nationalism, just as Duke had done. Derek read back through the forum thread, which now included more than a thousand emails, and this time, instead of feeling just hurt and vulnerable, he began to feel angry, even inspired.

I just want this guy to die a painful death along with his entire family; is that so much to ask?

Violence against white supremacists will send a message that white supremacists will get beat up. That's *very* productive.

He'll probably just transfer.

I bet the kid never comes back from Germany.

"I'm not running away," Derek wrote to a friend, and as his semester in Germany neared its end, he began making plans to return to New College. He wanted to speak to the school's Pluralism Committee about his beliefs and maybe recruit other students to become members of Stormfront. He planned to invite white nationalist writers and publishers to campus so they could present their scientific arguments about race. Most of all, he hoped to turn the forum thread into a lesson that would benefit other white nationalists, and late in the summer of 2011 he landed on an idea: an international conference for Stormfront members, the first of its kind, focused on verbal tactics to out-argue "anti-whites."

Derek proposed the idea to his father, and Don loved it. They had traveled to dozens of conferences together, so why not host one? Derek scheduled a date for that upcoming September, and Don booked a meeting space that could hold a few hundred people in Tennessee. "Verbal Tactics for Anyone White and Normal," Derek wrote on the invitation, promising that the conference would "give our people the offensive" after "decades of one-sided venom against White families."

During his last week in Europe, Derek worked to book nearly a dozen keynote speakers for the conference, including Duke. "Come learn how to stand strong against the enemy's abuse," Derek said then, on the radio. But first he flew back from Europe to begin the fall semester at New College, mindful of the abuse he expected to face himself.

He walked alone through campus that first night, retracing the familiar redbrick pathways until he bumped into a party of students spilling out from a dorm. He walked around them and hurried to his car before anyone recognized him. He drove a few miles south, checked into a Howard Johnson, and began looking on Craigslist for an apartment that felt far away. The best deal he found was a single bedroom in a working-class neighborhood of Sarasota known for its racial diversity. "What about safety?" Derek asked the landlord in his reply to the advertisement, and the landlord suggested he come visit the house at 11:00 p.m. to get a sense for the area at night. The street was dark and quiet. Flowers bloomed in the front yard, and a creek ran behind the house. The landlord mentioned that his neighbors sometimes came into the backyard to fish in the creek. Some of them were black and Hispanic, but none went to New College or knew about Derek's history. He told the landlord he would take it.

New College typically required all students to live in dorms, but Derek had been granted special permission to live off campus. Officially, Derek had requested extra living space to complete "craft and metalworking projects," but the mutual understanding was that both Derek and the college stood to benefit from greater separation in the wake of the forum thread. The administration had quietly looked into Derek's background in the weeks after the initial thread and then decided against any sort of disciplinary action. New College had always prided itself on encouraging student activism and radical free speech, even if it didn't anticipate that those values would come to benefit a prominent white nationalist. There was no evidence Derek had broken any laws or student conduct rules while enrolled at New College, and his faculty adviser wrote to the dean vouching for Derek's "academic integrity and excellence." Several members of the college board of directors concluded that the school was essentially stuck with Derek. If it kicked him out for exercising his right to free speech, it risked a lawsuit or, perhaps more damaging, a public spectacle that would attract wider attention to the white nationalist on campus. In fact, it seemed like a risk for the school to say *anything*, so instead nobody from the administration approached Derek to ask him about his beliefs, and no administrator spoke publicly about the issue to the student body. So long as Derek didn't threaten anyone's safety, members of the faculty and the administration concluded that his situation was strictly a "student-life matter"—and, as fall semester began, students were more divided than ever.

Juan, Derek's friend from the previous year, sent an email inviting Derek to his dorm for a beer. Juan had read through some of Derek's Stormfront posts over the summer—"all this bizarre and horrifying stuff about brown people," he remembered—but ultimately Juan trusted his own instincts more than what he read on the internet. If Derek truly despised brown people, why had he spent dozens of hours cultivating a friendship with a Peruvian immigrant? Juan decided to believe that Derek was already in the inevitable process of changing his views. "Glad you are indeed coming back," Juan wrote to Derek. "NCF can learn a lot from you, and you can learn a lot from it as well."

But most other students wanted nothing to do with him. Some vandalized a blue PT Cruiser they mistook for Derek's car, threatened to protest against him on campus, or dropped classes once they saw that Derek was also enrolled. One student, fearing for his safety, applied for a concealed-carry permit and bought a gun. Once again, a familiar debate overtook the student forum.

"Just try to reach out. Maybe he's a nice guy."

"Total rejection is the only option."

"There's nothing wrong with giving the kid a shot. Yelling at him won't change his current career choice."

Amid the chorus of the forum, one voice began to rise above the rest, equal parts indignant and insistent. James Birmingham, twenty-six, had already graduated from New College with a degree in anthropology, but he had stayed in Sarasota to work in the student affairs office, and he remained an active forum user and a staunch advocate for students of color. He was half Chinese, and in six years as a campus organizer he had helped coordinate rallies for veganism, marches for indentured farmworkers, and an annual anarchy conference called All Power to the Imagination, where radical leftists from around the world exchanged ideas for "breaking down the systems of oppression." One of those oppressive systems was white supremacy, which James had devoted himself to fighting ever since he was a sixteen-year-old heavy metal fan and skinheads in the mosh pit began calling him a "Chink."

He had done enough research in the years since then to learn what most experts thought about race: that it was a fluid, social idea, and not a scientific fact. No clear genetic boundary existed between races, no biological line dividing minorities from whites. James had studied anarchist theory and read that in English the concept of "race" didn't appear until the sixteenth century, as a way for colonialists to differentiate themselves from natives, and later for slave owners to differentiate themselves from their slaves. It was a man-made tool of oppression and exploitation. James had made himself an expert on the topic and traveled across the country to give presentations on the anthropological history of race. "Race is socially constructed and has no basis in the hard sciences, biological or otherwise," James had explained that year to one audience of anarchists in Baltimore. "But it has been structured into every part of society, conditioned into individuals and bonded to emotions from early on in life. Race itself isn't real, but it has real meaning."

Each fall at New College, James witnessed the very real effects of centuries of white domination. He led orientation workshops on race and privilege for first-year students, and one group exercise in the orientation manual began with students lined up side by side at the bottom of a wide stairway. Take one step up the stairs if you're white, James would tell them. Take one step if you're male. One step if you're straight; if your parents went to college; if you own a car; if English is your first language; if you have more than fifty books in your household; if your family has health insurance; if both of your parents are employed; if your high school taught the culture and history of your ancestors; if you're a citizen of the United States. And year after year, James had watched the most privileged group of students—the ones who looked exactly like Derek—fly right up the stairs, just as they typically ascended to the top positions in American society. Whites were much better off than any other social group by every statistical measure: income, net worth, life expectancy, home ownership, infant mortality, graduation rates, and on it went.

And now, as another school year was about to begin, James kept reading on the forum about Derek, who believed he was "oppressed and victimized by a lifetime of anti-white discrimination." The ignorance and hypocrisy was too much for James to bear. One night that fall, before his latest privilege workshop, James posted on the forum. "You may be correct that ostracizing Derek won't change his mind," he wrote. "But it will let me go about my daily business without having as much of an urge to vomit all over myself."

James had been visiting Stormfront regularly for the last several years, monitoring the site for white supremacist events in Florida that he could disrupt with other anarchists. For years he had been reading on the message board about Derek Black, the prodigal son of the movement, an elected politician, a zealot—and now a New College transfer student to whom so many classmates were giving the benefit of the doubt on the forum. Maybe Derek was just misguided, they wrote. Maybe he was confused. Maybe he had been indoctrinated with his beliefs. They said they wanted to reach out to Derek, to somehow change his mind, and to James it all seemed wide-eyed and naive. Derek was twenty-two, an adult and not a child, and he was now the one doing the indoctrinating. He was a public figure with a radio show and a long history of white nationalist activism. He had spent his young adulthood demeaning and excluding minorities and encouraging others to do the same. Why should his classmates be so worried about including him?

Before the fall semester began, James and a handful of other anarchists pushed back on the forum with their own advice: Ignore Derek. Heckle him. Make him feel uncomfortable. "Do not make eye contact or make him feel acknowledged at all. Make him as irrelevant as his ideology."

"There are rifts on the left for a reason," James explained on the forum. "May the best strain win."

For a short time that fall semester, their campaign of exclusion made Derek begin to disappear. He went to visit Rose at her dorm to try to make amends, and she told him not to come back. The German Club expunged him from its rolls. The Pluralism Committee asked him not to attend its meetings. Classmates flipped him off at the library and glared at him in the dining hall until he began to avoid trips to campus. He went home to West Palm Beach on some weekends. He did homework at an off-campus coffee shop or in his car while parked near the runway of the Sarasota airport, where he could watch planes take off. He stayed home at his rental house and played guitar on the back porch, often returning to the familiar chords of a song by the Avett Brothers called "Paranoia in B Flat Major."

I keep having this dream; I'm at a party
There's people throwing drinks and screaming,
Telling me that I don't belong.

One Friday early in the semester, Derek felt lonely and isolated enough to risk making a return to the social epicenter of campus, Palm Court, where he had spent many weekend nights the year before. New College had no fraternities or bars near campus, so instead each weekend a different group of students hosted a themed party in a courtyard surrounded by dorms. Derek was standing off to the side of the party, drinking water and admiring the decorations, when a small group of students approached him, led by a Hispanic woman. Some of them were self-described antifascists and anarchists, and Derek didn't know them. "How does it feel to be a neo-Nazi?" the woman yelled, and then a few others started shouting at him, too. They were drunk, and soon they were all shouting at Derek, surrounding him, moving in closer until another classmate stepped into the circle and pulled Derek away. Blair Sapp knew Derek from a history class they had taken together the previous year, but they hadn't spoken since Derek was outed on the forum. Blair had no problem with Derek being confronted or even ostracized for his beliefs, but now it looked to Blair as if Derek were about to get punched. He led Derek out of the courtyard, away from the party, and into the empty common room of a nearby dorm.

If ever there was a situation where Derek might feel vulnerable enough to question his beliefs, then maybe this was it, Blair thought. It was nearly 1:00 a.m. Derek was exhausted, shaken by the incident in the courtyard, and now in some ways indebted to a classmate whom he already respected. Like Derek, Blair had an expert knowledge of history. Like Derek, Blair had become active in politics, working for the Florida Democratic Party, joining student government, and helping to rewrite the New College constitution. Blair was still working up the courage to fully come out as gay to parts of his conservative family in a conservative part of North Florida, and he understood better than most how community pressures and a fear of rejection could hold someone's personal identity in place. Maybe, Blair thought, Derek had his own doubts about his identity. Maybe he was looking to break away from his past, if only he could find the right opportunity and a safe space.

They sat down across from each other at a table and talked about Derek's beliefs, debating the history of genocide, the racial implications of whites living in Africa, and social group variations in IQ scores. Blair mentioned many of the structural advantages whites enjoyed in America; Derek said those advantages were a result of whites' genetic superiority. Blair mentioned the concept of white privilege; Derek said it was nothing more than a conspiracy theory created to make whites feel guilty about their success. For each point Blair made, Derek had a practiced response. He was polite but firm. He didn't seem to be experiencing any self-doubt about his views. "I felt like I held my own against him, but he was way smarter and more compelling than I imagined," Blair said. "He knew history, and he had evidence to push back against everything I said. I went into it thinking maybe his mind was going to change, but I came out believing that maybe he was actually going to do some real damage on campus and bring more people to his side. It seemed like he was as likely to sway others as he was to change himself." After about an hour of conversation, Blair and Derek stood up and shook hands. Blair went back to his dorm. Derek took the long route back to his car, steering clear of Palm Court, before driving away from campus.

A few weeks later, in the late summer of 2011, Derek drove twelve hours north of Florida to the area he and his father had sometimes referred to on the radio as "friendly territory," up in the Smoky Mountains of Tennessee. It was one of the least diverse places in the United States, which also made it the ideal location for Derek's first Stormfront conference. He had obsessed over each detail, from the colors of the conference logo to the sandwiches in the sack lunches. The SPLC and a few anarchist protesters had come into the resort town of Pigeon Forge hoping to disrupt the conference. Derek didn't want to risk announcing the specific location, so instead he had reserved three different venues under a fake name. A few minutes before the start of the conference, he sent a direct message to all attendees with instructions to meet at a nearby gas station. From there, the group carpooled to La Quinta Inn.

Derek stood in front of the conference room to act as master of ceremonies, and before he could welcome the attendees, they began to applaud. It was like speaking at a family reunion: his parents standing in the front row, his young niece playing in the back of the room, his half sisters seated in the crowd alongside a hundred others whom Derek had befriended over the years. There were white nationalists who had traveled from Wales, Australia, Europe, and

Canada. They had watched Derek grow up at conferences like this one, and now he was back running a conference of his own. It felt, Don said then, like "a proud homecoming."

The mood was also made triumphant by the American political moment, which continued to be defined by the kind of dissatisfaction and agitation that typically pleased white nationalists. For the first time in American history, a new survey by the Pew Research Center showed that most whites believed their children would inherit a lesser country. "How can anyone deny at this point that white America is basically slipping away?" Derek had said on the radio in the weeks before the conference, and he encouraged his audience to "do something about it." He told his listeners about a new research study in which whites said they considered antiwhite bias a bigger problem in America than antiblack bias. Other polls indicated that working-class whites were experiencing surging feelings of anger, depression, and victimization—a tinderbox of disenfranchisement that had exploded into American politics. The Tea Party was continuing to grow into the millions in part because of a nebulous fear of immigration and shifting racial demographics. Alabama had just passed the harshest immigration law in the country, forcing public schools and landlords to root out and report undocumented immigrants. Obama's approval rating among working-class whites had dropped to 30 percent. They thought the president "didn't understand the real America," according to a Reuters poll, and Trump, the bombastic businessman, had gone one step further by insinuating that in fact Obama wasn't American but instead a Kenyan-born Muslim who had also fudged his transcripts from Columbia and Harvard. Don and Derek didn't much care about the legitimacy of Obama's birth certificate, but they were buoyed by the fact that by mimicking white nationalist rhetoric, Trump had amassed a massive following on the far right. He was polling near the front of the 2012 Republican presidential field, even though he repeatedly said he would likely only run as an independent and that he probably wouldn't run at all. For Derek, Trump's success was just more proof that a growing faction of whites regarded Obama as an outsider, a Muslim, a communist, an antiwhite radical. Many of those people had brought their conspiracy theories to Stormfront, where the chat rooms had grown from 30,000 users to nearly 100,000 in the last five years.

"It's time to adopt an attack strategy and take the moral high ground," Derek told the crowd at the Stormfront conference, and then for the rest of the day he rotated onto the stage to introduce nine keynote speakers he had recruited to Tennessee. There was Ed Fields, who had spent fifty years publishing a white power newsletter called *The Thunderbolt;* Paul Fromm, one of the leaders of an international white supremacist group called the Council of Conservative Citizens; and James Edwards, the host of a popular new white nationalist radio show in Memphis. Each speaker focused on the same topic: strategies for mainstreaming white nationalism by changing its rhetoric.

Out came Bob Whitaker, a segregationist known for writing a document called "The Mantra," an intellectual call to arms for white nationalists. "We are at war," he told the audience. "Wars are determined by words."

"Gen-o-cide," said Duke. "Say it with me now. This is the murder of our very genes. Repeat that over and over."

"One hundred repetitions make a truth," said Sam Dickson, a longtime lawyer who sometimes represented members of the Klan.

Don came onto the stage to speak last, and before he directed attendees to a party at the hotel's restaurant, he asked Derek to join him on the stage for one more round of applause. "This is all to his credit," Don said, and later he went on Stormfront and wrote a short testimonial to Derek's work. "I've attended well over 100 national conferences and many hundreds of local meetings in my forty-two years as a white Nationalist," Don wrote. "This was the best and most productive I've seen. Our surroundings were also inspiring, nestled in the Smoky Mountains, surrounded by friendly White people. Even the hotel maids were White . . . and spoke English. I've always believed a White Nationalist gathering should be held in a White area."

Derek wrote his own post on the message board. "Staying on the genocide message demoralizes/embarrasses antiwhites," he reiterated. "Stay on the offensive, because you are right."

And then, after a night on the couch of his parents' hotel room, Derek steeled himself to drive back toward New College—over the mountains, out of "friendly territory," and far across the ideological divide. Maybe this was the way college had to be, Derek thought: a two-way battle of exclusion; always staying on the offensive; hunkering down inside the rental house as he reinforced the divide between whites and minorities, comrades and enemies.

Then, a few days after he got back to campus, Derek received a text message on his phone. It was an invitation from two Jewish students he had befriended in an economics class the previous year. One of them, Matthew Stevenson, was the student who had sometimes sat in the courtyard of Derek's dorm and had sung along with him to Willie Nelson. The students hosted a few friends each Friday night for Shabbat dinner, and now they wrote to Derek hoping their group might include one more.

"Hey," the message read. "What are you doing on Friday night?"

4. "Push the Rock"

Matthew Stevenson had hosted Shabbat ever since his first months on campus, and the tradition began as dinner for two. Each Friday, Matthew and his close friend Moshe Ash carried challah bread and a kiddush cup to the small table in their dorm, where they could commiserate on their predicament as New College outsiders. Matthew was the only Orthodox Jew at a school populated mostly by atheists; Moshe was a transfer student from Tulane University, and he felt that his abstention from drinking and drugs limited his social options on Friday nights. Some weekends the two of them drove home together to Miami, where they had first met years earlier in the city's large Jewish community. But mostly they just drove to a Publix grocery in Sarasota and bought a large piece of salmon and the ingredients for a honey mustard glaze, which Matthew could cook in the dorm. The New College cafeterias were rated among the worst in the country, and soon a few other students started coming each week to share Matthew's food, if not his faith. Gradually, the Shabbat dinner became a social circle all its own: a rotating group of six or seven Christians, atheists, whites, and Hispanics. Each week they gathered in Matthew's dorm to listen to him say a few Hebrew blessings and then discuss life at New College, which lately meant talking mostly about Derek Black.

Matthew had spent time with Derek months earlier, during their first year on campus. They had shared a class and an affection for country music, but they hadn't spoken since Derek left to study abroad in Germany. Matthew had been home in Miami for Passover when the forum first erupted with posts about Derek's identity, and as part of Matthew's observance of the holiday, he avoided using a computer or a phone. Only several days later did he notice an urgent string of text messages from Moshe. "Matthew, I have something CRAZY to tell you," Moshe had written. "Do you remember Derek Black? The quiet transfer red head kid who always wore a cowboy hat? Well, turns out he is a huge and influential member of the neo-Nazi movement. And his father? Don Black, former Grand Wizard of the Ku Klux Klan and head of the Stormfront website!!!"

"Wow," Matthew responded. "I guess it's kind of hard to break 'I'm a Klansman' into the conversation. What's Derek's Stormfront ID?"

Together they found Derek's user name, Theodoric, and then began combing through his 4,257 posts, which stretched back over a decade. Matthew had first visited Stormfront years before, hoping to better understand the prejudice he had occasionally experienced since eighth grade, when he started to regularly wear a yarmulke. He had been chased by white supremacists on a trip to the Leaning Tower of Pisa and harassed on the street by anti-Semites while visiting rabbis in Ukraine and Poland. Each time, Matthew had heard versions of the same hate speech he now read in Derek's old Stormfront posts. "Jews are NOT white," Derek had written. "They worm their way into power over society." "They manipulate." "They abuse." "This has to be the cutoff that Jews are expelled and do not come back."

"Shocking and horrifying," Matthew wrote to Moshe, as they texted Derek's old quotes to each other. But over the next weeks, Matthew began to experience a different reaction, one rooted in his own faith. Maybe he could somehow influence Derek's thinking. A radical transformation was still possible. Matthew had experienced one himself.

As a boy he had been baptized Presbyterian, a Scotch-Irish redhead from a family of Protestants with roots in the Deep South. His mother had gone into treatment for alcoholism, and for several years Matthew went along with her to several AA meetings each month, until he began to feel more comfortable interacting with adults than with other children. At school, he tested several years above his grade level—a highly gifted student who nonetheless couldn't fit in with his peers. He felt both superior to his classmates and jealous of their relationships, and late in elementary school Matthew's feelings of exclusion and isolation were exacerbated by acute physical pain. His back started to hurt, then his joints, and then even his hair. He developed a sudden tic that reminded some doctors of Tourette's syndrome—a cough that built every few minutes into a reflexive shout or yell. Matthew's father, Michael, pulled his only son from school for several weeks at a time and took him to a series of doctors. Each one insisted Matthew's condition was more psychological than medical. They treated Matthew with a series of desperate prescriptions, each one stranger than the last. Heavy narcotics. Acupuncture. Meditation. Elimination diets. Holistic Chinese teas infused with scorpion poison. None of it worked.

Michael, a yacht salesman, had always been a spiritual seeker—"a taste of fulfillment from over here, bit of grace from over there," he said of himself—and lately he felt more wanting than ever. His son was sick. His wife was in recovery. Their financial security depended on his ability to sell million-dollar yachts in the depths of an economic recession. Michael enrolled in classes at the Kabbalah Centre in Miami, where rabbis taught the traditions of Jewish mysticism. Kabbalah had originated in the thirteenth century as a secretive part of Judaism, accessible only to devout, married men over forty, but in the 1990s it had begun spreading across the United States as a method of self-improvement available to anyone and popularized by celebrities like Madonna. "Improve your life through personal transformation and discover the hidden keys to the secrets of the universe," the Kabbalah Centre promised. Michael had been skeptical at first. For two years, he refused to invest in the basic set of Kabbalah books, called the Zohar, expecting that he would eventually abandon Kabbalah and resume his spiritual shopping elsewhere. But the classes helped him manage his anxiety and his anger. He felt lighter, happier. One afternoon, he decided to bring his son to the Kabbalah Centre.

Matthew was one of only a few children at the center. It was a place for adults, the world in which Matthew had always felt most comfortable, and within his first several weeks of ritual prayer he started to benefit from what his Kabbalah teachers sometimes called "the active work of personal transformation." His pain gradually began to ebb. His coughing tic disappeared. Over the next years, his jealousy of more popular classmates slowly abated, and his ego shrank as a hunger for Kabbalah grew in their place. He spent several nights a week studying at the center, and still he wanted more. He wanted to become Jewish so that he could experience not only the teachings of Kabbalah but also the faith in which it was grounded.

Michael had never converted to Judaism, and he tried to talk Matthew out of it. "Why would you want to make your life harder by becoming part of the most persecuted group of people in the world?" Michael asked his son, but Matthew couldn't be dissuaded. Instead of returning to his private school, Matthew enrolled at an elite, online high school run by Stanford University, which allowed him to devote much of his day to the Kabbalah Centre. Each morning he went to the center for prayer and then drove to the beach to take a ritual *mikveh* bath in the ocean. He began wearing a yarmulke. He started eating kosher meat. He taught himself Hebrew by reading the Torah in his bedroom. He helped his father buy and distribute copies of the Zohar, Kabbalah's holy text, at hundreds of prisons across the country. For a brief while during his senior year, Matthew even considered forgoing his admission to New College and staying in Miami to work as an assistant to a rabbi. He worried about putting so much distance between himself and the Kabbalah Centre, but his father and his rabbis encouraged Matthew to go. The purpose of Kabbalah, they reminded him, was less about being observant or pious than about putting his faith to practical use. They told him to set an example on campus by respecting human dignity and always seeking out the best in himself and others.

"Reach out and extend the hand, no matter who's waiting on the other side," his father had told him once, and now, on a Friday afternoon in September, Matthew wrote again to Derek.

"Looking forward to seeing you tonight."

•

The Shabbat group that night was smaller than normal. Only Moshe and Derek's friend Juan came over to Matthew's apartment and waited for Derek to arrive. Already they all had relationships with Derek, but still they had been studying him in some ways, listening to his radio show, and reading over his Stormfront posts to answer the questions echoing in their heads. Juan wanted to know: If Derek believed in racial purity, what did he make of someone like Juan, whose ancestry was part European, part indigenous, and part black? Moshe wondered: The Holocaust that his grandfather narrowly survived in the Bergen-Belsen concentration camp—did Derek and other white nationalists believe it never happened?

They waited around a small kitchen table and made jokes about how their Friday night deserved its own reality show tease line: "Watch two Jews and an immigrant befriend a white supremacist!" But in truth they all felt comfortable spending time with Derek in part because of their minority status. There was less risk that classmates would accuse them of sympathizing with Derek's beliefs or condoning his behavior. A few of their white classmates, meanwhile, had chosen to skip the Shabbat dinner or to cancel at the last minute. One of Matthew's roommates, a sophomore named Allison Gornik, had tried to dissuade Matthew from inviting Derek. "Even if you're not physically afraid of him, what he's doing is spreading bigotry that's actively hurting people," she told Matthew, and when he decided to proceed with the dinner anyway, Allison went into her room and closed the door out of protest. Shabbat dinner was one of her favorite parts of each week—a family meal with roommates who felt like her surrogate brothers, a safe and loving tradition. And now there was an infamous white nationalist on his way to their dorm, knocking on the door, waiting outside with a bottle of wine.

"Just don't be assholes. We want him to come back," Matthew said to the group, with typical bluntness, right before Derek walked in and sat down.

Matthew wore all white, as he always did on Shabbat. He said the blessings and toasted the group with his kiddush cup, which Derek complimented, mistaking it for some kind of medieval goblet. They stumbled around like that for a bit, trying to find a common language. Matthew had hoped he could pour Derek enough kosher wine to get him talking more freely about his beliefs, but Derek rarely drank, and he wasn't talking much now either. He was polite and quiet, and he seemed content to eat his salmon and listen, so Matthew decided to change his tactic. He didn't bring up white nationalism or Derek's ideology, and neither did anyone else. What good would come from berating him, Matthew wondered, if Derek simply left the table and never came back?

Matthew had already experienced enough shaming at New College to believe that exclusion only reinforced divides. He was an observant Jew among atheists, a political conservative in a place of radical liberals, an aspiring hedge fund manager in a school of rabid anticapitalists. The previous year, while his freshman roommate plotted radical protests to preserve the environment and composted dinner leftovers in their communal bathroom, Matthew had founded New College's first finance club and invited a speaker to campus to give a talk on Wall Street investing. "Oh great," one classmate had written on the forum. "Another shyster teaching how to shyst." And because Matthew was angered by that small-mindedness, he had made a point of inviting several more speakers to campus, growing the finance club to fifty people, and redoubling his own commitment to finance. Sometimes, after a few drinks, he had begun railing to his New College friends about the "Looney Tunes" socialism that he saw on campus and especially on the forum. In some ways, the incessant, in-your-face liberalness of New College had made him become more conservative.

"There is no better way to make sure Derek keeps these abhorrent views than if we all exclude him," Matthew said.

But nonjudgmental inclusion—Matthew believed that tactic had potential, and the more he researched Derek, the more convinced he became. On Stormfront, Matthew learned Derek had been homeschooled by his white nationalist family and therefore spent little time with people of color or Jews. By listening to snippets of Derek's radio show, Matthew came to understand that Derek was sharp, rational, and good at making arguments with outsiders. He could deflect anonymous callers who belittled him and questioned his ideology. He had spent the last decade practicing—and teaching—the verbal tactics of debate against the enemy. So what information could Matthew provide during the course of one Shabbat dinner that would reorder Derek's worldview? There was nothing. So instead of trying to build a case, Matthew began working to build a relationship in which Derek might be able to learn what the enemy was actually like. "The goal was really just to make Jews more human for him," Matthew said.

They sat at the table for a few hours and haltingly worked their way into a safe conversation, careful to avoid discussion of Derek, or his family, or his background, or his beliefs. Matthew was witty and sarcastic, and his jokes about New College culture made Derek laugh. They were both interested in history—in early Christianity, languages, and monasticism—and it seemed to Derek that Matthew had studied every conceivable topic. Derek thought Matthew was smarter than he was; Matthew thought Derek was the first person his age who understood history better than he did.

The dinner ended with the beginnings of mutual respect. Matthew invited Derek to come back, and he agreed that he would. For the last few months, Derek had been trying to condition himself to the idea of a solitary life on campus, but now he sensed the possibility of joining an established group of friends. It seemed to Derek as if Matthew, Moshe, and Juan had offered him an implicit agreement: They would pretend to be oblivious about his white nationalist convictions, so long as Derek treated them with respect and kept his beliefs to himself. It wasn't the kind of ideological compromise that Derek would have approved of from the podium in Tennessee—"Stay on the offensive!" he had instructed other white nationalists then—but now Derek decided it was harmless. Maybe every minority didn't need to be his ideological enemy. He decided he would stay quiet about his beliefs, return to Shabbat, and see where it went.

Early the next morning, Moshe texted Matthew, "So how do you think it went last night at the dinner?"

"Jews 1, Nazis 0," Matthew wrote.

"You think we made progress?"

"Definitely," Matthew said. "And we'll make more next week."

In between dinners, Derek retreated off campus to his rental house, where the landlord had become increasingly taken with his new tenant. Maynard Hiss, sixty, knew nothing about Derek's background, but there was an earnestness about him that felt unique. Over the years Maynard had rented the furnished bedrooms in his bungalow to all kinds of Florida itinerants—students and sun seekers, a traveling salesman, and a Jehovah's Witness. They often rented month to month and stayed mostly in their rooms, passing through Sarasota without laying down any roots, lonely travelers on their way from one place to the next. And then there was Derek, who signed up to volunteer for the local Habitat for Humanity, introduced himself to the neighbors, and used his weekends to visit every local science museum. Maynard mentioned he was vegan, and Derek offered to cook him a special vegan meal. He asked Maynard for tips on nearby state parks where he could sift in the sand for fossilized shark teeth and beaches that offered the most scenic kayaking. He bought four baby chickens, built a coop for them in the backyard, and then planted sundews, Venus flytraps, and sugarcane in the garden.

"Such a wonderful curiosity and ability to learn new things!" Maynard wrote to a friend, describing Derek. "So thoughtful and well raised."

And yet, on weekend nights, Derek was often alone in the sitting room that offered a view of the canal, teaching himself the chords to a new song or listening to lectures on tape about medieval history. Maynard began to wonder, where were his friends? One Saturday, as Maynard was getting ready to leave for a community contra dance, he decided on a whim to invite Derek along. Probably this sounds silly, Maynard said to Derek, and probably there are better options on Saturday night than to go dancing with a bunch of old folks. But, to his great surprise, Derek said yes and then offered to drive Maynard to the dance hall in Pinellas Park, fifty miles away. Derek had never tried contra, which is similar to square dancing. He had never met any of the seventy-five other dancers at the event. But by the end of the night he was moving easily up and down the dance line, falling into rhythm with one stranger after the next, charming each new partner with both his natural skill and his self-deprecation. "He made more friends in one night than I'd made dancing there in fifteen years," Maynard later remembered.

A few weeks later, when Maynard happened to meet another New College student in the checkout line at Home Depot, he couldn't wait to tell her about his impressive new tenant. Derek Black, he said. Did she happen to know him?

No, she said. She didn't know him—but she did know about his family history with the Ku Klux Klan, and his popular white nationalist radio show, and the fact that he believed Jews and minorities needed to get out of the United States. She knew about the New College forum threads and the fact that Derek inspired fear in many of his classmates. She told Maynard that Derek had been shunned from campus. She warned him that Derek might be dangerous.

Maynard drove straight back to the rental house, where he found Derek in the living room. They had just started a routine of going kayaking together in the canal behind the house. Maynard had begun wondering if maybe he should let Derek live rent-free, as a friend instead of as a tenant. Now he told Derek what he'd learned, and Derek sat with him on the couch and answered Maynard's questions. He always expected that Maynard would find out at some point, and he'd practiced versions of this conversation in his head. Yes, Derek admitted, he was a white nationalist. Yes, he was still doing his radio show. Yes, he did sometimes call in to the broadcast from his bedroom in Maynard's house.

Derek said he had never broken the law or intentionally threatened anyone's safety. He wasn't looking to physically hurt minorities on campus, he said. He just believed, in the long run, that America was better off as a country that put white people and their interests first. Derek apologized to Maynard for the way he found out. Maynard thanked Derek for his explanation and told him he needed to think about things. Derek went back to his room and started browsing apartment listings on Craigslist in case Maynard kicked him out.

Maynard's father, an architect, had been New College's first chairman of the board in 1960, helping the school acquire land from the Ringling family and the nearby airport, and Maynard still had friends in the administration. He called them to ask about Derek, and they told him the school had decided against expulsion because Derek was respected and well liked by his professors. As Maynard considered what to do, he tried to square the idea of this bigoted radical with the quiet tenant in his house. Was this person really hateful? The one buying baby chickens, naming them after Beatles' songs, petting them day and night, chasing them across backyards in the neighborhood as they learned to jump and flap, apologizing to everyone for the inconvenience, befriending the retirees down the block and the black woman next door?

It didn't fit. How could a true segregationist be so openly engaged with the world? It seemed to Maynard like an inconsistency that Derek was on his way to sorting out. He wanted Derek to live with him, regardless of his politics, and he said as much to Derek, who was grateful and relieved.

"You get along with all kinds of social groups," Maynard wrote to Derek once. "Naturally, you are very adaptable. You are good with other people and willing to take chances. That's the person I know."

Later that fall, Derek signed up for his biggest social risk yet: the New College talent show, a campus performance in front of about a hundred people on a Thursday night. In the last few months, he had begun to make a tentative reentrance into the campus community. He continued coming to Shabbat dinners at Matthew's apartment, and he decided to sign up for the small New College fencing club, where his presence each week prompted a few members to quit. But the talent show was a spectacle for the entire student body, where much of the audience came drunk and dressed in costume. Heckling was a likelihood for any performer, and much more so for Derek. But he had played at hundreds of open-mic nights in West Palm Beach. He was confident in his ability and comfortable in front of a crowd. "What's Derek Black's talent? Being a racist?" a student wrote on the forum, when the contestant list was published hours before the show.

Derek walked onstage that night to a smattering of boos, but then he started to play, and damn if he wasn't good. The song was somber and the crowd went quiet. Many of the other talent show contestants were amateurs—beat boxers and spoken word poets performing in public for the first time. Derek had the polish of a professional as he played "Adrian," a Mason Jennings folk song, varying his way from major to minor key. To Derek, it was a song about a hanging in the Wild West—an unjust execution—in which a father sang out his last words to his son Adrian about the importance of their shared righteous cause:

Looking down from the apple tree
My hands tied in back of me
With this rope below my chin
We don't fear death my Adrian.

His performance was affecting, good enough to end with some applause and a second-place prize. He went back to the rental house, savoring a small bit of redemption until the next morning, when a new email arrived in his in-box from the forum. A few classmates had been curious about the song Derek played, and so overnight they did a little research. The songwriter Mason Jennings? He had performed at civil rights rallies and written a tribute song about Martin Luther King Jr. The lyrics of "Adrian"? They were inspired by Toni Morrison's Pulitzer Prize–winning novel, *Beloved*, about the psychological effects of slavery. "That song he chose?" one forum email read. "It's a song about a LYNCHING. He's trolling us."

For the first time at New College, Derek decided to respond on the forum. It hadn't been his intent to insult or inflame his classmates, and he wanted to explain himself. "Honestly, I hadn't interpreted it as being about a lynching, per se," he wrote. "I imagine more of a 19th century Wild West scenario myself, sort of like a jeering town crowded all around. I hear it more as a poor person condemned unjustly and made an example of by a cruel and self-righteous crowd."

He saw it, in other words, as a song about himself.

"God. This is so fucking disturbing," wrote one class-mate, Bárbara Suárez. A few months earlier, Bárbara had been one of the students who cornered Derek when he came to the party in Palm Court, yelling at him until another student whisked Derek away, and now she and Derek began to have a direct conversation over email. Bárbara was Colombian, and she had fled to the United States in 2000 after her grandmother was kidnapped by a FARC guerrilla terrorist group. On her first day at New College, she had attended a privilege workshop with James Birmingham in which she continued to stand still while other students flew ahead of her up the stairs. Standing still because she had been poor and working class. Standing still because she had been born outside the United States. Standing still because she spoke with an accent. Standing still because she had experienced oppression and discrimination as a result of her race.

She knew how to recognize a lynching where Derek saw a tragic hero in the Wild West. It was a perspective Derek had never considered, and now he was hearing it over the course of a long email exchange. "Cruelty and inhumanity," Bárbara wrote to him. "I feel those are the very things you endorse. Don't take this as an attack or instigation. I'm more interested in hearing an explanation."

"I have always been very careful in interviews and the radio to condemn sociopathy and antipathy that ignores human suffering," he wrote.

"You choose to ignore anything that might point to your privilege," she told him. "You preach the values of individual responsibility, but you are quite keen towards dodging the bullet whenever any of your public statements shed some light on your real stance on race."

"I can only speak about my own view," he told her, but now more than ever he was beginning to hear other people's views, too, in a community so different from the one in which he grew up. A reporter from the student newspaper sent him links to a progressive feminist blog and an article about white privilege. He enrolled in a German poetry class, where he sat in a room with the student president of Hillel, a Jewish student group, and listened to Jewish poems about the Holocaust. A Haitian immigrant stopped him on campus and told him what it was like to grow up in a black neighborhood of Orlando, with policemen patrolling throughout the night, stopping and frisking whomever they pleased. A gay student wrote several times to ask Derek why the United States shouldn't, in fact, belong to Native Americans, the original majority. "Also," she wrote, "what is your great concern about a white minority?"

They made compelling points, and after hearing so many new perspectives, Derek began to question a few of his assumptions. He read an article on the forum that explained the concept of privilege. The story said, among many other things, that men automatically assumed conversational and societal power over women, and Derek thought that was probably true. Derek's half sisters had occasionally complained that Duke had bypassed them as potential white nationalist leaders and instead anointed Derek simply because he was a man. "I understand the concept of male privilege," he wrote to a classmate. But white privilege? Derek had always dismissed it as a conspiracy to make whites feel guilty about their success. "Always stick to the talking points," Derek had instructed other white nationalists. And so rather than opening himself up to a series of unpleasant debates, Derek decided to follow his own advice with his classmates, many of whom began to feel as if they were debating against some kind of robot.

"The concept of 'racism' is used to demoralize White people," he wrote to one.

"These government policies are frighteningly anti-White," he wrote.

"Once again, my concern is White genocide."

If Derek wasn't really listening to their concerns as people of color—if, on some days at New College, it seemed as though *nobody* were listening—then the only recourse was to do something drastic. That winter, a group of about thirty students, mostly minorities, began to meet each Friday afternoon to discuss possibilities for some kind of organized resistance. Maybe a boycott of some kind, they thought, or a campus march. It felt to the people in the room that New College's problems with race had metastasized far beyond Derek. In some ways, he had become a distraction, the overt racist who pulled attention away from other aggressions and micro-aggressions on a campus that was more than 80 percent white. A few days earlier, two students had hung a gigantic Confederate flag in the window of their dorm that was visible from across the grassy quad. On a poster in the cafeteria, someone had written, "I own a nigger." And meanwhile Derek had been back on campus for months, continuing to broadcast his radio show while the New College administration said and did nothing as fall semester rolled into spring, each day another step toward normalizing Derek's presence on campus and lulling the school back into its routine.

A shutdown. That was the answer. The student activists

could close the school for a day and force their classmates to listen to their concerns about racism and oppression in all its forms. That winter, the group delivered a letter to the school president. "We feel our institution falls short in fostering a safe space," it read. "Do not underestimate our determination and ability to organize as well as our continued commitment to see our demands met."

Canceling a day of classes required faculty consent, so, in early February, five students and recent graduates spoke at a staff meeting, including James Birmingham. They said they wanted New College to add a new requirement mandating all students take at least one class about oppression. They described their vision for a shutdown: every class canceled, all buildings closed, students and employees gathered together on the grassy lawn to discuss possible antidotes to prejudice and discrimination. "How many are opposed?" one student asked the staff, and a few professors raised their hands. The last New College shutdown had come in May 1970 in response to the shootings at Kent State, when the Ohio National Guard opened fire on unarmed students protesting the Vietnam War. Four dead, nine injured, a historic tragedy. By comparison, a few faculty members said, this was hysteria over some hurt feelings. But the students were unrelenting, and one Hispanic teacher stood and spoke on their behalf. She said racism was a corrosive problem on campus, and students who felt marginalized and unsafe were in no position to learn. At the end of the meeting, the faculty vote was unanimous, and the shutdown was approved for Valentine's Day the following week. The students arranged to fly in an employee of the Southern Poverty Law Center to help lead the event.

"It is of course highly unusual for New College to suspend

normal activities in this way," the college president wrote in an announcement to students. "But this fact only underscores the importance of this campus-wide issue affecting all students, faculty and staff. We strongly urge you all to take part."

Derek was unnerved, and he asked to meet with the student body president a few days before the event. He particularly dreaded having the SPLC on campus; the organization had published his online "extremist file" alongside a collection of domestic terrorists, and it had spent the last three decades working to dismantle Derek's ideology and his parents' professional lives. The SPLC had launched a magazine called *Klanwatch* in 1981, when Don was the Grand Wizard, using the publication to monitor Don's every move. It had publicly called for Chloe's firing from her job at the sugar company, alerting her Cuban American bosses to her white nationalist beliefs. In the pantheon of people Don and Derek had publicly ridiculed, the employees of the SPLC were the most despised of all. "Liars," Don had called them. "Spiteful opportunists." "Vile predators." "Anti-whites." "Jewish supremacists."

"The SPLC's presence on campus offends me," Derek wrote to the head of the New College Pluralism Committee. "They use dirty tactics to personally attack anyone they want. Their modus operandi is defamation."

But nobody much cared about Derek's complaints, and on Valentine's Day an instructor from the SPLC was on campus to lead a discussion for students and staff on the campus lawn. "Speak your truth," the SPLC organizer told them, and a dozen people rotated to a microphone to read anonymous statements submitted by those who felt persecuted on campus.

"I hear transphobic statements more often than you would believe," one person had written.

"The lack of diversity on this campus is highly problematic."

"Ninety-nine percent of the housing staff is black. Ninety-nine percent of the faculty and administration and student body is white. That's institutional racism, hands down."

"In regards to Derek Black, I've found myself deciding to not enroll in classes that I'm interested in because of fear of being in the same classroom with him. At what point will his free speech be less valued than my education?"

Because there was nothing else to do that day—and nowhere else to go with classes canceled—Derek wandered by the event on his way to lunch and stopped at the edge of the quad to listen. In front of him he saw a few of his professors, Matthew, Moshe, and at least two hundred other students. For a brief moment, he wondered: If this many smart people were so affronted by his beliefs, could they all be wrong? He listened to a succession of minority speakers tell stories about the ways in which racism affected their feelings of safety and self-worth. All this time, Derek had dismissed his rejection on campus as an overreaction from hysterical classmates, but now he began to consider if there was truth to what they said. The moment felt significant to him, so he took out his phone and snapped a photo of the crowded quad.

Some of the activists saw him there at the edge of the crowd and sensed a glimmer of possibility. Maybe he was listening to their message. Maybe Derek was opening himself up just a bit, beginning to consider other ideas and perspectives, if only someone could break through.

Derek lingered for a few moments and then walked away to have lunch with his friend Moshe. A few days later, Derek returned to campus for another event conceived with him at the center. It was his birthday, and Matthew was throwing him a party.

It had begun for Matthew as a strictly tactical relationship—to change Derek, who in turn could change the thinking of other white nationalists about Jews and minorities—but now a friendship was growing in its place. They met some nights to play pool at the student union. Matthew bought a cake and threw Derek his birthday party. In return, Derek invited Matthew and a few other friends to his rental house for dinner. "It would be a true pleasure to host you," Derek wrote, and then he cooked them a three-course meal, making sure that each ingredient was kosher. And so after a while Matthew decided he knew Derek well enough to stop scorekeeping their relationship. He gave up on monitoring Derek's morning radio shows to see if his language was somehow softening. He stopped waiting for some kind of public apology or a grand renunciation. "I actually just enjoy spending time with him," Matthew explained to his father. "He's surprisingly genuine and kind."

Most of Matthew's friends gradually returned to his Shabbat dinners, after Matthew assured them that Derek was not physically intimidating or dangerous. Matthew's roommate Allison occasionally came back to the table to join her roommates, but even if she was no longer sequestering herself in her room, she was still wary of Derek. As her own act of personal protest, she tried not to speak to him directly. Each week, Matthew said the Hebrew prayers, toasted with kosher wine, and carefully guided their conversations away from white nationalism, until after a few hours the other

students at the table began heading off to party or play soccer, leaving Matthew and Derek alone at the table.

Derek had nowhere else to go. Matthew could do little
else on Shabbat but sit in the dark and talk. Observing the
Sabbath meant that from sundown on Friday until sundown
on Saturday he was not allowed to work, drive, write, use
his phone, turn on lights, or do much of anything beyond
read the Zohar and pray in the dark apartment. The chaos
of a school week gave way to stillness—perfect for the kinds
of contemplative discussions Derek and Matthew liked best.
They played a board game. They drank wine. Matthew made
Derek laugh with ridiculous stories about the New College
Potluck Club and its naked dinners, or well-off students who
had taken up dumpster diving behind the dining hall in an
effort to challenge their own privilege. Derek shared bits of
the world history he had learned at white nationalist conferences; Matthew talked about the religious philosophy he had
come to understand at the Kabbalah Centre. Some nights,
when Matthew's roommates finally returned from a party
in the early morning hours, they found Matthew and Derek
still seated across from each other at the dinner table, right
where they had been five hours earlier, continuing to talk
with an intensity nobody else could quite match.

When some of Matthew's other friends privately denigrated Derek's character, calling him a racist and an oppres-
sor, Matthew insisted on treating Derek with respect, even
compassion. "In some ways, he just has way bigger versions of
the same hang-ups we all have," Matthew told a friend once.
He believed it was human nature to separate into groups, to
define oneself against the other. He had noticed it happening all the time in Judaism, in which prejudices ran thick
between different sects and orthodoxies. Matthew liked

to tell a joke about a devout Jewish man who was stranded alone for a decade on a remote island. When rescuers finally found him, they discovered the man had built not one but two synagogues, and they asked him why, as the only resident on the island, he needed both. "This is the synagogue I go to," the man said, pointing to one. "And this is the synagogue I *don't* go to." For Matthew, the point of the joke was that it was natural for people to define themselves partly by what they were not. Everyone had prejudices, Matthew thought, even if Derek's were much more extreme and pronounced.

Matthew's father and a few of his friends began to worry Matthew had crossed some sort of line. Maybe it was noble to reach out to a white nationalist, but it seemed naive to befriend one. What if Derek was using their conversations as practice to better argue his points? What if he was cultivating a Jewish friend to protect himself against charges of anti-Semitism, in the same way David Duke had once befriended members of the Neturei Karta, a small sect of Orthodox Jews who oppose Zionism?

Even though Matthew had stopped listening to Derek's radio show, other students continued to monitor it. Derek never spoke about his own life or his experience at New College. Each day, it was two more hours of political analysis and white nationalist talking points, and students on campus would repeat some of Derek's latest quotes to Matthew. He said that Obama was the "minority welfare candidate," and because he believed all minorities would inevitably vote for Obama, he told his white audience that it was their cultural responsibility to vote against him. "It's the third-worldization of the United States," Derek said one day. "It's an erosion of our culture. It's Jewish control."

Midway through the school year, one classmate wrote

to Matthew and suggested abandoning outreach to Derek—calling it "a good idea that clearly didn't work."

But Matthew was resolute. "The basic principle is that it's our job to push the rock, not necessarily to move the rock," he replied. "That's the only part we can control. Just give it time. We don't know where it will go, but I think he's already started softening."

5. "Solid and Unshakable"

Whatever his classmates might have mistaken as the first hints of softening—Derek's civility, his intellectual curiosity—were the exact characteristics that made Don more certain than ever about his son's potential as a white nationalist leader. Every slur Derek never said, every enemy he never made, every minority he somehow managed to befriend, was all more proof of what Don already believed: Only someone like Derek could lead white nationalism beyond its violent history of swastikas and white robes and into the multicultural mainstream of twenty-first-century politics. Only someone who possessed discipline, patience, tact, and control—the qualities Don had spent his life trying and sometimes failing to master. "Too much zeal," he said of himself. "Too much brash stupidity during my youth." But now, each day at New College, Don thought that Derek was demonstrating his restraint and redeeming his father's mistakes.

Don was about to turn sixty, with his only son away at school and his wife working long hours for the sugar company. He fought back against the long silence of his days by listening to news on both the radio and cable TV, and lately so much of what he heard sounded vaguely familiar. Derek had always insisted that the best way to expand white nationalism was to reinforce feelings of white grievance and victimhood—to pit whites against minorities by hammering home what he saw as the travesties of cultural erosion and white genocide—and during President Obama's first term that tactic had also become increasingly popular on the far conservative right. Andrew Breitbart, a conservative media mogul, manipulated the tape of a speech by Obama appointee Shirley Sherrod to make it look as if she were racist against whites. Radio host Rush Limbaugh went on the air to warn his listeners, "In Obama's America, the white kids now get beat up with the black kids cheering, 'Yay! Right on.'" Don monitored the news as Lou Dobbs railed to his CNN audience about "rampant illegal aliens" who were "overtaking the country" and as Newt Gingrich, a 2012 presidential candidate, said Spanish was "the language of the ghetto." Don heard Glenn Beck tell his viewers on Fox News that Obama had a "deep-seated hatred of white people," and he watched as U.S. representative Steve King, of Iowa, said Obama was "on the side of black people."

Don, meanwhile, mostly stopped speaking in public, except for during his daily radio show with Derek. He had spent most of his life forcing his way in front of a microphone to create more enmity between whites and minorities, but why risk the backlash when more mainstream voices had begun doing that work for him? So instead Don monitored Stormfront and spent twelve hours each day alone in the house, left with only the blaring TV to drown out the ghosts of his life: the dusty punching bag and treadmill that had taunted him in the living room ever since his stroke; the drawers filled with nutritional supplements that never quite restored his energy in the way the infomercials promised; the strewn cardboard boxes filled with old white power newspapers, Klan manifestos, and conference agendas—artifacts of a revolutionary movement still anticipating its revolution. Forty years now Don had been waiting, and the wear had carved deep pathways across his forehead and dulled the wild blue of his eyes. He was still broad shouldered and handsome, but the stroke had left him leaning hard against a cane, slumped down from six feet three to six feet one. His had been a difficult life, a messy life, and even though Don still felt certain about the rightness of his ideology, so many of his memories were clouded by doubt and regret. Lately he believed that the process of aging forced people to choose between two divergent outlooks. Maybe some thought back on their lives and felt mostly nostalgia, a desire to experience everything again. And then there were people like Don, who saw mostly a series of mistakes and bad choices he wished to do over.

"If I could go back to a point in history, like rewinding a tape, I would do it all different. I really would," he said, and in some ways his model for a better approach had become that of his son. "I would take a much softer path from the very beginning. I would be less confrontational. I would try to have fewer enemies. I would work more from within the system, rather than escaping from it. I would be patient about taking people where they were politically and then slowly moving them in my direction, rather than just shocking or scaring the hell out of them, which is what I usually did."

The first people Don frightened as a teenager in the late 1960s were his parents, steady conservatives who were committed to both the Church of Christ and the segregated social norms of small-town Athens, Alabama. Don's father ran a small construction company, relying on business loans from the town's Jewish banker and cheap work from crews of black laborers. The groups seemed to coexist well enough in the rural quiet of Athens, at least from the perspective of the white boss who could afford to buy a house in one of the subdivisions his company built. "My parents were content going along with the status quo," Don said.

But Don was both inquisitive and ambitious, with plans to become a nuclear physicist, and he spent his days reading at the library across from their house. The newspapers on the rack told the story of dissension sweeping north across Alabama on its way toward Athens: fire hoses in Birmingham, two hours to the south; a march on Selma, just as Don prepared to begin high school; the desegregation of his high school during Don's junior year. The new status quo in the late 1960s was constant turmoil, so Don started searching the library for possible solutions until one day he found a slight paperback titled *Our Nordic Race*, written by a Virginia preacher named Richard Hoskins. "Today the entire world is seething with unrest," the introduction read. "The line of conflict is found wherever our civilization comes into contact with the belligerent and aggressive nations of the colored world. It is a critical problem which will be solved not by emotion but only by the cold processes of intellect."

Our Nordic Race led Don to a publisher called the Noontide Press, which specialized in books it described as "dissident, provocative, and politically-incorrect." Don ordered everything out of the catalog when he was fourteen and fifteen, devouring the writings of white supremacists like Willis Carto, William Pierce, and George Lincoln Rockwell, until he became convinced that globalism and desegregation were making whites an endangered species around the globe. Once he exhausted the Noontide Press catalog, he began sending postcards to far right organizations requesting more information. One group, the National Socialist White People's Party in Arlington, Virginia, sent him several dozen buttons and copies of a newspaper called *White Power*, with a story across the front page that read, in part, "It's time to wake up and fight back!" Don took the extra papers to his public high school and distributed them to friends, until one day when he was sixteen he came home to find his parents waiting for him outside the house with Limestone County sheriff Buddy Evans and an agent from the FBI.

It wasn't necessarily that any of them disagreed with Don's opinions on desegregation. Polls showed that more than 80 percent of people opposed the Civil Rights Act in Athens, a cotton town of ten thousand near the border of Tennessee. But just because the "colored" sign had come off one of the water fountains at Gilbert's Drug Store on the downtown square didn't mean the white race was beginning its slow march toward extinction. Athens was still 93 percent white, with an all-white police force and an all-white town council. George Wallace, the governor of Alabama, was still traveling around the state and repeating his most famous campaign slogan: "Segregation now! Segregation tomorrow! Segregation forever!" The infrastructure of white supremacy remained very much in place in Athens and elsewhere. Few other whites saw the logic in trying to spark a white national-ist revolution.

The sheriff gave Don a warning about instigating racial unrest. The FBI agent visited his high school later that month and spoke at an assembly about the dangers of hate speech. Don's parents scheduled him an appointment with a psychologist and encouraged him to go back to therapy each week.

Their collective goal was intervention, a gentle push back toward the mainstream, but the effect proved opposite. Now Don knew the FBI was monitoring him. There went any possible government security clearance. There went his chance of working as a nuclear physicist. So instead of heeding their warnings, he began mailing newsletters to his classmates rather than distributing them at school, and he joined the National Socialist White People's Party as a youth member. Then, midway through his junior year, he took the first radical step down the path he would one day wish to start over: He told his parents he was leaving for a conference, his first, a gathering of young Nazis and white supremacists in Arlington, Virginia.

Don was prepared to hitchhike to the conference, but instead his parents gave him a ride to the Birmingham bus station, where Don had arranged to carpool to Virginia with two other teenagers who had also been writing postcards to the NSWPP. He didn't know their names or what they looked like. He had never met another committed white nationalist. Don, sixteen, held on to his suitcase and waited at the bus station with his parents, who refused to leave until they met his travel companions. Finally here came one, nineteen, well mannered, and offering his outstretched hand, with a telegenic face that would help make him the most famous politician in Louisiana. And here came the other, also nineteen, getting off a bus from Mobile with shaggy clothes and a crude swastika tattooed onto his shoulder, which would later be used to identify him as a serial killer responsible for murdering more than fifteen people in an attempt to start a race war.

Don Black. David Duke. Joseph Paul Franklin. Together they would come to define the white supremacy movement for the next several decades, but now they were three teenagers in Duke's family car. They ate pretzels and listened to a compilation tape of twangy southern rock called "Head Bang Music" as they drove up Interstate 81. The highway had opened a few years earlier, the latest link between the old South and the North, and out the window cotton fields gave way to the Great Smokies and then to the Blue Ridge Mountains. Their car engine overheated in southern Virginia, and they sat in the heat and talked about their beliefs as they waited for another member of the NSWPP to come help with repairs.

Don thought Duke could be a little shrill and preachy, a college student who turned down the music every few dozen miles to offer monologues about racial science. Franklin, meanwhile, was a high school dropout who cussed, leered at female drivers on the highway, and seemed to delight in repeating the racial slurs Don mostly tried to avoid. But it was fourteen hours from Birmingham to Arlington, plenty long enough for strangers to become allies. Don had never spent so much time with people who shared his racial conclusions, and hearing their certainty reaffirmed his own. They had each arrived at the idea of white supremacy through books. Franklin had grown up with an abusive father in an all-white housing project in Mobile, and he escaped to the library first for fantasy novels, then for books on Christian extremism, and then for *Mein Kampf*, Hitler's autobiography. Duke, an aspiring naturalist, had followed a reading trail of books about genetics and biology until he stumbled into a segregationist title, *Race and Reason: A Yankee View*, which argued that integration resulted in more crime.

The three teenagers traded book recommendations in the car, circling back over the course of the day to the central ideas on which they all agreed: Whites were biologically superior to other races because of evolutionary differences, they thought. They believed their white ancestors had been forced to learn survival skills in cold northern climates, whereas blacks had been able to lounge in the heat of Africa. As a result, Don thought whites had become smarter, more disciplined, and more resourceful. And now the great white gene pool was endangered by desegregation, immigration, and a rising Jewish political influence. By the time the three teenagers finally arrived in Arlington for the conference, a transformation had taken place. Don no longer felt like a lone extremist searching for answers. He was part of a movement, a soldier for a cause.

He spent about five days as the youngest attendee at the conference, studying political organizing and eating lunch on the National Mall with white supremacist authors he admired, until eventually his parents mailed him a plane ticket to fly home. He had never flown on an airplane before, but his parents were rattled by his absence and eager to have him back. Duke and Franklin planned to stay in Virginia for a few upcoming white power demonstrations, and Don promised to join them soon.

"That was the trip that convinced me to jump all the way in," Don later remembered. "I had kind of been the lone guy, going out and preaching about all this, and I came back with strong relationships and better ideas. That car ride gave all of us a big push forward in our commitment."

Duke would go back to LSU the next semester and finally summon the courage to stand up and speak at Free Speech Alley, until his crowds of dissenters grew so big he hired a security guard to protect him on campus. Franklin would begin privately planning his self-described effort to "spark a race war," eventually bombing three synagogues and using a sniper rifle to shoot "as many evildoers" as he could: an interracial couple outside a shopping mall in Madison, Wisconsin, in 1977; another interracial couple in Atlanta in 1978; *Hustler* publisher Larry Flynt, as payback for publishing photos in his magazine of interracial couples; a black Pizza Hut employee in Tennessee; a Taco Bell manager in Georgia; civil rights activist Vernon Jordan in Fort Wayne, Indiana; two young black boys in Ohio; two more in Pennsylvania; and on and on it would go for more than three years, until finally Franklin was caught, convicted, and executed after killing at least fifteen people and wounding at least twelve others.

And Don would go quietly back to Alabama, back to the library, back to the same worn copy of *Our Nordic Race*. He lacked the ego and the confidence to be a political demagogue like Duke. He didn't believe in sparking a revolution through violence, murder, or detonating bombs like Franklin. But in the pages of *Our Nordic Race*, Don found the outlines of another kind of racial soldier. "A problem to be solved by the cold process of intellect," the book had instructed, and that was the kind of leadership Don hoped to provide.

But he was also zealous and impatient, and a few months later Don made another one of the mistakes he would soon come to regret. He went to Georgia for the summer between his junior and his senior years of high school for what he described to his parents as a six-week internship: volunteering for the gubernatorial campaign of J. B. Stoner, a segregationist and a Ku Klux Klan member once convicted of bombing a black church. One of Don's colleagues that summer persuaded him to break into the office of a rival white power organization to steal its mailing list. Don had neither a weapon nor any experience as a thief, but he was just about to get away with the mailing list when Jerry Ray, the brother of Martin Luther King Jr. assassin James Earl Ray, stopped Don at the door and shot him in the stomach with a .38 hollow point.

Don stumbled into a nearby Laundromat and collapsed as a few women dialed 911. Because he was still a minor, the hospital notified his parents, and they scrambled to find a charter flight from Athens to Savannah. Their only other child was a daughter twelve years older than Don, a talented writer who moved away to become a beatnik in California. It had seemed at the time like an act of extreme rebellion, but now they had Don, who was being followed to the hospital by a caravan of FBI investigators and TV news anchors as he went into emergency surgery a few days before his birthday.

He turned seventeen in the hospital, already a proven warrior for a racial movement. At nineteen, he was back to distributing white power pamphlets, this time to classmates at the University of Alabama, where the student newspaper described him as the "campus 'Nazi.'" At twenty-two, he was initiated into the Knights of the Ku Klux Klan by his close friend Duke, who had taken over the Klan as a side job while he and his new wife, Chloe, ran a day care in the basement of a Baptist church. At twenty-five, Don was already declaring his long-shot candidacy for mayor of Birmingham, running as the city's most famous white nationalist in an election that would eventually result in the city's first black mayor.

It seemed to Don as if whites were always losing, each day another step deeper into the abyss. How could he sit patiently by, relying on the cold process of intellect as increasing rates of immigration and interracial marriage polluted the gene pool? For much of the nineteenth and twentieth centuries, America's racial demographics had remained steady at about

90 percent white. But by 1960 that percentage had begun dropping down to 87 percent, then 85, then 80 percent by the end of the next decade—an accelerating decline that demographers said would make white children a minority by 2020 and all whites a minority by 2045 unless someone or something forced the country to reverse course, and soon.

"People will begin waking up here in the next few years," Don told one reporter in 1970. "The tide is going to turn," he said in 1975. "It's just about to happen," he said in 1978, and yet all the while Don was mostly driving in circles around the same rural territory of the Deep South, from Virginia to Louisiana to Alabama and then back again, lighting up crosses at KKK rallies in the same parks of Birmingham and Nashville, giving the same speech to the same audience of a few hundred supporters. Duke left the Klan in 1979 to pursue a political career and anointed Don the Grand Wizard. He ran the group as an unpaid volunteer while he worked as a medical assistant at an Alabama doctor's office. "We are a non-violent Klan," Don said then, but there were also several more militant Klan organizations at the time, like the White Knights of the Ku Klux Klan and the United Klans of America. Those groups attacked and killed civil rights leaders, Vietnamese immigrants, and four elderly black women in 1980. No matter how often Don condemned those killings and spoke about his own group as the "family-friendly, more educated Klan," they were all co-opting the same Klan history of fear and violence. They were all ultimately dressed in the same hoods and robes.

The Klan was a dead end, Don decided. The movement was going nowhere. He had spent fifteen years trying to awaken white people to his revolution, and still they seemed as complacent as ever. "I was at a desperate point in my life,"

Don remembered of that time. "I wanted to do something. I had all this true belief and conviction, and I was tired of waiting around. I wanted to push things forward." So, when another white nationalist offered Don a Hail Mary solution in 1982—a chance to join a ready-made revolution that was already under way—Don went against his better judgment and decided to take it.

The plan, which they referred to as Operation Red Dog, was to overthrow the tiny Caribbean island nation of Dominica with a small army of white supremacists from the United States and Canada. Don had never heard of Dominica, a new country of sixty thousand people. He'd never been to the Caribbean, and he didn't have a passport. He went to the library to research the country and found an old story in *National Geographic* with a series of double-page nature photographs. The island of Dominica was only twenty-nine miles wide and sixteen miles long, but it had white sand beaches, active volcanoes, lush green valleys, unspoiled rain forests, and some of the world's most pristine rivers. Geologists considered it the one remaining territory in the New World that its discoverer, Christopher Columbus, would still be able to recognize. If America had become a multicultural mess beyond saving, Don thought, then here was an immaculate, isolated place to begin a new white utopia.

As the operation neared, that fantasy compelled Don to look past all the glaring flaws in their plan: that their white supremacist army consisted of only ten men; that many of those men were alcoholics or petty criminals with no military experience whatsoever; that their hope was to invade Dominica by water, sailing from Louisiana across the choppy Gulf of Mexico on a leaky, hurricane-battered boat; that their success in overthrowing the government depended on teaming up in Dominica with a group of local mercenaries, black soldiers who also wanted control of the country and had no interest whatsoever in turning their island into a white nationalist paradise.

"I got too swept up in the romance of it to see the stupidity of the whole thing," Don said, and so he went to a store a few days before their departure and bought a semiautomatic pistol. He had served years earlier as a medic in the U.S. Army Reserve and the National Guard, but this was the war he had spent his adult life preparing to fight. He climbed into a van with nine other white supremacists in April 1981, and they began driving toward their boat in the New Orleans marina. A few miles down the road, federal agents surrounded the van. They had learned about Operation Red Dog while working undercover, and now they searched the rear of the van and unloaded crates of Jack Daniel's, a Nazi flag, military fatigues, dynamite, tear gas, ten shotguns, ten handguns, and several automatic rifles.

At their arraignment a few days later, many of the white supremacists were already beginning to cave. A few offered to testify against their co-conspirators. Six pleaded guilty in exchange for a lesser sentence. Most disavowed their white supremacist ideologies and said they had been motivated mostly by money or greed, believing that explanation would improve their odds with a jury. At the arraignment, they lined up together in ragged T-shirts and jeans, dressed like the fools they had been—all of them except for Don, who wore a navy blue suit, pleaded not guilty, and vowed to defend himself in court. The jury was just another audience for him to convert, another group of white Americans in need of waking up. "Perhaps we were naive," he told the jury. "Perhaps we were stupid. Perhaps I was duped. But what we

were doing was motivated by the highest principles, by patriotic motives."

The jury deliberated overnight and then found Don
guilty of violating the obscure Neutrality Act of 1794,
which makes it illegal for Americans to wage war against
countries at peace with the United States. Like most of his
co-conspirators, Don was sentenced to three years in federal
prison.

The warden assigned Don to the highest-security cell at
Big Spring federal prison, right next to the prison guards'
office, and the guards prepared for the possibility of a race
riot. Don was the most high-profile inmate in a diverse,
low-security prison, and he had told a few journalists that
he planned to continue running the KKK from his cell. "A
tireless rabble-rouser," was how the court file had described
Don, but now under the watch of the prison's security
guards he couldn't do much beyond write letters and make
occasional phone calls to Duke and members of the Klan. He
had nowhere to go each day but back into the inmate lineup
for morning count, back into his cell for sixteen hours, back
to the asphalt of the prison courtyard for ninety minutes
of exercise and sunlight. Out beyond the prison's twenty-
foot, razor-wire fence, the sun-scorched desert of rural Texas
stretched out in every direction for fifty miles. For the first
time since Don began handing out white power pamphlets
at age fifteen, he had no choice but to slow down, reflect,
and reassess.

Most of the 450 inmates at Big Spring were white-collar
offenders with no previous criminal history, and they sub-
divided into groups of blacks, Latinos, and whites. The self-

segregation reinforced Don's conviction that people tended to align with their own race when they wanted solidarity and safety, but the close-quarters living of Big Spring also required that he treat everyone with respect. "I wasn't going to get jumped by someone looking to make a statement against the KKK," Don said, so he learned to moderate his beliefs in mixed company, saying less about race as he worked in the commissary alongside inmates who belonged to Mexican gangs or the Nation of Islam. His longest conversations were the ones he had with his cellmate, Rex Cauble, sixty-seven, who had earned millions as an oil wildcatter before his arrest for helping to import 106 tons of Colombian marijuana into Texas. Don came to believe that Cauble was sympathetic to many of Don's beliefs, but Cauble had never advocated publicly for white supremacy. Instead, he'd used his wealth to make five-figure political donations, befriend the Texas governor, advise his campaign, and become an honorary member of the Department of Public Safety. During his friendship with Cauble, Don absorbed an important lesson: If Don wanted political power, it was sometimes best to maneuver through back channels.

Don signed up for the prison's computer science classes, spending a few hours each day on an early-model TRS-80 microcomputer from Radio Shack. Within a few years, he'd learned enough about operating systems and coding to become convinced of the machines' potential. He'd grown up handwriting postcards to P.O. boxes asking for white power literature, and here was a shortcut that might one day allow him to manage databases and even send electronic messages to potential allies around the world. It made him think back to the introduction of the first white nationalist book he read, *Our Nordic Race*. "We must mold public opinion," the introduction read. "We must distribute literature on our racial history in as large of quantities as possible." Maybe the computer was the back channel Don had been seeking all along. By the time he was released from prison in 1984, he felt more optimistic about the movement than he'd been in the last decade. Duke met Don outside the prison gate at Big Spring, and together they flew to Alabama on Cauble's private jet, arriving at a bar for a homecoming party with a few hundred white nationalists.

"We're here to build the greatest white regime this country has ever seen," Don said that night, with Duke standing by his side.

They changed tactics together over the next several years, focusing less on Jews and more on third-world immigration, swearing off the Klan, and starting the National Association for the Advancement of White People. Their goal was to reposition white nationalism not as a hateful cause but as a modern civil rights movement for whites. Don traveled around the country to market that message, and he reconnected with Duke's ex-wife, Chloe, while doing a radio interview in Florida. Don and Chloe married in 1988, and she became pregnant a few months later—just as Duke launched his first serious run to represent Louisiana in its state legislature.

For the next six months, Don split time between his pregnant wife and his closest ideological ally, repeating the fourteen-hour drive between West Palm Beach and Louisiana a few times each month to help build voter databases for Duke and hone his campaign platform. They decided not to make race a talking point, but instead to make it the subtext to every issue. Duke blamed Louisiana's high murder rate on black aggression. He said he was against minority set-aside programs, against welfare culture, and against affirmative action. "We demand an America based on merit," his campaign brochure read. "Equal rights for all. The truth is that today, better qualified white people face racial discrimination."

It was a relatively small race to represent thirty-five thousand constituents in Louisiana's House of Representatives, but Duke's long history with the Klan made his campaign "perhaps the most important state or local election of our time," according to one news report. President George Bush sent thousands of signed letters into the district to remind voters of Duke's connection to the Klan, and former president Ronald Reagan campaigned against him, but still the Duke headquarters overflowed with six thousand letters from well-wishers. "Thanks for speaking out for all politically-incorrect white Americans," one letter read. Don used his nascent computer programming skills to build better databases for the campaign, the earliest version of Stormfront, and white voters in Louisiana's most well-educated district turned out for Duke's campaign rallies by the thousands. Three days before Duke won the election with the largest turnout in state history, Don received an urgent call at campaign headquarters. It was from Chloe. She said she was in labor. Don rushed out of the office and onto the highway, but before he crossed into Florida, his early-model cell phone was ringing again. Chloe said the baby had been born, a healthy boy. She asked Don for a name.

It was something he had been thinking about during the last few months. What would be a name with both history and meaning? A name that reflected his beliefs? Don had always admired Theodoric the Great, the Ostrogoth ruler who restored the Roman Empire to glory in the late fifth century. He also loved *The Song of Roland*, an epic, fictional French poem about an eighth-century Frankish commander who dies in battle after being ambushed by Muslims from Spain. In the story, Roland fights for Charlemagne's army not only with a sword but also with his mouth, shouting louder and louder to warn his comrades of the Muslim attack until finally his temples burst and his brain explodes on the battlefield.

"Derek Roland Black," Don said, lingering on each syllable years later, on Derek's twenty-first birthday, as they reminisced together on their joint radio show. Derek in honor of Theodoric, the great Aryan leader. Roland in remembrance of a white martyr who died speaking out for his cause. "There's something about that name I really liked," Don said. "It's the name of a Viking in many ways, a real fighter. Solid and unshakable. When you say it, you can almost hear the sound of clashing steel."

6. "A Million Questions"

"Derek. Hey, Derek!"

He was on his way out of the New College library late one afternoon in April 2012, exiting onto a campus where he'd learned to walk quickly and ignore his own name. A classmate had just flipped him off on his way into the library a few hours earlier, and then Derek had hidden himself away at a corner desk where he could work without being seen. But now he was outside the library again, and the shouts of his name were getting louder and closer. He looked up to see a golf cart spinning back around in his direction, with half a dozen students hanging off every side. In the driver's seat was Mike Long, the popular student body president, who pulled the cart up to Derek and stopped. Mike said he and the other students were on their way to the marina for a sunset cruise on his sailboat. "Hop on," he told Derek. It sounded less like an invitation than an instruction, and Derek didn't have time to think up an excuse. He climbed onto the cart, and Mike drove toward the bay.

Mike had befriended Derek before he was outed on the forum as a white nationalist, just as Mike had befriended almost all of his classmates. As a freshman, he had become student body president based in part on sheer extroversion, hosting parties, launching a sailing club, and introducing himself to most of the eight hundred students on campus. Maybe it was partly the inherent privilege that came with being a self-described "straight, white, straight-talking man" that fueled his social confidence, but Mike had never been afraid to talk to anybody, including a white supremacist. At a school where so many other students engaged in theoretical conversations about politics and ideology, Mike had twice been elected president with the same action-oriented campaign platform. "Stop all the hand-wringing and just deal with the issues," he said.

That was how he had transformed from a high school dropout in juvenile drug court into a graduate with an A average, after retaking four years' worth of credits in his final two years. That was how he had afforded to attend New College, trading his old Jeep Cherokee for a battered sailboat where he could sleep rent-free. And that was how he had decided to invite Derek onto his boat for this sunset cruise, never stopping to ask what anybody else thought, never pausing to debate the benefits of exclusion or inclusion or where any of it might lead.

They sailed out into the calm waters of the bay, moving west toward Longboat Key as the manicured shoreline of campus receded behind them. Sunset was still at least two hours away. Mike was preoccupied with sailing the boat. Derek knew only one other person onboard, Matthew's roommate Allison, and what he knew about her was that she had been avoiding him at Shabbat dinners for the last six months. At first she had stayed in her room, and she had continued to make herself scarce in his presence. It was one thing for Juan, Matthew, or Moshe to befriend Derek; they would never be mistaken on campus for white nationalists. But Allison was a white descendant of Italians, English Protestants, Germans, and Hungarians, and she had come to

New College from the lily-white, conservative town of Mentor, Ohio. Nobody knew her politics, and she didn't want to risk being mistaken for a racist sympathizer.

But the boat was only thirty feet long, and it was more awkward to avoid Derek than to speak to him. After making a point of protesting Derek's presence at the first Shabbat dinners, Allison had slowly acclimated to his presence. She knew he wasn't violent or confrontational in person, and now she made small talk with Derek about their mutual friends—Juan, Moshe, and Matthew. Allison was curious about the ecology of the bay, and Derek had grown up kayaking each day in the ocean, building his own saltwater fish tank, and raising baby clown fish hatched from the egg. He talked about his love for reptiles, photosynthesis, the history of Florida waterways, and the best way to pick up a hermit crab without getting pinched. He gave Allison his phone number and offered to teach her how to sail later in the semester. She thought he seemed quirky, gentle, and interesting—nothing like the extremist she had expected—and before long the sun had set and they were arriving back at the marina. They said good-bye and Allison went back to her dorm, but she was still thinking about Derek. "I'm wicked curious about the kid," she wrote to a friend on Facebook. "I'm like a detective."

If Derek liked science, history, and reptiles, for Allison it had always been people who fascinated her most—their motivations, feelings, behaviors, and beliefs. Her parents had installed dial-up internet when she was eleven, and from her family room in Ohio she had begun to cultivate a network of friends from chat rooms around the world. Each night she talked to people from Australia, Israel, the Netherlands, England, Oklahoma, and Louisiana, learning how to ask them questions about their lives and their homes without inserting her own assumptions or judgments. She was naturally good at thinking outside herself, at empathizing, and she had come to New College to study psychology. "I just like people," she once wrote to a friend. "I like trying to make sense of them." And now there was Derek, whom she found impossible to understand. How could there be such a chasm between how he acted and what he believed? How could someone who seemed mild and kind promote something so hateful and oppressive?

A few weeks later, Derek invited her to come to a Friday night contra dance with Moshe and a few of their mutual friends. It was a big group, so she agreed to go. She had never been to a contra dance, and for a few hours she rotated her way through the dancing line, gradually finding her feet, moving a bit clumsily from one partner to the next until eventually she came to Derek. The song was a waltz. Derek took the lead, and she began to follow. His rhythm and his footwork were excellent. He told her not to obsess over the steps or the choreography or how she looked in the floor-to-ceiling mirrors as she was performing the moves. The best way to learn, Derek said, was to block out every possible distraction until the only thing left to feel was the music and his lead.

Close your eyes, he told her, and eventually she did.

"You didn't crash me into anybody when I had my eyes closed," she wrote to him later, once she was back on her computer, chatting on Instant Messenger.

"I'm glad I didn't," Derek wrote back. "So many dangerous moments that if they didn't happen just right would have destroyed the universe!!"

"Oh hush. ☺ I don't know. I think it was more the

whole close-your-eyes thing. To me that sort of indicates some degree of trust there (like, I don't do trust falls). And, hmmm, I'm not sure how to word it, but I guess at first I was like, 'Yeah right kid. I'm not closing my eyes. I don't even know you.' But then I did."

At the same time, she worried: Was this really someone she was willing to trust? Was this a lead she wanted to follow?

She began researching Derek on her computer, reading news articles about him, and listening to his radio show. She signed up for an account so she could see Derek's posts on Stormfront, where some of the discussion that spring was about the ongoing trial of Norwegian right-wing terrorist Anders Breivik. He had massacred seventy-seven people the previous summer, most of them teenagers attending a government-run summer camp outside Oslo, because he wanted to attract attention to his fifteen-hundred-page manifesto about the genocide of the white race, the ills of multiculturalism, and his feeling that Norway had become a "dumping ground for surplus births of the third world." His manifesto sounded like many of the typical posts on Stormfront, and in fact Breivik had once been a registered Stormfront user, posting four times in 2008. Derek and Don both publicly condemned Breivik's massacre and expressed horror at his methods. "We attract too many sociopaths," Don had written on Stormfront. "This makes me want to pull the plug on this place and never look back." But on their radio show, Don and Derek also sympathized with Breivik's assertion that the Norwegian government was partly at fault for the massacre. If races were kept more separate, they said, everyone would be happier, safer, and better off.

As much as Allison wanted to dismiss the Stormfront community as a cesspool of extremists, she had heard subdued versions of the same racial beliefs every day growing up in Mentor, Ohio. Her childhood was shaped by some of the same assumptions.

Her mother, Julie, had grown up in inner-city Cleveland, where she spent the tumultuous decade after desegregation in an impoverished neighborhood that was half white and half black. Racial tension erupted at schools like Collinwood High, where in 1970 four hundred white students threw rocks at the building, shattering fifty-six windows while two hundred black students huddled inside the third-floor cafeteria, breaking legs off chairs to arm themselves against an attack until finally a SWAT team arrived at the school. "Bomb City USA" was what politicians from around the country called Cleveland back then, so Julie ran home each day from junior high, propelled by fear. Her desire to find a safe, stable place took her first to an elite private college and then to the exurbs of Cleveland as one of the first people in her family to arrive firmly in the middle class. She wanted to raise her own children in what seemed to her like the safest place of all, which also happened to be the whitest place: on a quiet road in a rural subdivision in Mentor, Ohio, once voted the Whitest City in America, where she never worried about leaving her car unlocked, keeping the garage door open, or walking alone at night in the cool air blowing off Lake Erie. Her husband worked for a company that designed airline parts and they both tended to vote Republican. The oldest of her three children, Allison, went to a private Catholic high school on 425 acres of wooded land, which Julie managed to pay for despite a tight family budget. Julie taught her children what she believed to be true from her own life: that everyone in America had equal rights and equal opportunities, regardless of race, and that hard work was the primary determinant of success. Her America was a place of self-determination, an ultimate meritocracy in which you deserved whatever you got.

Julie had provided Allison with a safe childhood, a loving childhood, and because Allison rarely needed to fear for her own basic needs, she grew curious about the world around her, becoming confident, open-minded, independent, empowered. When her parents told her at the last minute that they didn't have enough money to pay for college, she researched the best bargain schools in the country and discovered New College of Florida at the top of several lists. She moved to Sarasota by herself and worked at a grocery store for a year so she could establish residency and qualify for in-state tuition. Then she enrolled in New College and began devouring every post on the student forum, growing her social conscience as she learned about privilege, systematic oppression, and structural bias—all the ways in which whites were unfairly advantaged and America was not at all a meritocracy. And then she started going back home on vacations to Ohio and sharing those ideas with her mother, who was brave enough to acknowledge her own prejudices and listen.

"You helped open up my mind about all of these things," Julie had told her once.

And now Allison wondered about Derek. Could she push him to challenge his beliefs? Should she?

Allison told her mother about Derek, and Julie went on Stormfront herself to research his views. What Julie read terrified her—"a whole other level of ugliness," she said—but she also had complete faith in Allison and in her ability to influence others. She encouraged Allison to trust her own instincts. "The thing is I'm really conflicted," Allison said then. "Even if I could have some direct, positive impact, I'm not sure it is morally okay to befriend someone like this."

Late that April, before she saw Derek again, Allison went kayaking on the bay with her closest friend at New College to ask his advice. Bennet Bastian was kind and judicious and destined for the Peace Corps, and she trusted his integrity as much as her own. They paddled out into the water toward the Ringling Museum as she laid out her doubts. Just because she liked spending time with Derek, did that make it okay to prioritize a friendship with a white nationalist over vocally supporting the victims of that oppression? She thought it seemed presumptuous and naive to think she could somehow change Derek's thinking. Even if transformation was possible, how could any true friendship begin from a place of such calculation?

Bennet had never researched Derek's beliefs, and he typically avoided reading the forum. He had little patience for pettiness or drama, and to him Allison's decision seemed clear. She enjoyed spending time with Derek. She was in no danger of becoming a white nationalist herself, so what was the potential downside?

You two should be friends, Bennet told her. Even if Allison never tried to change Derek's beliefs, her influence could only do him good.

As their friendship grew over those next few weeks, it sometimes seemed to Allison as if she were the one benefiting most. Every day spent with Derek meant another spontaneous adventure. Allison was used to scheduling her time on a desktop calendar, plotting out daily goals as she advanced down the road map she had drawn for her life. She was smart and ambitious, with plans to earn a doctorate in clinical psychology, and sometimes instead of watching *Game of Thrones* in her free time, she read books about dialectical behavioral theory and built a database of potential graduate programs, making lists of the pros and cons for each one. "So thorough!" Derek wrote to her, because he had never kept a schedule or a calendar. Some days he thought he still wanted to become the leader of white nationalism. Other days he also wanted to get a doctorate in medieval history, or volunteer on yachts in the Caribbean, or become a carpenter, or move to Fiji to work as a scuba-diving instructor. He tended to write his best school papers not on a schedule but in a burst of inspiration, and until that moment arrived, he did whatever else seemed interesting or fun, whether that meant studying Latin, visiting faraway farmers' markets, or mapping out his favorite constellations. He had explored much of central Florida on spontaneous road trips, and now he began inviting Allison to come with him.

They waded out to a sandbar in the middle of the night to watch the moon set into Sarasota Bay. They mapped constellations in the night sky, explored hidden beaches, and snuck onto the Ringling Museum property after it closed. Once, a few days before the end of the semester, Derek suggested they borrow one of the college's sailboats to venture out into the Gulf of Mexico, but the wind died in the night before they could make it out of Sarasota Bay. They pulled the boat onto a desolate beach infested with sand fleas and shivered through the night before turning back for New College the next morning. "Now we share the trauma of being stranded at sea!" Derek later wrote to her.

"What's our next big adventure?" Allison wrote back, because she felt most comfortable spending time with Derek away from campus, far from the stares and rumors about her that were already beginning to spread. For the last two years, she had enjoyed the widespread respect of her peers, who admired her schoolwork and also her ability to set it aside for a party or soccer game on Friday nights. She could be both studious and fun, with a social openness that won her friends from a wide cross section of student cliques, but now a few classmates started to wonder if that openness could also make her naive, or even gullible. A few people saw her getting into Derek's car one morning and decided to unfriend her on Facebook. Others emailed her quotes from Derek's radio show and warned her about enabling a charming white supremacist.

She was worried about the same things, so each time she began to feel closer to Derek, a series of familiar questions echoed in her head. What was she doing? Why, instead of confronting this infamous white nationalist and challenging his beliefs, was she making his campus life more pleasant and comfortable? Sometimes she would tell herself to back away, and she would decline one of Derek's invitations, only to then change her mind and join him on an adventure at the last minute. She liked him. She trusted him. She was attracted to him. She felt increasingly convinced that he was inherently different from the overt racists whose hateful messages she read on Stormfront. And yet she was in no way willing to let their relationship become romantic. That would be tantamount to aligning herself on campus with Derek and all he'd chosen to represent.

Derek was infatuated with Allison. She was intuitive and kind, and it seemed to Derek that she understood him, even if they had never talked about his family, his childhood, or his increasingly conflicted feelings about white nationalism. But Derek could also sense Allison's reluctance, so he kept his feelings quiet. He didn't want to push her away, so he contented himself with friendship and with conversations that ranged from whimsical to contemplative. They talked about internet penguin videos, their shared affinity for the Oxford comma, the discrepancies between American and British grammar, seventeenth-century monasteries, *Game of Thrones*, and theoretical destinations for future time travel. "Allison is one of the nicest people I know," Derek wrote to a friend late that spring. But the one subject they rarely talked about was Derek: His parents. His politics. His beliefs.

It was obvious to Allison that he didn't want to talk about white nationalism. He had yet to respond to more than two thousand posts about his views on the student forum, and he had successfully avoided the subject over the course of at least a dozen Shabbat dinners. Allison encouraged her roommate Matthew to talk directly to Derek about his beliefs. Matthew was the one person on campus who still knew more about Derek than she did; he also knew more than she did about U.S. history, religion, and anti-Semitism. Maybe Derek would listen to him, she suggested. But Matthew told her that his friendship with Derek was primary and also potentially transformative in and of itself. He wasn't willing to risk it on an intervention about Derek's beliefs.

Allison had always believed in drawing her friends out—in deepening trust and intimacy by discussing big issues rather than avoiding them—and her directness had made her a confidante to more than half a dozen classmates. "By let's

talk more, I usually mean I'm going to ask 6 million questions," she once explained in a message to a friend. "It's a way
to avoid talking about me. Ninety-five percent of the time
it's because finding out more about the other person is more
interesting to me than talking about myself." And now the
other person was Derek, whom she found more perplexing
than anyone she had ever met. "I need to talk to him about
his beliefs to see exactly where he stands," Allison wrote to
a friend, but she also worried the intensity of her curiosity
might scare Derek off, so she continued to wait until the
moment felt right.

Late one night, before they parted ways for summer
vacation, Allison led Derek up a maintenance ladder and
over a railing to the stucco roof of her dorm. It was one of
the quietest places on campus, a private platform amid palm
trees, with views on a clear night of Orion to the south and
Gemini above Sarasota Bay. Up here there was no chance of
interruption. Allison asked Derek if they could talk about
his beliefs.

Despite all of his lectures about verbal tactics and dis-
arming the liberal enemy, Derek had virtually no practice
talking about white nationalism with people who explicitly
disagreed with his ideology. "Why waste the time?" Don had
told him once. Instead, Don had taught him to spread their
ideas by recruiting whites who said things like "I'm not racist,
but . . ." Several years earlier, they had raised ten thousand
dollars on Stormfront to record CDs of white pride songs,
and they had distributed those CDs outside an Alan Jackson
concert at an amphitheater in South Florida. The audience
of twenty thousand was almost exclusively white, and the
parking lot was crowded with pickup trucks and Confederate flags. This was the audience Derek had always been after:

whites who naturally gravitated toward spending time with other whites and believed their values to be at the true core of America—people living out many of the tenets of white nationalism without even realizing it.

Derek knew Allison was not one of those people. She had written posts on the forum about the corrosive danger of male privilege and micro-aggressions. She valued diversity, and her friendships on campus reflected that. He dreaded the possibility of a confrontation with her, because already she was the one person on campus who made him feel vulnerable. She gently teased him about the black-brimmed cowboy hat he often wore, and Derek finally agreed to take it off for good. Once, when Allison offended Derek by saying he could sometimes be avoidant, he had let the slight pass without comment and then privately vowed not to speak to her for three weeks, which only proved her point. His way of dealing with tension was to avoid it, but now they were alone on a roof, and there was no place else to go. Maybe by talking to Allison and hearing her perspective on his views, he would learn more about how to better disarm the liberal enemy. He said she could ask whatever she liked.

So she began to unspool some of the questions that had been mounting in her head over the last months: about whether he believed in the Holocaust (yes, to some degree); and if he would be okay with having a mixed-race marriage (no); or biracial children (absolutely not). Already some of his positions had begun to soften since arriving at New College, and Allison felt reassured that Derek's views differed from some of the rhetoric she read on Stormfront. Derek didn't use any slurs, and he told Allison that he respected all people. In part because of his relationship with Matthew, Derek said that he had begun to like and accept Jews. He now considered them white, and he no longer understood why other white nationalists saw them as such a problem. He said he wasn't a white supremacist, because he no longer believed whites were necessarily better than other people. He was simply a white nationalist, which meant he thought whites needed to be protected within their own border, like an endangered species.

Derek told Allison that he still thought races had inherent biological traits. He mentioned his belief that whites had a slightly higher average IQ score than minorities and that blacks had higher levels of testosterone, which he thought led to a greater propensity for violence. He explained his fear of a white genocide and his belief that the death of a white, European culture would weaken the world. He had spent much of his life honing a rational case for white nationalism, and Allison thought he presented his arguments as mostly dispassionate and factual. He based his prejudice not on an intractable gut feeling but on what he thought to be a logical theory, and for Allison that realization brought a wave of relief and then a sense of possibility. Maybe she could show him the ways in which his theory was wrong. Maybe she could dismantle his logic, if only she had more information.

"What happened with Derek?" a friend wrote to her later, once she was back down from the roof.

"I talked to him about his less than ideal beliefs," Allison wrote back. "I'd like to be able to argue against them, and as of right now I can't do that effectively at all."

There was so much more she still needed to know, so she decided she would continue to talk with Derek about white nationalism sometimes. Their conversation on the roof had remained mostly civil and productive, largely because Allison also had the advantage of being white. Derek didn't feel implicitly challenged by her racial identity; Allison didn't feel personally threatened by his beliefs. Because she wasn't the one he hoped to oppress or deport, she could also engage with him in discussions that were less emotional than logical. She could present herself not as an enemy armed for battle but as a confused and curious friend who hoped to better understand Derek's racial conclusions. One night, she wrote to him again on Instant Messenger.

A: If you ever think I'm prying, you're always welcome to tell me to butt out. I won't take it personally.

D: Don't worry. I feel more comfortable burdening you with all this stuff than anybody else.

A: So if I were curious about details about what your opinions are/what you personally believe/etc. re: WN, could I organize my discombobulated (I love this word) thoughts and send you an email sometime? Or should I wait until we're on a rooftop or at sea or camping or some such?

D: I'm a little concerned I won't be able to stop feeling like I'm talking to a journalist. I'd prefer talking in person, but I dislike making everything something we'll do months from now at the red-letter date.

A: Ouch. Okay. I definitely wouldn't want you feeling that way.

D: The thing is that I've never talked in depth about my political stuff with anyone who I was close to who wasn't a WN. So my fallback is my experience explaining it to journalists.

A: We talked on the roof of Z Dorm about it. Or do you mean more in depth than that?

D: Yeah, I definitely mean plunging the depths of my

soul. It's such a conflict. On one hand I consider it just one of the things that I've done or been involved with, and on the other hand I consider it the one thing I'm involved with that has the most impact on the world.

A: That sounds like an issue of importance. Would you be okay with "plunging the depths" as you say?

D: I'd prefer not to see a psychologist named Dr. Allison ☺. But, yeah, we can talk about anything.

That summer unfolded in one long conversation: Allison back home in the exurbs of Cleveland, Derek perched under the umbrella tree outside his parents' house in West Palm Beach, each of them curled into a phone or hunched over a computer as they sometimes talked for six or seven hours in a single day. Allison usually called each morning during the bus ride to her internship working with families in crisis in downtown Cleveland. Derek usually called again before he and Don started their morning radio show and then continued to text from his cell phone during commercial breaks on the air. During the day, Derek worked on his New College senior thesis, retiled his parents' kitchen, and kayaked or bodysurfed in the ocean, but by 5:00 p.m. he was usually back at his computer, messaging Allison.

"Evening," he wrote.

"Hey you!" she responded.

Some nights they stayed on Instant Messenger until they went to bed, narrating their lives to each other through dinner and dessert, competing to see who could message the other one more, or stay up the latest, or be the last to say good-bye at the end of a chat. "We're approaching 9 hours," Derek wrote one night, as 1:00 a.m. turned to 2:00 a.m. and he continued to type away in the lofted water bed he had built for himself as a child. "We need an alternate dimension with 30 hour days," Allison suggested, because they still had so much more to say. They took internet quizzes to see who could identify more countries in Europe and then plotted itineraries for hypothetical trips to each country they didn't know. They sent each other links to old family photos and made diagrams of their family trees. Derek told her about his parents, describing his mother as impassioned and his father as rational and "all theory"—two people linked by a common philosophy that "keeping the house clean or getting upset about missed chores pales in comparison to changing the hearts and minds of the world."

Allison told Derek about her father, who had died suddenly from an allergic reaction to a bee sting when she was five. She sent Derek a link to her personal online journal of short stories, which she had never shared. "Very impressed," he told her, after reading one recent story. He sent her the link to a duet he had written and then recorded with his young niece. "Oh, Derek, this is awesome," she told him. She wrote that she missed the ocean, so he went to the beach and collected seashells and sand and mailed it to her in a care package. They spent dozens of hours plotting out weekend adventures for the next school year: river trips to sift for fossils, camping excursions to North Florida, road trips across North America, nights spent visiting random dive bars in St. Petersburg.

"I want to go on our adventures nownownow!" she wrote.

"I was just thinking the same thing today," Derek said. "Why are we separated?"

"Right!? I'm already getting claustrophobic in Ohio."

They were trying to make sense of each other, and as

the summer wore on, they used each online chat to examine their differences, searching out the possibility of common ground. Before they could debate about things like ideology or race, they had to agree on the merits of debate itself. One night, during an IM chat, Allison told Derek that she thought any worthwhile relationship depended on communication and compromise.

> D: I don't like the idea of compromise. I kind of prefer the battlefield "concession" terminology. You give ground 'cause you know the other person's idea is better or their will is stronger.
> A: No. I was talking about compromise.
> D: Compromise is just sad, like no one will be happy. You do it just to get through the situation. Conceding is like, "I surrender. You win!"
> A: Compromises are good things. It means you're listening to another person's viewpoint, taking it into account. Compromises can be happy!
> D: You only compromise if you want to maintain a relationship even though you think the other person is wrong.
> A: That is SO false. You're unwilling to compromise to see compromise as a not-terrible thing.

Even when Allison disagreed with Derek, he made her laugh. He made her think. She began referring to him as "mon ami," French for "my friend"; then sometimes as "sweet friend"; then as "sweet boy." It was so easy to be charmed by him—to feel, during those hours of conversation, as if they were the only two occupants of a fantasy dimension built from their own ideas and adventures—until inevitably each chat ended and she returned to her internship in Ohio with Derek still on her mind. She sometimes listened to his radio show; Derek, realizing as much, often called in sick to the show or dialed in and offered only filler while his father did most of the talking. Allison looked online for arguments against white nationalism and checked out books from the library on the history of racism in the United States. She read several IQ studies so she could pinpoint the scientific flaws in Derek's conclusions. She watched documentaries about the Klan and read through hundreds of messages on Storm-front. It was all so upsetting, so ugly and revolting, that some days it made her nauseated at her desk. In the chat rooms of Stormfront, Hitler was a misunderstood hero, Muslims were terrorists, and all racial minorities were subhuman species. Gays were degenerates, and women were possessions to be won. It made Allison furious with Derek for participating in a community with such reprehensible beliefs, even if he had stopped posting on the message board. She was angry with herself for associating with him. What was she doing? Whom, exactly, was she choosing to confide in? What kind of friendship was she trying to build? And her doubts would multiply until their next conversation, when she could disappear back into their happy, alternate dimension until inevitably the ugliness of white nationalism pushed its way in again.

Late in the summer, another news alert of a "Stormfront shooter" flashed across cable news. This time, the shooter's name was Wade Michael Page, forty. His target was a Sikh temple in Oak Creek, Wisconsin, on August 5, 2012. His motive was ethnic cleansing, six dead and four wounded in the name of white supremacy. For the last decade, he had been a registered user of Stormfront.

Stormfront's audience had grown over the years to

include at least half a dozen murderers—incidents Don referred to as "a series of very unfortunate coincidences." There was Richard Baumhammers, who searched for love on the Stormfront Singles dating page in 2000 before launching on a shooting spree that killed five. There was Richard Poplawski, who bragged on Stormfront about his "AK" under the user name "Braced for Fate" and then used that AK-47 to kill three Pittsburgh police officers in 2009. There was Luka Magnotta, a twenty-nine-year-old Canadian, who in May 2012 filmed his killing of a Chinese immigrant and then dismembered the body with an ice pick, mailing out limbs to politicians and elementary schools.

And now, just months later, there was Wade Michael Page. On a message board with more than seven million posts, he had posted only seven times, mostly to promote his white pride band, End Apathy. His left shoulder was tattooed with a Celtic cross, a white power symbol that Stormfront used as its logo. His body was also marked with a fourteen-word white supremacist motto that was no different from Don and Derek's own political motivation: "We must secure the existence of our people and a future for white children."

"These kind of things absolutely hurt us," Don said on the radio the next day, condemning the shooting on Derek's show. But then, instead of empathizing with the victims of that Sikh temple massacre—five men and one woman who had been preparing the temple's food for a Sunday service— Don and another co-host known as Truck Roy began to rationalize the shooter's motives.

"We think Sikhs belong back in Punjab, Mexicans back in Mexico," Don said. "All of these third-world immigrants belong back in their own countries instead of here."

"Take this Punjab region of India," Truck Roy said. "If

somebody was flooding that with tens of millions of non-Indians and overrunning their neighborhoods, I bet you'd have more than one Sikh that snapped every once in a while. The most logical explanation is you have a white genocide going on. You see our young white men, especially the ones that have nothing to lose, and they are sitting around watching their neighborhoods getting eaten up, watching white kids getting forced assimilated in their schools and workplaces, and eventually you are going to reach a breaking point. That's probably what happened here."

Derek didn't say anything on the radio that day, and Allison wasn't listening to the show. But somebody else at New College did hear the justifications made on behalf of the shooter on Derek's show, and that student sent a message to Allison, who later emailed Derek. "Hey, not my business and I'm sure you know this anyway, but be careful of things you say/how you say things," she wrote.

"To my recollection, I've said nothing about that guy," Derek responded. "Not to say I disagree with anything Roy or my dad said. I also sometimes wonder why you'd put up with being my friend when so many people at our tiny school think these things about me. With friends who don't seem affected by it, I just presume the benefits trump the negatives or that they're just impervious to self-righteous posturing by people who act out against me on campus."

She received his email at her internship in the early afternoon, and she spent a few hours reading more about the Sikh shooting and listening back over Derek's radio shows. She wanted to calm down before she responded to him, but no amount of time was making her feel any better. *He didn't disagree with anything Roy or Don said.* No matter Derek's sweetness—no matter how great their alternate dimension—

Allison now felt linked in a terrible chain of events: Another racist mass murderer had spent time on Stormfront, which was run out of Derek's house, where he was spending his nights chatting with her. She wrote back to him late that night:

> I'd say I fall into the first category that the benefits of our friendship trump the negatives. But I do take issue with this—"or that they're just impervious to self-righteous posturing." Maybe because I'm extremely tired, or maybe because I feel like our friendship is strong enough that I can call you out on things, but "self-righteous posturing"? C'mon. That's not fair at all.
>
> You've never clarified, Derek. You've never said "Hey all, this is what I do believe and this is what I don't." These other students have nothing to go on. What they *do* have to go on is your family, and Stormfront, and your radio show.
>
> Point is, these NCF kids can do their research and make their conclusions and that's all they can do, because *you haven't given them anything else to go on.* The impetus is not on them to approach you. It is not the job of someone who's potentially scared/intimidated by someone else to approach that person to see if they are in fact scary/intimidating.
>
> As it is, I'm pretty close to you, and I have a million questions.

"You're naturally right that I deemphasize my own role," Derek wrote back. And if Allison wanted to keep asking him more questions about white nationalism, he had already begun thinking about the best way to provide her with answers. His second annual Stormfront tactical conference was coming up in a few weeks, back in the woods of eastern Tennessee. Derek would be leading one of the seminars. So would Don, David Duke, and a dozen other white nationalist leaders. If there was one place where an outsider could come to understand the pull of white nationalism in Derek's life, maybe it was among his family and his allies at the conference he'd created.

A few weeks after they returned to school for fall semester, Derek sent a copy of the conference invitation to Allison.

"I think you should come," he told her.

7.   "This Is Scary"

The invitation to the Stormfront conference promised a secretive gathering with "no disruptions and no outsiders," and to ensure that level of security, Don decided to change the location of the conference a few days before it was set to begin. He moved the event out of the whitewashed town of Gatlinburg, Tennessee, and into the surrounding Smoky Mountains—up several miles of winding mountain highway, down an unsigned dirt road, past a gate, and into a retreat of log cabins obscured by a forest of yellow birch trees. *USA Today* had recently published a front-page story about the upcoming conference, and Don hoped to avoid the disruption of would-be protesters or spies from the SPLC. "Nobody will find us way out there," Don said on the radio, a few days before the event. "We can recharge among our own people. Even the air is still pure and clean in this one little corner of the country." He opened registration to 150 attendees, most of whom were committed Stormfront members who would wear name tags displaying their Stormfront IDs. Security guards would stand at the main gate. Volunteers would monitor the incoming roads. "It's just going to be the true, die-hard white activists," Don said. "The people coming are the ones we know and trust."

And now there was the possibility of one more. Derek called Don a few days before the conference and mentioned that he might invite a classmate, leaving out any other details. Then he followed up with Allison and urged her to come.

The two of them had begun arguing about white nationalism with increasing frequency during the first weeks of the semester, and Allison still felt unsure about exactly what Derek believed. His prejudices could be difficult to pin down. She sent him articles about the corrosive effects of white privilege, and he wrote back saying only that "overt prejudice can be really bad." She sent research showing racists were usually also sexists. He said, "I respect women and have tried to push for their equality." Allison thought Derek was being dishonest about his beliefs, watering down the true extent of his racism in order to preserve their friendship. He had been socialized on Stormfront, but he didn't sound like most Stormfront users, and for that reason alone Allison was tempted to go with him to the conference. She wanted to see if he offered the same dispassionate arguments to an audience of skinheads and neo-Nazis that he articulated to her when they were alone on the roof of their dorm. Only then could she know for sure if he was telling her the truth about his views, and only once she knew his actual views could she possibly begin to dismantle them. She researched more about the upcoming conference and then wrote to Derek one night on Instant Messenger.

"This is scary," she said.

"I think you can handle yourself," Derek wrote back. "Theoretically, if you could handle attending something like my family reunion, then this would be easy enough. Lots of people from all over who know me from various times and adults I've known since I was little. Just a family reunion where people have also come to hear speeches."

"This is going to be an exercise in self-composure and calm when really I'm just freaking out," Allison told him.

The more she read about the conference, the more hesitant

she became to go with him. The 2012 presidential election was two months away, and racial hate crimes in the United States had ticked back up to the historic levels of 2008. In the Republican Party, the 2012 primary had become a race to the far conservative right on immigration issues, with one candidate after the next proposing ideas that were once popular only on forums like Stormfront. Rick Santorum tried to please Tea Party activists by saying he wanted to make English the country's official language, mandatory for all residents. Herman Cain suggested building an electrified border fence, twenty feet high and coiled in barbed wire, with enough voltage to kill a human being. Michele Bachmann said she could do one better by building a "secure double fence" along every foot of the border. Even Mitt Romney, the party's eventual nominee, had moved away from his centrist roots and suggested an immigration policy of "self-deportation." His idea was essentially that lawmakers could make life in America so difficult for immigrants—by withdrawing government assistance, eliminating their jobs, and increasing police patrols in minority neighborhoods—that they would become miserable and choose to leave on their own.

In 2012 the Republican Party had essentially decided to forfeit the minority vote. It had chosen, as Derek once predicted, to become an overwhelmingly white party, and now the decisive question of the election was whether enough white voters remained. The white share of the electorate, which was 87 percent in 1992, had dropped down to just over 70 percent. "We will see if white people begin sticking together now like a typical minority bloc," Don said on the radio a few weeks before the conference began.

The political climate in the run-up to the election had turned the small Stormfront gathering into a major national story. *USA Today* wrote that the conference reflected another "resurgence in right-wing extremism." Louisville's *Courier-Journal* reported that conference goers would include neo-Nazis, skinheads, Klansmen, and Christian identitarians who believed God favored whites. Maybe Derek considered the event no different from a family reunion, but to Allison it sounded nothing like her own large family gathering from earlier in the summer, which she had described to Derek during one of their online chats: a dozen cousins playing a card game called euchre at a park alongside the Rocky River in Cleveland, competing for prizes in a water balloon toss, and setting up a tripod to take a chaotic family picture with children and dogs under the picnic shelter. "We put the fun in dysfunctional," Allison had written then.

But Derek's idea of a family reunion seemed so much more dysfunctional. Allison wanted to quiet her anxiety enough to make a logical decision, so she began writing out a list of reasons to go. She trusted Derek enough to believe he wouldn't put her at risk. Because she was white, she could blend in without fearing for her own safety. Most of all, she thought the best way to make an effective argument against Derek's beliefs was to first make a legitimate effort to fully understand them. Only that way could she earn his complete trust. Only then could she build a case against white nationalism using not just her values but also his values and his vocabulary. By going to the conference, she would earn her way into those conversations. Maybe one of those conversations would trigger a shift.

She decided to approach the conference with the meticulousness of a research project, so late one night she began peppering Derek with questions during an online chat. "Is your mother going?" she asked. "What do I wear?" "What's the agenda for the day?" "Are there assigned seats?" "What happens after dinner?" Allison decided she would tell her mother and her close friend Bennet she was going to the conference—"so somebody knows where I am, just in case," she explained. But she would give everyone else an alibi for the weekend about visiting an old friend in Jacksonville, Florida. Together Derek and Allison came up with an alias for her conference name tag, Alice Bailey. "A pseudonym. Weird, weird, weird," Allison wrote, as they continued sorting out details, until 3:00 a.m. turned to 4:00, and finally they arrived at the questions Allison feared most of all.

What should she tell people when they asked if she was a white nationalist? And how would she explain her relationship to Derek, which they were still figuring out themselves?

A few weeks earlier, Derek had finally summoned the courage to ask Allison out. He didn't want to pressure her in any way, so rather than asking in person, he had sent her a formal-sounding text message: "Allison, would you like to go out with me, or is that something I shouldn't think about?" And ever since then, she had been trying to decide exactly how she felt about him. She respected him. She enjoyed him. She cared about him. "It has very much crossed my mind, too. I won't deny it," she wrote back to him. But she also didn't want to tag herself in pictures with him on Facebook or be seen walking across campus holding his hand. As much as she hated to admit it, she cared about what her classmates on campus would think, and some of them would think she had lost her mind. She still had doubts about whether she had made the moral choice in befriending him. In no way was she ready to publicly date. She rejected his offer as kindly and as honestly as she could. "Things are nice now," she had written to him. "Can't we just let it be nice?" Derek had quickly agreed: "If it's not natural and comfortable, it's not right. But, in any case, I'm glad I asked and continued my personal record of sharing with you the important things that cross my mind."

Now, over Instant Messenger, Allison suggested posing at the conference as Derek's "curious friend."

> D: Curious will lead into "What do you think of all of this?"
>
> A: "Thanks for asking. I'm processing. So, where are you from?"
>
> D: That seems effective. Don't talk about controversial things unless you want to raise tension.
>
> A: "TELL ME YOUR BELIEFS. TELL THEM TO ME."
>
> D: Yeah. That would be weird.

They decided that Derek would drive and she would stay with him and his parents at their rental cabin. She would sleep in a bedroom, and he would take the couch. They would stay for two nights and then drive back to New College. "You are absolutely going into my territory," Derek wrote to her, but even if she was attending the conference as an outsider, in so many ways she and Derek had already become co-conspirators.

"I'll likely be ready to burst with the amount of questions I have," she wrote to him. "I will keep my freak outs to zero until we're alone, in which case you might have to deal."

Don and Chloe started traveling north toward the conference in a separate car, driving up the Florida coast until they crossed into Georgia. The trip required thirteen hours in the late-summer heat with a tired air conditioner, but Don still looked forward to the drive. He had traveled to more than 130 white power conferences since he first drove to Arlington, Virginia, as a sixteen-year-old with David Duke and Joseph Paul Franklin in the late 1960s. Over the ensuing decades, racial conferences had become the epicenter of his personal and professional life, providing him with vacations, intellectual nourishment, and his only time with many of his closest friends. Most conferences lasted for one or two days, but Don tended to stretch his trips out over several weeks, grateful for the excuse to leave South Florida. He no longer needed a map to navigate his way around much of the Deep South. He could follow roads from memory as he let his mind wander. Each highway rest stop reminded him of another old story, and lately so many of those stories revolved around Derek. About halfway to Tennessee, Don pulled over and called in to their radio show to reminisce. "Back on the road," Don said. "It's a good time to reflect, to think things over. I remember when Derek started going along with me to these conferences when he was nine years old. Together we did a lot of driving."

At first Don had thought of those joint trips mostly as required babysitting. They had pulled Derek out of the diversifying public schools, which meant he was home all day under Don's care. Chloe needed to work at the sugar company. If Don wanted to leave town, the only solution was to take his son along with him. There were usually a few other children at the conferences, and most kids played with Game Boys in the back of the conference room or stayed at the motel swimming pool. But Derek liked listening to the speakers, and he recognized many of their names from his father's stories. He asked Don questions about their choices of language and their ideas, and he stayed at Don's side each day when the conference migrated from the meeting room to the lobby bar. Derek sat with the adults, quietly sipping his lemonade as they downed pitchers of beer. He gravitated to the speakers with the best academic credentials, like Canadian psychologist Philippe Rushton or California State professor Kevin MacDonald, and Derek accepted as fact their theories about whites having larger brains than blacks and Jews possessing a unique psychology that allowed them to manipulate other groups.

But what Derek learned about most on those trips was his father—a man in many ways different from the solitary person Derek knew so well in South Florida. At home, Don was often tired, burned-out, pessimistic about the movement, and burdened by the daily logistics of Stormfront. For his own mental health, he forced himself to walk away from the computer each afternoon for twenty minutes and sit outside in the yard, where he could close his eyes in a chair facing into the sun. But at conferences Don was energized and popular—a white nationalist icon equally capable of debating eugenics and skull sizes with racial academics and trading war stories with militant skinheads. He brewed his own beer and drove the after party late into the night. Among white nationalists, Don was revered for his loyalty and generosity. He had once put his family home up as collateral to pay the jail bond for a young skinhead. Another time, he allowed an itinerant Stormfront chat room moderator to park his trailer in the family driveway and live on their property for two years. "There's nothing to recharge your batteries like joining arm in arm with your allies," Don said. "That's where I get my energy. That's where I get my best ideas. I'm always happiest when I'm surrounded by people who fought alongside me in the bunker."

Derek had climbed right into the bunker with him, aligning himself as his father's greatest ally. Both of Derek's half sisters had rebelled in their teens—one running away for a brief time, the other shaving her head and joining a group of skinheads out west—but the only time Derek ever acted out was when Don threatened to go to a conference without him. For more than a decade, Derek rode along with Don to two or three conferences each year, driving thousands of miles across the South. They became fixtures at the Council of Conservative Citizens Conference in Nashville and at American Renaissance in Louisville, the most academic conference and also Derek's favorite, where racial scientists talked about genetic destiny and the possibilities of forced sterilization for minority women. They stopped during their road trips to stay with Don's best friends—"an extended family of comrades," Don called them—and they adopted Derek, too. He learned how to catch fireflies at the Mississippi trailer of Joe Daniel Hawkins, who had plotted with Don to overthrow Dominica. He had one of his first crushes while staying for a few weeks at a KKK compound in rural Arkansas. He went to see the movie *Sleepy Hollow* at a theater in Washington with an undercover FBI informant named Todd Blodgett, who had infiltrated the higher ranks of the white supremacy movement and then taken a liking to Derek. "An exceptionally bright kid being brainwashed into the realm of racist hatred," Blodgett said of Derek then, so Blodgett made it a part of his job to occasionally take Derek away from conferences for short outings, hoping to give the boy's mind a break.

After only a few years on the road, Derek was as well

known among white nationalists as his father. Red Dog, many white nationalists called him, and together they watched him grow up. There was Derek at nine, posing for a photo with then Mississippi governor Kirk Fordice at the Council of Conservative Citizens Conference, looking at the camera not with a child's smile but with a resolute stare. There he was at sixteen, seated behind his first radio mixer board, broadcasting speeches live on his internet radio show. There he was at twenty, an elected politician, playing guitar onstage in an attempt to cheer up a conference crowd after Obama's election, performing a cover song from 1972 called "The Monkey That Became President."

After a decade of conferences, Don had come to trust Derek more than anyone else in his bunker. For years he had kept the Stormfront administrative passwords to himself, not wanting to write them down for fear that someone might use the passwords to dismantle the website, but eventually he chose to share them with Derek. Don thought of his son as a partner and eventual successor. Even if they rarely talked about it directly, Don always assumed Derek would eventually take over Stormfront and build out the brand—adding more video components to the website and more original reporting, increasing the site's fund-raising, expanding the business into politics and social media and conferences, just as he was beginning to do now.

"The Second Annual Derek Black Conference," Don said on the radio, just hours before he and Chloe arrived in Tennessee. They pulled up to a rental cabin with a stone fireplace and a view of the mountains and waited for Derek to arrive.

•

Allison had prepared herself for skepticism, but instead, when they arrived at the cabin, Derek's family was already lining up to greet her with hugs on the front porch. Chloe carried out a tray of grapes, Derek's favorite fruit. His young niece jumped up onto Derek's shoulders, and he carried her around, pretending to be a dinosaur. One of Derek's older half sisters pulled Allison aside to brag about Derek's leadership ambitions and his white nationalist pedigree, assuming that would impress Allison. Only Don remained the slightest bit wary. "So, what do you think about all of this?" he remembered asking Allison that night. But when she gave her practiced response—"just curious," she said—he was kind enough not to press her.

Their cabin was enormous, with a hot tub on the deck and floor-to-ceiling windows in the living room, and before long their greeting party had expanded to nearly a dozen relatives and friends who had traveled to Tennessee for the next day's conference. They played pool in the living room and drank beer on the porch. As the night wore on, Derek pulled Allison aside to tell her more about each guest—one of whom was a white nationalist donor who had written Derek into his will, another who had babysat for him as a boy, another who had donated to his first political campaign. "I forgot you were famous," Allison told him, and now some of that glow extended onto her. Derek's family worked to make her feel comfortable and asked thoughtful questions about her studies. Where she had expected to find only bigotry and nastiness, she also recognized something else.

"These people genuinely love and adore you," she wrote to Derek later.

Most of them assumed Allison also identified as a white nationalist, because why else would she be there with them in the woods of Tennessee? She sat next to a few of Derek's relatives that night as they sorted name tags for the conference and talked over their usual gripes: the "brown people" and their high birthrates; Obama's radical, antiwhite policies; the Jewish insistence on media control and political correctness. "Interesting. Very interesting," was about all Allison said in response. Everything about the conversation disgusted her, but what good would it do to speak out? She was alone in the woods of Tennessee, and she wasn't going to persuade dozens of the country's preeminent white nationalists to change their beliefs. But she did hope to influence Derek, if only she could continue to earn his trust. She had promised him that she wouldn't have a panic attack or cause a scene with his family, so she continued to smile politely as the night wore on. She tried to imagine herself as a duck, placid and unruffled on the surface, even as her legs churned frantically beneath the water. "She was very pleasant," Don later remembered of that night. "There was nothing about her that was outwardly hostile, but I could also tell that she wasn't exactly one of us. She was very difficult to read."

At the conference the next morning, she wore a sundress and her "Alice Bailey" name tag and found a seat next to Derek in the middle of the room. One attendee was taking photographs of the event, and Allison made sure to stay away from the camera so her picture wouldn't end up on Stormfront. She carried a notebook as she listened to all seven speeches, looking down as often as she could, writing questions she hoped to ask Derek later. What was with all the Holocaust denial and the Germany worship? Why so much militant terminology? Why was everyone so obsessed with Jews? And didn't Derek notice all the condescending code words for minorities that littered every talk, like "their kind," "others," "insurgents," "third-worlders," "infiltrators," and "enemies"? She listened to Don speak about "securing a future for the conquering white race" and heard Duke talk about the treasonous ills of interracial dating, which he said would only accelerate white genocide. The speakers took turns insulting Jews, Hispanics, blacks, and immigrants, often to rousing applause, but what Allison dreaded more than the presentations were the casual coffee breaks that came in between. Standing alongside Derek meant she had no place to hide. It seemed as if all 150 people at the conference wanted to speak with them about race and white genocide, and after a while she began excusing herself to the bathroom, waiting until she was alone and then locking the door. "Breathe. Breathe," she coached herself, as she swallowed the urge to scream. She turned on the sink to drown out the noise of the conference and ran cold water over her hands, washing them over and over until finally she felt calm, clean.

Derek's speech came last, and he pushed back the podium and sat down in a chair close to the audience next to his friend and radio co-host, Truck Roy.

It was the first time Derek had ever felt dread before giving a speech. After months of conversations with Allison, he was slowly becoming less secure in his beliefs. Whereas before he had catered his message exclusively to white nationalists, he now was at least aware of another perspective. Each time he caught a glimpse of Allison in the audience, it was a reminder of everything she had told him: His words could often hurt, alienate, and oppress. Derek said nothing about minorities or enemies during his speech but instead focused on the demographic decline of whites in America. "The primary issue is conveying the moral rightness of our opposition to genocide," Derek told the crowd.

He instructed the audience on how to use wordplay to take the offensive in conversations with what he called "anti-whites," and Allison took notes in case he was practicing for an argument he planned to have with her. She thought Derek sounded much the same to her at the conference as he did when he was talking about white nationalism on the roof of the dorm. He said white nationalists were the "true multiculturalists," because they were trying to protect the white race from extinction. Anyone who opposed that cause was in fact advocating for a kind of mass murder, he said. Therefore, if anyone could be accurately described as evil or racist, it was not white nationalists but "anti-whites" who essentially supported genocide.

Allison thought his speech was absurd and upsetting. She also thought it was consistent with what Derek had been telling her in private during the last several weeks. She now felt reassured that he had been honest with her about his views, and also that those views differed from the majority of people on Stormfront. But Allison also listened to his talk and made note of all the fundamental ways in which they disagreed. She had grown up with the understanding that a privileged group of white people essentially ran the world; Derek thought the white race was facing imminent decline and singular racial persecution. She believed minorities had a harder time in the United States because they were victims of structural racism and oppression; he believed people of color were more likely to struggle because of their own biological deficiencies. She thought greater diversity made for stronger communities; he found diversity so threatening that, at least theoretically, he wanted to separate people by skin color onto different continents, even if that meant disrupting millions of lives.

Derek's talk ended with a long ovation, and then Don offered a toast to what he called "the next generation." Allison listened as the applause built around her and wondered, even if she could somehow convince Derek of the flaws in his ideology, how could she ever compel him to give up all of this? His parents were glowing. A line of admirers had begun to form near his chair, a dozen people waiting to compliment Derek on his talk. "They really loved and cared about him," Allison said. "Derek was so much more at the center of everything than I'd realized."

There was another event planned for the next day, a nature walk led by Duke in the Smoky Mountains, but Allison was ready to get home. She and Derek started driving early in the morning, and she turned up the radio and rolled down her window for a blast of mountain air until finally she experienced something like relief. She told Derek that a conversation about her questions and impressions could wait for another few days. "I just wanted to get someplace far away and feel more normal," she remembered thinking. They stopped on the way home to visit Allison's aunt, and then fifteen hours later Derek dropped her back off at her dorm. The space looked delightfully mundane, and Allison felt so at home back with all of her roommates: one Jewish, one gay, one headed off to work for the Peace Corps in Africa. Matthew asked about her weekend visiting friends in Jacksonville, and Allison told him it had all been great. Then she went to her room and tossed her Stormfront name tag into a pile on her desk, eager to be free from it.

A few days later, Matthew was talking to Allison in her room when he spotted a small name tag on top of a pile of papers. "STORMFRONT," it read, and beneath that logo was a name Matthew at least partially recognized: Alice Bailey. He asked Allison about it, and she began to confess about her trip to the conference, telling him about staying with Derek's family and listening to Duke's anti-Semitic talk.

"A research trip," she called it, but Matthew was confused and then upset that Allison had lied to him. What more could she possibly need to know about Derek and his beliefs? What was so ambiguous about white supremacy, bigotry, and oppression? Matthew had always trusted Allison's instincts, but he thought her trip to Tennessee was reckless. It was one thing to reach out to Derek from the safety of campus in a gesture of inclusiveness; it was much more risky to turn herself into the outsider by traveling into Derek's community. What if an undercover FBI informant had been at the conference taking photos of attendees? What if the government now thought Allison was a potential white nationalist recruit? Matthew had studied demagogues like Hitler and Duke enough to know they could be charming and convincing, and he warned Allison to be careful. She told him not to worry, that she could take care of herself. "I didn't necessarily think she was going to the dark side, but it was the first time we weren't on the same page," Matthew said. "There was a little distance there. It was hard to tell exactly where she stood."

But this second Stormfront conference did reaffirm for Matthew exactly where Derek stood: at the forefront of the white nationalist movement, right where he had been a year before, when he first started coming to Shabbat dinners. Matthew and his close friend, Moshe, logged on to Stormfront together to read about the conference, hoping to find some hint that maybe Derek's views were beginning to change.

Instead they read about how Derek had spoken again about his belief that whites were the true victims of racial genocide. They saw pictures of Derek posing arm in arm with Duke, offering him another conference podium from which he could spread his racial bigotry and Holocaust denial.

For Matthew, who had come to Judaism through the Kabbalah Centre, the new evidence was a frustrating setback. "New year, same Nazi-esque speeches," he said. But for Moshe, Derek's zeal was beginning to feel like a personal affront. Moshe's identity was built on the very history that white nationalists were trying to erase.

His grandfather Chaim Grosz had been born in Hungary in January 1944, the last of nine Jewish siblings in a family of prominent rabbis. The Nazis had invaded Hungary a few months later, and Chaim had become a prisoner of war before he could crawl, detained in the city of Debrecen along with his mother and many of his siblings. Most of Hungary's 800,000 Jews were sent directly to Auschwitz: forty-five jam-packed cattle cars on each train, another train departing every five hours, each day an estimated 10,000 Hungarian Jews dropped off inside the gatehouse and marched directly to the gas chambers. More than three-quarters of Hungarian Jews were killed that year, accounting for about one out of every six Holocaust deaths. And then there were the lucky ones, like Chaim, a baby who for whatever reason ended up on a train with his mother and seven of his siblings bound not for Auschwitz but for Bergen-Belsen, a camp of about 120,000 prisoners in northern Germany. Their train trip lasted five days in an overcrowded car with no windows, no ventilation, no food, and no water, and about a third of the passengers died along the way. The rest arrived at Bergen-Belsen, a work camp where there were no gas chambers but where Nazi guards kept prisoners in fear for their lives by instituting a policy of random hangings and shootings. Chaim and his seven siblings were assigned to share two lice-infested bunks and four slices of bread per day. The camp had minimal food rations, limited freshwater, no medical supplies, and narrow, three-story bunkhouses where the only life-form that managed to thrive was infectious disease.

Tuberculosis, typhoid fever, typhus, and dysentery killed more than thirty-five thousand prisoners in the first few months of 1945, and somehow Chaim was not among them. He was not one of the several hundred prisoners who starved to death each week in the bunkhouse. He was not one of the thirteen thousand corpses lying unburied on the ground when the camp was liberated a few months later. He was not among the twelve thousand or so prisoners who died after liberation, still too sick or too starving to recover. Instead he was one of about fifty thousand Bergen-Belsen survivors—malnourished, underweight, displaced, developmentally stunted, but still somehow alive at the end of his first year. *Our Miraculous Survival*, was how Chaim's older brother described it years later, in the title of a self-published book about their experience.

From Bergen-Belsen, Chaim was sent with his mother and siblings to a refugee camp in Italy and then on to begin his childhood in New York, where he became a U.S. citizen and then a rabbi at age eighteen. He was angry with God and conflicted about religion, but he wanted to respect his family's rabbinical tradition. He started a printing business with his brothers, married, and then had his first child, Moshe's mother. They moved to Miami, where eventually Moshe was born and where on many Friday nights the extended family gathered at Chaim's house in Miami Beach to welcome in Shabbat.

Much of Moshe's childhood had been built on honoring his family history—on identifying both religiously and culturally as devoutly Jewish. His mother spoke Yiddish before she spoke English, and she taught Moshe the correct, Orthodox way to cut his nails and tie his shoes. He attended Hebrew school, ate at kosher restaurants, and lived in a neighborhood of Eastern European Jews who shared his family's sense of oppression and displacement. Moshe saw Chaim every week, and they talked about almost everything except the Holocaust. Chaim didn't remember much about it, nor did he want to. Many of his cousins had died at Auschwitz. He never traveled back to Europe, and he avoided buying any products made in Germany. The malnourishment that began in his first year led to health problems for much of his life, until he died at sixty-nine. "Mostly because of my grandfather, the Holocaust was at the root of lots of things in our family, but it was also taboo," Moshe said, and so of course he had become fascinated by it.

He taught himself German in high school, researched the Holocaust, and slogged through Hitler's *Mein Kampf.* When he was seventeen, he traveled with his brother to Bergen-Belsen, stopping at Anne Frank's gravestone and then walking down the camp road into the memorial, where he could see the sandstone foundation of the old barracks and the burial mounds pushing up against the dirt, each one adorned with a sign that read, "One thousand buried here." He looked at the camp's alphabetized roster of prisoners, flipping through until he saw his grandfather's name, but even more sobering for Moshe was the list of names that followed. There were more than fifty people on the roster with the last name Grosz, some listed as victims and others as survivors, an extended family tree that went on for page after page.

Moshe returned to Miami and watched documentaries about modern-day anti-Semitism, learning about Stormfront, Don Black, and David Duke. Moshe read Duke's autobiography, which contained passages about Duke's own visits to concentration camps, which Duke considered mostly a hoax. Duke said gas chambers in the camps were designed only to disinfect clothing so that Jews would not get lice. He said Holocaust survivors were evidence that the Holocaust hadn't really been so bad. He said the Holocaust was mostly just "a device used as the pillar of Zionist aggression, Zionist terror and Zionist murder." He said Hitler was a great leader and Nazi Germany was in many ways the ideal country. "They had a greater sense of gaiety, national purpose, unity and true brotherhood among their people probably than any nation's ever had," Duke wrote.

And then Moshe brought all of that knowledge with him to New College, where Duke's godson happened to be in his first banking class, and instead of confronting him or dropping the class, Moshe had somehow found it in himself to befriend Derek, to invite him over for beers, to join him at Shabbat dinners, and to sometimes speak with him in the German they had both decided to learn because of their divergent family legacies. A full year now. That was how long they had been sitting together around the table on Friday nights. That was how long Moshe had been buying Derek's salmon, pouring his kosher wine, hoping for some kind of a transformation, believing again and again in the essential goodness of humanity. The backlash caused by his friendship with Derek had made aspects of his campus life miserable. At the beginning of one year, Moshe had offered to live with Derek, and even though Derek had opted to stay off campus, Moshe had been unable to fill that empty room. "People associated me with Derek or saw me getting in and out of his car, and that made me hugely unpopular," Moshe said. One student wellness survey suggested "expelling Derek Black and Moshe Ash" as a way to improve the New College community. And so Moshe wondered, all of that sacrifice, and for what? So Derek could talk with them about music, or religion, or contra dancing at Shabbat dinner and then go back to Tennessee for the weekend and speak to another audience of neo-Nazis and anti-Semites?

Matthew and Moshe had sometimes relieved their frustration by sharing inside jokes about Derek. They signaled to each other with Sieg Heils when Derek left the room, or they talked about how Derek was just another college student who liked 4/20, because the marijuana holiday was also Hitler's birthday. Moshe had mailed postcards from his travels around Asia to Derek's home address in West Palm Beach, delighting at the thought of Don Black going to his mailbox and pulling out a photo of a beautiful brown woman. "At first, spending time with Derek could be this thrilling, scary adventure," Moshe said. But now he thought the jokes were getting tired as the reality of Derek's ideology held strong. On some Friday nights, what Moshe really wanted to do was stay home. "He's still basically a Nazi after all this time," Moshe told Matthew once.

For so long, Moshe had worked to remind himself of all the reasons why Derek could still change. He was smart and self-directed. He was kind. On a campus that was 85 percent white, he had forged a diverse group of friends. Moshe understood how hard it could be to break away from the past. He had begun having his own intellectual doubts about Orthodox Judaism early in his teens as he began to learn more about science and theories of evolution, and yet it had taken him several more years to move away from the religion that shaped so much of his identity, his community, and his family. "The hardest thing I've done," he said, and the memory of that transition gave him empathy for Derek.

But now Derek was almost twenty-three, an adult who had been living apart from his parents for a few years, and he was still just as devoted to spreading their ideology. Moshe worried: What if all he had done by befriending Derek was to enable him, to provide him with cover from the social justice activists on campus so that he could continue to promote a racist ideology while living a comfortable college life? What incentive did Derek have to change? He had a standing invitation for Friday nights. He had a group of friends who would sit with him in the cafeteria. And now he had a new friend, Allison, who was willing to go with him from their liberal college to a white nationalist conference in Tennessee.

Maybe she was on her way to becoming a white nationalist, too, Moshe sometimes thought. Maybe, all this time, it was actually Derek who had been doing the persuading.

8. "Another Debate, and Another Midnight"

Allison had spent much of her childhood learning how to debate, usually against her mother. Julie Gornik did not believe in instituting rules just for the sake of rules—in what she called "because-I-say-so parenting." Other parents in suburban Ohio built a path for their children walled by incentives and punishments, directing them to adulthood by paying them as a reward for good grades and grounding them for missing curfew. Julie wanted to give Allison freedom to think critically and advocate for her beliefs. Rules about bedtime, computer limits, and curfew were all up for rational debate. Julie thought the most salient argument should always win, even if that argument sometimes came from her young daughter. Once, in high school, Allison said she wanted to stay home from school because she felt stressed and tired. Julie told her no; Allison had no fever and no obvious symptoms. So Allison argued her case in a long, handwritten letter, citing her stellar GPA, her perfect attendance record, and all the reasons why this day in particular was one she could miss without repercussion. She wrote about the importance of physical *and* mental health and the correlation between rest and peak performance. Julie read over her daughter's letter, followed her logic, and then conceded that Allison could take a day off on rare occasions when she needed it. "Respectful but also relentless," was how Julie described Allison's debate strategy, and in that way she had gone about dismantling the rules of her child-hood, one cogent argument at a time.

Now Allison felt more prepared than ever to begin debating Derek in earnest. After her trip to the Stormfront conference, she was confident she understood his beliefs. She cared about him enough to invest herself. In their discussions so far, Derek had justified his ideology not with emotional arguments but with science and theory. What she still needed was more scientific counterevidence on which to build her case, and luckily during that fall semester of 2012 she was enrolled in a New College course called Stigma and Prejudice. "How do we assess the accuracy of stereotypes?" the syllabus read. "How can stereotypes be changed? Although many of us feel strongly about these issues, this is not a course for promoting our personal ideologies. This is a course for gaining science-based insight on the processes and implications of stereotyping, prejudice and discrimination."

The professor was in her first semester at New College, but she had taught the course at other universities for the last several years. As part of her introduction each semester, she sometimes showed a 2000 HBO documentary called *Hate.Com*, about the rise of bigotry on the internet. One of the first faces to appear on-screen was Don Black, described by the narrator as "the godfather of hate on the net." Next came his eleven-year-old son, Derek, sitting down for an interview in a baseball cap adorned with the Confederate flag, explaining that "nonwhites do not have the same values, ideals, and beliefs that I have."

This time, the professor began showing the documentary to Allison's class but then stopped it after only a few minutes, before Don or Derek appeared on the screen. It

seemed to the professor that many of the New College students in her class had already seen *Hate.Com,* and later one
of them pulled the professor aside and explained that Derek
attended their school and that *Hate.Com* had been posted
on the student forum. The professor had always tried to
connect her course to current events, but never before had
her syllabus been put to such practical use. Each Monday
and Thursday, there was Allison returning to her seat in the
semicircle with sixteen other students, taking notes about
their discussions on psychological science to arm herself for
the next conversation with Derek.

The two of them had been spending even more time
together since their trip to the Stormfront conference. Derek
was still living in his landlord Maynard's house a few miles
from campus, but he was often at the dorm with Allison.
They played chess, watched *Game of Thrones,* and did homework side by side at a Sarasota coffee shop. Derek, who typically liked having space to himself, rarely tired of being with
Allison. "I'm fine with a couple close friends even if the world
is collapsing," he wrote to her. "But it's not that way when
I'm spending time with you." The same was true for Allison.
"I'm my best self with you," she told him, and in her experience that wasn't always the case. With one former boyfriend,
Allison had sometimes felt as if parts of her were being sub-
sumed into the relationship—her individual friendships, her
autonomy, and bits of her confidence gradually swallowed
up by the codependency of coupledom. Derek, meanwhile,
encouraged her to do whatever she felt like doing most,
whether that meant going dancing with friends or playing
intramural soccer. He brought her food late at night while
she worked on school papers and then left her alone to finish

her work. Spending time with Derek never felt to Allison like an obligation. It was always the choice she wanted to make.

The more time she spent with Derek, the more convinced she became that a full transformation was possible. She also believed Derek's identity was far from fixed. In her course work, Allison had learned about a stage of cognitive development called emerging adulthood, a phase that ranges from about age eighteen to twenty-five. Psychologists believe those years mark a time of transition away from parents and toward greater independence. In studies, emerging adults demonstrate higher cognitive flexibility and more openness to new ideas. If Derek was ever going to reconsider his worldview, Allison thought, the most likely time for that transformation was now.

Every few days, Allison worked to inject white nationalism into their conversations. But Derek dreaded interpersonal conflict, and at first he preferred to talk about his ideology with Allison mostly online, where even a heated argument could feel somehow remote and dispassionate. One night, while they chatted on Instant Messenger, he began to explain his fears about how immigration could lead to white extinction.

D: Only white countries have this prospect of not existing.

A: But if they're functioning the same or better . . . what does it matter what you look like?

D: There will still be plenty of majority black countries in the world. China will continue its tradition of being Chinese. I see no evidence that bringing in massive immigration will make the West function better.

A: I feel like you sometimes cross that line into

playing the victim in representing/discussing white people, like they're so damaged/oppressed/in need of protecting.

D: They/we shouldn't be minorities. This stuff about oppression is your word. What world do you think will exist in 200 years? Whites will be minorities, but what else will be different?

A: Hopefully the world will have progressed, will have developed, will be more accepting of differences and be much more of a global community.

D: Why will that have happened?

A: Because people will have mixed together more, instead of being so segregated.

D: Diversity typically means strife, and clever people take advantage of it. America should be vastly majority white.

Allison began to send him studies from her own online research and also from the scientific journals in her Stigma and Prejudice syllabus, and she targeted her evidence at the basic pillars of Derek's beliefs. He thought of different races as subspecies that had evolved over time to have clear biological differences, so she sent an article from *American Psychologist* about how race itself was a fluid, unscientific concept. The only thing anthropologists agreed on was that *Homo sapiens* of an unknown color had evolved in Africa from *Homo erectus* about 200,000 years ago. The idea of race was a modern, sociopolitical concept that was impossible to define because there was no one exact metric. In South Carolina, someone one-sixteenth black could be categorized as black, whereas someone in Brazil who was fifteen-sixteenths black could still be considered white. Some Asians in America were categorized as blacks in Britain. "At what point is White Black or Black White?" the article read.

Derek also thought most other races were biologically inferior to whites, with the possible exception of Asians. He had often cited as evidence the small differential in average IQ score between whites and blacks that he had read about in books like *The Bell Curve*, by Richard Herrnstein and Charles Murray. Derek believed minorities were genetically less intelligent than whites, and therefore he thought that a rising minority population also meant a dumbing down of America. But through her psychology course work and her own research, Allison had learned more specifics about the IQ test and some of its shortcomings, and she began to send Derek several more recent IQ studies based on better data. Allison's studies showed that any nominal differentials in IQ score between whites and minorities could be explained by implicit cultural bias in the IQ test itself and also by confounding factors for test takers like poverty, educational discrepancies, health, and poor prenatal nutrition—all of which were statistically more likely to affect minorities. She sent Derek research on a well-documented phenomenon called stereotype threat, which happens when a person fears his test score will confirm a negative stereotype and then that fear itself negatively affects performance. She sent Derek a recent study from Johns Hopkins University about how first-generation immigrant children performed better in school than other American students. It wasn't that other races were biologically less intelligent than whites, Allison told Derek. It was that, in America especially, other races faced more obstacles and had fewer opportunities, which was sometimes reflected in test scores.

But Derek believed it was whites who were oppressed in

America by policies like immigration and affirmative action, so Allison began bombarding him with data and studies that proved the opposite was true. She sent him research about the overwhelming white representation in state government and how whites were more likely to be promoted over similarly qualified minority candidates at work. She emailed evidence about how blacks were twice as likely as whites to be suspended from school for the same behaviors; twice as likely to work for minimum wage in the same jobs; three times as likely to live in poverty; and five times as likely to go to prison. She provided readings from her Stigma and Prejudice class about how whites enjoyed an advantage over minorities in everything from lower prices at car dealerships to better fruits in their grocery stores. It was still very much a white person's country, she told him, at the great expense of everyone else.

"Follow the evidence," Allison said, and even if Derek rarely conceded her points, he was at least reading her links and continuing to engage.

> D: Anyway, yet another debate, and another midnight.
> A: Oh man. ☹
> D: I've never debated so much with someone as you.
> A: How do you feel about that?
> D: I don't exactly wake up in the morning and look forward to it. I consider it healthy though.
> A: I think this qualifies as our least-emotionally-charged WN debate.
> D: Yeah, we're definitely getting out our argument jitters.

•

But sometimes Allison wanted their conversations about race to be emotionally charged. White nationalism wasn't just some academic thought experiment. It was a caustic, harmful ideology that was causing real damage to people's lives, so Allison began to send Derek links about that, too. She emailed him medical research from Harvard about how psychologists considered racism a chronic stressor with the power to alter brain chemistry. Derek clicked through Allison's links and read about how minority victims of prejudice were more likely to suffer from high blood pressure, elevated heart rate, suppressed immunity, depression, and heart disease. White people in those same studies did not show any physical response to prejudice, which made Derek begin to wonder if in fact he had been wrong in his theory that actually it was white people who were discriminated against.

For years Derek had been hearing about the abstract evils of racism, which he had always dismissed as empty rhetoric from his enemies on the liberal left. But he didn't consider Allison an enemy, so now he spent hours on his computer reading through raw data, doing his own research, and debating the evidence with Allison. She wrote to him, saying that even if his intellectual theories about the future of a multicultural America were correct—which they weren't—that still wouldn't justify the damage his racism was inflicting.

"It's not just that you're wrong," she told him. "It's that you're actually hurting people."

Allison repeatedly pushed their conversations from theoretical to intimate, hoping to make Derek confront the reality of his beliefs. Where did someone like his friend Juan fit in white nationalism's hypothetical ethno-state? What about Moshe and Matthew? Would they be deported? To where? She challenged Derek to consider how he would feel if the situation were reversed. "What if people didn't think you deserved to be a full member of society?" she asked him. Didn't he understand how that would impact his sense of security? His self-esteem? Derek told her that he didn't want white nationalism to cause damage in the lives of people he actually knew. "I consider all of this more like a really interesting thought experiment," he said, and he tried to avoid her questions about specific friends by resorting to vague, theoretical answers. "I don't expect us to go back to being a whites-only country," Derek said. "Maybe there are ways in which that might be good, at least in theory, but it is obviously unrealistic."

Allison wanted to know what Derek thought about the possibility of having interracial family members, or moving to a place like Africa, or living in an urban community of nonwhites. Their most intense debates sometimes ended for both of them with sulking or tears of frustration, because increasingly the hypothetical future they were arguing about was actually their own.

Their friendship had gradually evolved into a romantic relationship during the last few weeks, and that relationship was quickly becoming serious. Derek moved some of his clothes out of Maynard's house and into a drawer in Allison's dorm. After months of insisting on a friendship and nothing else, Allison decided it was best to be honest, and the truth was that she was falling for him. Whether she wanted to or not, it was happening, and she cared more about Derek than about what anyone else might think.

Allison told her mother about her new relationship with Derek, because he was becoming such a big part of her life. Julie completely trusted Allison, but she had also spent time researching Derek on the internet. "Some of it's a little scary," Julie told Allison. "I wish I could see him the same way you see him." So, a while after they began dating, Allison tried to explain her feelings for Derek in an email to her mother:

> Can we talk—*just for a second*—about how much I absolutely adore Derek? He is such a stable human being, and I don't ever feel insecure around him. He has a great work ethic, so we keep each other in line academically. And he also likes to do things. So the Longboat Key Gourmet Food Festival, the Stonecrab Festival, the Sarasota Bay Festival, going to the beach, going to Mote Aquarium, walking around downtown St. Pete, going to Selby Gardens, going to a Laura Marling concert—they're just all really great, fun things to do.
>
> And I love how he treats me—he's so kind to me, but not in an I-am-going-out-of-my-way-to-make-you-happy way, just a this-is-who-I-am-and-this-is-normal-for-me way. And he thinks I'm crazy smart, which is really nice. He respects what I do, thinks my work ethic is admirable, believes in the dreams I have, etc. I can write him emails about virtually anything, and I know that even if we differ in opinion, he'll consider mine seriously and my opinion holds a lot of weight.
>
> We're just very much on the same page about almost everything. More or less anything I find fun, he'll find fun, and vice versa, no matter how ridiculous it is. I'm so, so, so comfortable with him. It's sort of crazy.

"I'm so glad you're happy with him in your life!" Julie wrote back. And Allison was happy, almost blissfully so, except that her compatibility with Derek also accentuated their one glaring disagreement. Both of them believed ideology was at the core of personal identity. So how could she be falling for someone with so much rot at that core? Sometimes, she would allow herself to forget about white nationalism for a little while, and then she would get angry with herself for being so permissive. She would punish herself by going back onto her computer, back onto Stormfront to read through the message board. Most of the Stormfront posters made her feel physically nauseated. They made her resentful of Derek and also of herself. Derek could tell whenever she had been reading Stormfront because her tone would become distant and sometimes she would leave him alone in bed, choosing instead to sleep on the floor. "They are crazy," she wrote to him, describing her impression of most Stormfront members. "They are angry. They are full of hatred." And how could Derek not take that personally? Because these were people to whom he'd given his complete trust.

The summer before coming to New College, Derek had taken a four-week road trip across America with his niece to visit national parks. They had no camping gear and little money for hotels, so once they arrived in each city, Derek would look up the local Stormfront contributors and send them private messages, asking if he and his niece could stay for the night. He gave each one of his hosts a copy of his favorite white nationalist book, a collection of essays called *Race and the American Prospect*. Most of the people Derek messaged were strangers to him, and yet they had shown him their cities, taken him for hikes, invited him for dinner, and allowed him to sleep on their couches. Derek found a wide cross section of America hidden behind the anonymity of Stormfront user names: a lonely businessman in Kansas City, a karaoke singer in Vegas, a millionaire in Montana. These people weren't evil psychopaths, Derek told Allison. They were his community.

"We sort of argued all night and this morning," Allison wrote to a friend once. "It was rough. Derek's pretty terrified it's going to be the thing that splits us."

Once, late in the fall, Allison and Derek were driving back from a day trip to Honeymoon Island State Park when she decided to bring up white nationalism again. The beautiful, white-sand beaches of Honeymoon Island had been smoldering hot and crowded with mosquitoes, and now Allison was tired and itchy and ready not just for an argument but for a fight. Knowing that it would upset Derek, she imagined a scenario in which he ended up having a child with a black woman. What would be so wrong with that baby? Would Derek love it? Would he care for it? Would he deport it and send it away? Derek said his concerns would be for the child, who he thought would inevitably be a misfit in some essential way, cursed to a life of confused identity, and then Allison began listing off the names of their multiracial friends on campus, none of whom seemed unhappy or confused. "Your stupid theory makes no sense," she said to him.

She told Derek about two of her friends in the Hillel organization on campus who remained fearful of Derek because they still thought he might be dangerous or even violent. Derek said he thought that was ridiculous—an example of the emotional hysteria so typical of the American Left. What had he ever done on campus to make anyone afraid? Whom had he ever threatened at New College? He told Allison that he had never intended for anyone to fear him.

And so Allison started to unwind his logic, just as she had done in debates with her mother years before. Didn't

Derek promote an ideology that aspired to send Africans back to Africa, Jews back to Israel, Indians back to India? Didn't white nationalists want to deport those minorities and uproot their lives? How, exactly, did Derek believe a concept like that could be humane or in any way reasonable? Did he somehow not understand why that idea would be threatening for Rose, or Moshe, or Matthew? Or for Juan, who was just now in the final stages of getting his American citizenship? When the great deportation came, would Derek himself be willing to break into their homes and force them out? Or would he stand by and watch as his father and other Stormfront members did it for him?

Derek tried to equivocate. He said that he didn't necessarily think the end point of white nationalism was forced deportation for nonwhites, but maybe gradual self-deportation, just as Mitt Romney was suggesting, in which nonwhites would leave on their own. He didn't believe in self-deportation right *now*, at least not for his friends, but just eventually, in concept.

Allison thought the solution was simpler. "If you don't want people to be afraid of what you're advocating," she told him, "then maybe you shouldn't be advocating for it."

My beliefs about white genocide remain essentially the same," Derek insisted on his radio show during the fall of 2012, but his behavior was beginning to change, and Don had noticed. Derek had all but stopped logging in to Stormfront or posting on the message board, even as the political conversation intensified in the last weeks of the 2012 presidential election. Don called Derek and told him he needed to remain active on the message board, reminding him of his responsibility as both a moderator and a public leader of Stormfront. "You're an essential part of this," Don remembered telling him, because Derek and Stormfront had always been paired together in Don's mind. They were the two major creations of his life, and for twenty years he had watched them grow side by side.

Don had built his first dial-up internet bulletin board for David Duke supporters in 1990, the year after Derek was born. Next came *Stormfront* magazine a few years later and then the Stormfront website in 1995, just as Derek started school. Don had chosen the name Stormfront, he said then, "because turbulence is coming, and afterward there will be a cleansing effect." Within a few years, the site had amassed an international following and helped coalesce the fractured white supremacy movement. Only on Stormfront could neo-Nazis and racist academics plot strategy for a white take-over in French, German, or Russian. "I've done a thousand times more for our cause in three years than I did in the last thirty," Don explained during a television interview in the late 1990s. "The expansion of our message on the web is exponential."

The problem for Don was that the responsibilities of Stormfront kept expanding, too: tens of millions of visitors to the site during the next decades, thousands of posts each day, and all of it dependent on him. There was no paid staff, and he sometimes struggled to raise enough money from the site's sustaining members to keep it online. The site was under constant attack from hackers, so Don began waking up to check the board several times each night. There was no one else he could trust to keep the site alive, no one who understood the history of Stormfront or shared in his commitment.

No one but Derek, and so, after a while, a plan coalesced

in Don's mind. The website would eventually need a new leader. Derek would eventually want platforms from which he could extend the reach of white nationalism. He had already launched the Stormfront children's page and the radio network. "My assumption was that he would take over the site, and he would be the heir," Don remembered thinking.

Derek's new disinterest in Stormfront concerned Don, but he told himself it was only a stage. Don himself had gone through stretches of fatigue and depression about the white nationalist movement, when the country's changing demographics made the whole enterprise seem pointless; maybe that was Derek's problem, too. So when Derek began coming up with school-related excuses to get out of the radio show for weeks at a time in the fall of 2012, Don played along, explaining away Derek's absence to listeners each day on the air. "Hopefully we'll have Derek calling in a little later," Don said one day. Or: "You know Derek, always off doing something important." Don said Derek was busy working on his thesis. He was researching the great medieval European societies. He was perfecting his German. He was giving those liberal professors hell. But sometimes, unbeknownst to Don, what Derek was really doing was going alone to Sarasota Bay with his kayak and paddling far out from shore until he was alone with his thoughts. What did he believe anymore? Which life did he want to lead? Don wanted Derek back on the radio show—*Derek's* radio show, Don reminded him, to spread *Derek's* ideas about white genocide. He was supposed to be making history, spreading the family gospel, and saving the white race from genocide. But now Derek's brain was also crowded with new ideas, backed by data and dozens of studies, which suggested white nationalism was both dangerous and flawed. If he returned to the radio show, he knew

Allison and his other New College friends would be listening
and parsing every word. Suddenly he cared about both audiences. How could he possibly appease both?

Late that October, he took Allison with him on a family trip to Key West for three nights. They stayed with Don
and Chloe in a rental house owned by Sam Dickson, a family
friend and a prominent white nationalist from Atlanta. Don
and Chloe slept in the bedroom downstairs; Derek and Allison took the loft. Derek's parents enjoyed Allison's company,
and even if they didn't entirely trust her, they still trusted
Derek. "Since he was spending so much time with her, I fig-
ured she wasn't entirely hostile," Don said.

During the days in Key West, Don monitored the news on
cable TV and did the radio show alone. "The SPLC is pushing
their hateful antiwhite agenda, their gay agenda, their immigration agenda," he said, and meanwhile Derek and Allison
were off on adventures, exploring the tourist shops on Duval
Street, swimming, and going to a sunset festival. "The best
place ever!" Allison wrote to her mother. But then, in the
evenings, Allison and Derek reunited with his parents and
Dickson at high-class restaurants in Key West, where each
night the conversation turned into another eulogy for white
America. Don mourned the immigrant takeover of South
Florida. Dickson wondered about the intellectual capabilities
of blacks and minorities as compared with whites. For years
Derek had studied Dickson's speeches, read all of his writing, and admired his intellectualism, but now, seated next to
Allison, he thought many of Dickson's views sounded cruel
and extreme. Derek tried to discreetly steer the conversation
away from politics and watched as Allison sat quietly in her
chair. She had made an active decision to remain both polite
and silent about her opinions at these dinners, because she

didn't think she had any chance of persuading Don or Dickson. Instead she picked at her shrimp and listened to their ideas with private disgust as she made plans to push back against those ideas later with Derek.

"Having to sit through some of that literally makes my skin crawl," she told Derek later.

"Parts were borderline crazy," he agreed. "Sorry you had to sit through all that."

She traveled with him again to see his family in West Palm Beach a few weeks later, just after President Obama was reelected with 51 percent of the vote. Derek and Allison brought a pie and went to Derek's grandmother's house for Thanksgiving dinner, and the conversation that night was mostly ideological. Despite Romney's defeat, Don thought the election had been "mostly encouraging," and he had good reason to think white nationalism was beginning to take hold. Whites had voted for Romney by a 20 percent margin—59 percent compared with just 39 percent for Obama—the largest white support for a single candidate in twenty-eight years, whereas 83 percent of minorities had voted for Obama. "We are more segregated than ever as a country along racial lines," Don said, and he believed the aftermath of the election had only furthered that divide. Hundreds of white students at the University of Mississippi rioted on election night, including some who chanted racial slurs and burned Obama's campaign signs. Trump mourned Obama's election on Fox News and then tweeted, "We can't let this happen. We should march on Washington and stop this travesty."

The idea of some kind of revolution or mass secession had begun on Stormfront during the hours after the election and then metastasized across the internet, until more than ninety-five thousand Texans signed an official petition requesting that their state secede from the United States. "White folks are now officially the oppressed minority," one poster on Stormfront wrote, and what Don found most encouraging was how mainstream that idea had become. On election night, Bill O'Reilly explained Romney's defeat to his massive audience on Fox News by saying, "It's not a traditional America anymore. There's 50 percent of the voting public who want stuff. They want things and who is going to give them things? President Obama. Whereby twenty years ago, President Obama would have been roundly defeated by an establishment candidate like Mitt Romney, the white establishment is now the minority."

Don thought the election represented the fulfillment of Derek's earliest predictions: Whites would begin identifying as a minority. They would band together and exert greater power. But now, at the Thanksgiving dinner, Derek didn't seem all that interested in talking about the election or politics in general. When his parents asked what he thought about four more years of Obama, he said that he didn't really know, which was true. A part of his brain still reflexively believed America was slipping into a multicultural abyss. Another part felt personally relieved that Romney's immigration policies wouldn't unravel the lives of some of his friends on campus, like Juan. "Are you even a white nationalist anymore?" one of Derek's half sisters asked during dinner. And if Derek was mostly trying to stay silent and neutral because he was concerned about Allison, she was also beginning to worry for him. "It's constant scrutiny and pressure on him from both sides," she later told a friend, and even that very moment, at 8:00 p.m. on Thanksgiving, another thread about Derek was beginning on the New College forum:

Happy Thanksgiving reminder. Just thought you guys might like to know that Derek Black, son of former KKK grand wizard Don Black, goes to our school.

Guys, leave Derek Black off the forum. I came to New College expecting tolerance and acceptance, and thus far Derek Black has done a better job of that than the people attacking him.

Social justice is not about making the world a nicer place. It's about taking back rights and opportunities denied to us.

Did you know that Hitler was actually a pretty decent artist? And Charles Manson wrote some pretty songs.

This asshat started a CHILDREN'S PAGE on a white supremacist HATE website. How can you guys not sit there and seethe over just how fucked up that is? Are you all seriously saying lets not hurt the white supremacist's feelings? I hope your feelings get hurt Derek Black, because you are not welcome here and, sincerely, fuck off.

Derek and Allison read through some of the thread together that night. Allison felt protective of Derek and also angry with him; Derek felt hurt and also defensive. They argued for a little while before going to bed, and then early the next morning Derek dropped Allison off at a coffee shop in West Palm Beach and went alone to his parents' house. They needed his help fixing the roof, and they didn't want Allison to come. Theirs was a ramshackle house, built bit by bit by Derek's grandparents in the 1940s, with mismatched windows and a patchwork roof. Don and Chloe didn't usually show it to outsiders, and that still included Allison. So instead she waited at the coffee shop and clicked open the forum thread again, reading as the vitriol built from one post to the next, until finally the student administrator wrote to say that he was considering closing down the thread because of its offensiveness. Allison decided she wanted to write a public response. She thought she knew something that nobody else on the forum understood: Derek had already begun the gradual process of reconsidering at least some of his views, and she worried the outrage on the forum would discourage him and hold his identity in place. She addressed her message to the entire forum, and then for the first time in public she began to tentatively defend Derek.

So . . . as far as the person himself goes, a little research—

1) He's been known to go to Shabbat dinner that a Jewish student hosts every weekend—and that Jewish friend is one of Derek's closer friends.
2) He's dated a Jewish girl.
3) He considers a Hispanic student here to also be one of his closer friends.
4) He's posted on Stormfront a total of once in the last year.
5) He's been way, way more off the radio show than on it ever since he's been here.

But *regardless of anything about him personally*— Attacking a person, especially a person who is not fighting back and has never fought back, is not productive to anybody. What *is* productive is engaging in meaningful dialogue about how to change these oppressive structures here and elsewhere. Participate in diversity talks, be upset and *give a damn*, but in a positive way, not in a hostile way. Attacking him as a mass gang is not the way to change his views (so throwing things at him in the library, etc., which is what happened the semester after he came back, is not acceptable human behavior either). Talk about it, shed apathy, get involved, but do it constructively.

Derek drove them back to New College the next day as Allison read through the forum responses out loud. Derek thanked her for publicly defending him, but he also felt guilty that his issues on campus had now also become Allison's. A few of her friends had responded with notes of support, but others dismissed her as "biased," because by now some people on campus knew they were very close. "This is a potentially dangerous person," one student had written about Derek. "Disgusting," said another. "Pure hate," said a third, until finally late in the afternoon the forum moderator announced he was closing the thread. "If you post here, you get banned," the moderator wrote, but Allison felt increasingly certain the thread still needed one final post. "You have to respond to this," she told Derek. People on campus were still afraid of him, she said, and if Derek wasn't in fact dangerous, then it was his responsibility to allay their fears.

Derek agreed it was time for him to say something publicly to his classmates. What they knew about his views came mostly from three-year-old internet posts and archival radio shows in which he had denigrated Jews and minorities, and now many of those comments also made Derek cringe. After poring over so many of Allison's psychological studies, Derek no longer believed the white nationalist myths he had propagated about "Jewish manipulation," "testosterone-fueled black aggression," or larger brain sizes for whites. He was becoming unsure that his theory about IQ discrepancies held up to the best modern science. During his time at New College, Derek had gone from believing whites were a superior race in need of an exclusive homeland, to thinking all races were equal but should be preserved by living separately, to thinking that segregation wasn't really necessary, so long as whites weren't forced to assimilate.

He still considered himself a white nationalist because he remained concerned about the demographic decline of whites in America, but he now believed there was room to clarify his position to classmates without upsetting his family or disavowing his beliefs. He and Allison drove to their regular coffee shop in Sarasota and went up a spiral staircase to a quiet table on the second floor. Derek took out his laptop, and together they began to debate the language of his response. Derek told Allison that he was still a *white nationalist*, but he insisted that he wasn't a *white supremacist*. He told her he had friends who were *neo-Nazis*, but he felt comfortable publicly rejecting Hitler-era *Nazism*. Allison didn't necessarily understand all of his distinctions, and sometimes she still felt confused about exactly where Derek stood in his beliefs, but she pushed him to keep writing. She wanted others on campus to understand what she had already learned: that Derek's beliefs differed in significant ways from other white nationalists on Stormfront. They spent the afternoon going back and forth over the language, and finally Derek polished it into a final draft:

> I know this thread is closed, but I wanted to address it anyway. I haven't defended myself on here because I've discovered it's a no-win, very hostile situation all around. Posting this goes against my general judgment, because I don't think that people have an obligation necessarily to explain themselves for anything. It's been brought to my attention that people might be scared or intimidated or even feel unsafe here because of things said about me. I wanted to try to address these concerns publicly, as they absolutely should not exist if they don't need to.
>
> I have done my best since arriving to New College to stay out of people's hair. Since returning after the big thread about me while I was abroad, I have tried hard to not do anything of note whatsoever. Before I competed in the talent show last year, I debated whether I wanted to live with the potential forum war resulting from me singing a folk song. I always have to weigh whether I want to attend a public lecture for fear of the glares, and a couple club leaders have expressed that they'd prefer I not attend their meetings. During my first semester back I would go sailing to escape the occasional middle finger in the library, the murmurs when I'd get food in Ham, and the occasional threatening emails. An easy response to this from someone who's never talked to me could be along the lines of, "Well, that's the type of discrimination you've advocated against minorities!"

I do not and would never support discrimination or unfair treatment against anyone insofar as my privilege allows me to identify it. I am not a white supremacist, nor do I identify with white supremacy. I don't hate anyone because of race, religion, or anything similar. I am not a Nazi, nor do I identify with Nazism. I am not part of the KKK, nor do I identify with the KKK. As far as Stormfront goes, it's my dad's website, and though I have moderator privileges, I don't moderate. And as should be understood for both the radio and the website, only things I've said myself are things I can be held accountable for.

I don't want people to feel uncomfortable here because of me, but I also do not want to outline every belief system I have. If people want more information about what I actually believe as opposed to what people frequently say, then message me privately to set up a conversation. Making these statements obviously does not instantly create comfort or security for everyone who's uncomfortable, but I hope it might help slightly.

He sent it from the coffee shop that night, and Derek and Allison watched as the students around them began clicking open their email. Derek was worried his note to the forum might somehow find its way onto Stormfront. "He's pretty concerned about it getting out, 'cause it can cause a lot of trouble for his family," Allison wrote to one of her friends. But, instead, the immediate response was private and mostly supportive. "I commend you," one student wrote to him; and "Thanks so much"; and "I simply wanted to apologize." Even Rose, the Jewish classmate whom Derek had dated before being outed on the forum, decided to contact him for the first time in several months. "I thought your forum post was good," she wrote, and for at least a few weeks so did almost everyone else. Nobody flipped him off on campus. Nobody posted anything more on the forum. The semester came to a quiet end. Derek readied to leave Florida for a three-week language school in Europe, and Allison packed for a winter internship in Australia. "Seriously I am so, so, so glad he posted that," Allison wrote to her friend.

But something was still bothering her: the SPLC's "extremist file" about Derek, which was one of the first results that came up whenever Allison typed her boyfriend's name into Google. She thought Derek's contributions to white supremacy—while significant—were fewer than many other people on the list. She also believed Derek would have more freedom to continue changing his views if he wasn't publicly tied to an extremist identity by the SPLC. Without telling Derek, she decided to create a Yahoo email account and write an email to the SPLC using a fake name. She told them Derek no longer belonged on a public list of terrorists and demagogues, and as evidence she attached his recent post on the New College forum. She asked that the SPLC remove Derek's profile, but instead an employee wrote back and said the SPLC wanted to publish Derek's full post. Allison panicked and said no, that they couldn't, that Derek's post was private and they could ignore her original email, but it was too late.

Derek received a message from the SPLC a few days later, just before Christmas. The SPLC had written to Derek several times before, usually to ask about his father's activism or Stormfront's connection to mass murderers. This time, a reporter from the SPLC told Derek they were planning to write a story about his "changing ideology," and the reporter asked if Derek had anything more he'd like to say.

"Your views are now apparently quite different than what many people thought," the email read. "We're planning to write something today."

9. "I'm Torn"

By the time Derek received the SPLC's email, he was on his way to David Duke's European apartment in the Alps, where he planned to celebrate Christmas before continuing on to language school in France. Derek wrote back to the SPLC to explain that he was traveling, bargaining for more time so he could consider his options. "I consider this personal, but I'll give some sort of comment," he wrote. He assumed someone at New College had leaked his forum post to the SPLC, maybe James Birmingham or another campus activist, and now Derek felt trapped and tempted to backpedal. It was one thing to clarify his beliefs in a private email from a coffee shop on his liberal campus, with Allison at his side to arm him with psychological studies and scientific logic. It was much scarier to sit on Duke's couch and consider hedging against his white nationalist beliefs in a public response to the SPLC, which many white nationalists monitored daily and which Duke had once called "the hateful, disgusting propaganda machine of our enemies."

"I'm torn about how to deal with this," Derek wrote to Allison, because more and more he felt in every decision that he was weighing the possibility of two distinct futures, one devoted to white nationalism and another removed from politics.

At Allison's urging, he had recently taken the Graduate Record Examination and scored in the ninety-seventh percentile for verbal reasoning. His New College professors regarded him as a talented linguist and a promising historian, and despite Derek's ideology they believed he belonged in one of the country's elite graduate programs for medieval studies. "As a student, he was very respectful and curious," remembered Susan Marks, a religious history professor and an ordained rabbi who taught Derek during his final year. "I was nervous when I saw he was in my class, because his background was common knowledge, but he was kind and engaged. He would stay after class because he was excited about a text and wanted to ask more questions."

Based on his professors' recommendations, Derek had taken several graduate applications with him to complete in Europe for schools like Yale, Western Michigan, and the University of Toronto, and he told Allison his chances of acceptance were "good, so long as nobody googles my name." In their online chats, Derek had begun to imagine the possibilities of an anonymous life removed from white nationalism: earning a PhD, teaching at a university, and raising a family in a quiet college town.

But then there were the other parts of Derek—the zeal and ambition Duke helped to nurture, which had propelled Derek to become the young face of white nationalism for more than a decade. In his late teens, he had prepared for his own television interviews by re-watching one of Duke's early appearances on *Meet the Press* in 1991, studying how Duke smiled politely through confrontational questions, how he stuck to his simple talking points and flattered the interviewer for twenty minutes until she conceded, "Sir, you speak beautifully, and you have a wonderful polish about you." Derek had molded parts of his public identity in Duke's image, and as Christmas neared, Duke continued to instruct

Derek about all the ways in which he should embody the archetypal European ideal by eating gluten-free, keeping a clean house, and lifting weights.

It was just the two of them staying together for the week in a small apartment that belonged to Duke's girlfriend. Duke was persona non grata in Italy, and technically he wasn't supposed to be staying in the apartment, so each day he and Derek avoided the landlord on their way out. They walked Duke's dog in the nearby mountains, skied at a resort, and ate pasta in the mountain lodge on one of Duke's gluten-free "cheat days." Duke had a new daily radio show and his own YouTube channel, and when he wasn't discussing politics with Derek, he was often lecturing into a small microphone in the other room while Derek filled out grad school applications on the couch. "Finally, we are waking up!" Duke told his audience that week, because in the wake of the 2012 election he believed whites felt increasingly threatened by record levels of immigration, a two-term black president, and a sluggish middle-class economy. Duke hoped to grow white nationalism in part by co-opting the Tea Party movement and making it more explicitly racial. The Tea Party had diminished slightly in size and power since the 2010 midterm elections, but polls showed more than 15 percent of Americans still identified as part of the populist movement. Tea Partyers were demographically more likely than most Americans to be white, married, conservative, religious, and elderly. The movement's fractious leadership was careful to avoid explicit prejudice, but Tea Party rallies and protests had often become exercises in white grievance and resentment, featuring racist signs, Confederate flags, anti-immigrant chants, and hundreds of yellow flags bearing the Tea Party slogan, "Don't tread on me." At one protest on Capitol Hill

in 2010, Tea Partyers yelled epithets at members of the Con-
gressional Black Caucus and spit on Representative John
Lewis, a civil rights icon, as he walked through the crowd on
his way into Congress.

Duke had good reason to believe many Tea Partyers
instinctively identified with white nationalists on racial
issues, so he had announced a national speaking tour aimed
at connecting the two groups. "Tea Partyers believe we in
America have a right to preserve our heritage, our language,
and our culture," he said, in a YouTube video. "They are
called racist because they want to stop non-European immigration from turning America into a crumbling Tower of
Babel. The movement is made up of American people who
have watched in silent anger while the nation of our fore-
fathers has been destroyed. It is about preserving our heritage and our freedom. My friends, now is the time."

Duke sounded so convinced about the future of white
nationalism in the days leading up to Christmas that it made
Derek recall a bit of his own certainty. Of course whites
were being demographically wiped out in their own country.
Of course it was genocide. These were the facts to which he
had devoted the first part of his life, and now he thought of
them again as he opened his email to respond to the SPLC.

Waiting in his email that week was another new message—
one more reminder of just how much he risked losing if he
distanced himself from his family's ideology. It was a chain
email about the "illegal Mexican invasion" of the United
States sent along by Derek's parents. For the Black family,
white nationalism wasn't just a belief system; it was the glue
that held together friendships and family.

"My forum post and my racial ideology are not mutually

exclusive concepts," Derek wrote to the SPLC. "Everything I said is true, and I also believe in White Nationalism."

The SPLC posted his response the next day, and for a while Derek believed he had managed to appease both of his audiences. The New College forum remained quiet. Duke and Don both thought Derek had publicly reestablished himself as a committed white nationalist. Stormfront posters wrote that Derek had managed the impossible by reframing the tenets of white nationalism in a way that even liberal college students didn't find offensive. "A hero," one Stormfront poster wrote of Derek. "I wonder if he knows which one of his classmates is the mole."

Derek forwarded the SPLC story to Allison in Australia. She was disappointed he had publicly reaffirmed his commitment to white nationalism, but she also knew that for Derek rejecting that label was likely to be the last and most difficult part of any transformation, because the identity was so central to his family connections. She believed his evolution was still under way, and she understood the inherent pressure he felt from his parents and Duke. "White nationalism is basically their life's work, and I'm an essential part of that," Derek told her one night, and because he was always so candid with her, she also thought she needed to be honest with him. From her computer in Australia, she decided to confess to Derek that she was the one who had emailed the SPLC in the hopes that it would remove his extremist file. "I'm sorry for being so naive," she told him, but she also explained she had been motivated by a desire to protect whatever was left of Derek's public image. "You are not that same person anymore," she told him. "Your views are way different than they used to be." Derek felt surprised Allison had emailed the SPLC, but not betrayed. He had always expected his forum email might be leaked to the public, and he didn't doubt Allison's intentions. He also agreed with her conclusion that his political views had begun softening. "It's behind us," he told her, and they went back to trading photographs from their travels and sending each other their college essays to edit. Derek traveled by train to Slovenia and then went on to Serbia, Bulgaria, and Germany. Allison explored Sydney and the interior of Australia. Derek sent Allison a CD of his favorite songs for Christmas. She made him an online scrapbook with memories of their adventures. "It's been a good few months, so here's a recap," she wrote to him, before listing ninety-five of her favorite moments they had spent together.

A few days after Christmas, Allison logged on to her New College email account to write a travelogue to Derek, and at the top of her in-box she noticed a new thread about Derek on the student forum. Classmates had finally seen his response to the SPLC. "This is the truth we needed to hear from Derek, still a committed racist," one student wrote, and the responses were more indignant than ever before. Now Derek's classmates weren't just speculating about his views. They knew he was still a white nationalist—and, worse, a "snake" who had attempted to sanitize his ideology for his college classmates. Allison forced herself to read through the thread. Then she wrote to Derek on Instant Messenger:

> A: Forum thread about you again re: the SPLC arti-
> cle. Hate this hate this *hate this* and it's not even about
> me. It's about you. I want to go running or I want to curl

up and do nothing or I want to lose myself in Sydney. I disagree so strongly with this shit. And it's not like this is something like abortion or some more misguided moral thing where both sides are equally good people. It's that this is harmful and illogical and twisted. I want to be home.

D: Why?

A: Because I am having trouble being happy here in Australia, and then this WN shit just makes me want to go and hide somewhere. Usually I consider you a safe/supportive place but when I get into this, I don't see you like that. You become part of this bigger thing and not you. It hurts, because I care about you too much, you know?

D: I care about you. But don't do it for the wrong reasons.

A: I don't know what qualifies as a "wrong reason" to care about somebody.

D: You should do what's good for you. Wrong reasons end up hurting people.

A: What is good for me is what improves my work, what makes me smile, what makes me laugh, what makes me think and what makes me feel safe/secure. And you fulfill those qualities, and therefore in that sense you are good for me. Anything dealing with white nationalism and racism makes me sick and want to cry and is decidedly not good for me, which you are involved in. It's not a cut and dry thing.

D: I don't like to be the cause of pain for you. I try not to be.

A: I know. I just very much wish you weren't involved in WN.

Allison tried to lose herself in Australia and her internship, but her conscience continued to nag at her. Was she making the right choice in getting so close to Derek? She still wasn't sure. If Derek had been a men's rights activist, she thought she would have been too furious and disgusted to ever speak with him. She didn't believe she had the same courage as Juan, Matthew, or Moshe, victims of Derek's prejudices who nonetheless chose to become his friends. So Allison wondered, if sexism would have been a deal breaker for her, then why wasn't racism? Had her own privilege— and her childhood in a conservative, all-white community— somehow made her more capable of forgiving or overlooking racism? Sometimes, to punish herself, she wanted to feel disgusted with him. She went online and listened back to the audio from the most recent Stormfront conference. She again read over the latest forum thread, where now dozens of people were ridiculing the person she cared about most. As much as she disliked their tactics, she could empathize with their anger and their logic.

James, the anarchist organizer, had started the latest thread, in part because he felt in some ways vindicated by Derek's statement to the SPLC. Of course Derek was still a white nationalist, James wrote. In a decade of activist organizing, he had come to believe that America's systems of oppression only changed, if ever, after a long, painful fight. How many forum posts had he read during the last years from classmates who thought the remedy for Derek's views was open-mindedness and inclusion? Just be nice. Go talk to him. Give it time and the truth will prevail. James thought there was a naive assumption among some of his liberal classmates that the world was a fair marketplace of information, in which the best ideas naturally won out. But ideas didn't fight political battles; people fought them, and in James's experience people who were systematically oppressed—by gender, by class, by race—always had to work harder to get their ideas heard. The concept of civil discourse was the creation of a privileged class that didn't want their lives disrupted by protests or emotional arguments. "Revolutions don't happen at polite dinner parties," James wrote, and as the forum thread continued, he posted again and again:

> Can anyone give me an example of any radical (and yes, white supremacy—the notion not the movement—no longer being the ruling ideology would be a radical change) social change that was primarily the result of "cooler heads prevailing"?
>
> Do you really think Women's Suffrage and the Civil Rights Movement happened via "calm heads," via sterile debate and civil discourse? Because they didn't. They happened by putting blood, sweat and tears and rage into a social movement through a diverse range of tactics both "violent" and nonviolent.
>
> You cannot just chime in with "civil discourse" without understanding that "civil discourse" has historically been the arena of the ruling classes and a defense mechanism against listening to the "uncivilized."
>
> I am not arguing for violent tactics. I'm arguing against this fantasy that "calm, cool-headed arguments" through "legitimate" means can achieve radical change.

James posted an image of a kickboxer pummeling a Nazi, and hours later Allison saw it on the forum and decided to write a public response. She had spent the last year sitting with Derek, Matthew, Moshe, and others at polite dinner parties. And even if the result wasn't exactly revolutionary, she believed those conversations had opened Derek's mind and begun to change his thinking. What she worried now was that the forum would undo that goodwill and push Derek back into a corner, where he would again see the campus as his liberal enemy.

> The way to fight perceived hatred is not with hatred. These threads make me sick.
>
> If you have a problem with white nationalist ideology (which I certainly do and I think it's safe to say the vast majority of people here do) then *go fight oppressive structures*. Or at the very least, educate yourself about privilege and racial issues and classism and discrimination and *get informed*. Educate others. Those are helpful, positive directions to go in.
>
> What is *not* a positive direction to go in is to attack a person. If the aim is to draw attention and awareness to him, then that mission has been accomplished so many times the NCF community is *saturated* in knowledge. If the aim is to try to change or challenge his belief systems, the way to accomplish that is *not* through public contempt or ostracism. There has been enough discussion about this one person to last a lifetime, and all it's doing now—and all it's been doing for a long while now—is harm. Leave it be.

Derek read the forum posts at a hostel in Belgrade and then went out alone into the city that night. It was cold and quiet and he didn't know where he was going, but he wanted to walk. During the last year, he had mostly been able to dismiss the forum attacks against him as generic and uninformed, but this time he was hurt. He had taken the risk of posting about his ideology to his classmates, joining in for the first time on their private forum conversation about him, and now their rejection felt somehow more personal. He had made a small effort to embrace the New College community, and it had shunned him. The loneliness made him wonder about his future, and whether a public role in white nationalism could ever be worth so much exclusion.

He also could no longer quiet another alarm that had begun to go off with increasing frequency inside his head: What if so many of his classmates on the forum were valid in their criticism and righteous in their anger? What if white nationalism was inherently flawed and morally indefensible? It had been easy to dismiss their forum posts when he felt convinced of his beliefs, but now his certainty had shrunk down into something he could no longer define. He had publicly told his classmates that he wasn't a white supremacist, wasn't a neo-Nazi, wasn't a racist, wasn't a bigot, wasn't in support of discrimination or unfair treatment of any kind. So then what exactly was he? "You need to identify with more than 1/50th of a belief system to consider it your belief system," Allison wrote to him once, and when Derek tried to fall back on his one remaining defense about the ongoing white genocide, she obliterated that, too. "Oh, *Genocide*," she wrote. "Let's talk about that for a second. Like white people are *so persecuted* and poor, poor, poor victim white people. Like white people aren't absolutely in the positions of power. The concept is incredibly, horribly insulting and degrading to real, historic genocides against Jews, against Rwandans, against Armenians, etc."

For years Derek had taught other white nationalists the
tactics of verbal debate, but now he thought his old talking
points sounded callous and ill-conceived. "Is there anything
still holding me to this beyond loyalty?" he remembered
thinking. He needed time to sort out his thoughts, so he
walked by himself through the center of Belgrade. He continued into Kalemegdan Park and toward the Belgrade Fortress, lit by streetlights and perched high above the Danube
River. The thick stone towers cast shadows across the park
as Derek walked along the hulking fortress walls, which told
the epic history of the city. It had been built in the first century by the Celts, conquered by the Romans, and besieged
by the Goths and the Huns. For more than two thousand
years the fortress had been constantly occupied by one civilization after the next—by Serbians, Hungarians, Ottomans,
and Yugoslavs; by Byzantine Christians who carved crosses
into the walls and by Arabic Muslims who called it Dar al
Jihad. A dozen civilizations had risen and then fallen on the
fortress grounds, a succession of races always battling each
other for supremacy, destroying the castle walls again and
again so they could rebuild society on top of the same damaged rubble. What remained of the fortress was a beautiful
amalgamation: Serbian ramparts on top of Roman walls, with
Turkish and Austrian fortifications. Derek climbed to the
top of the fortress, took some photos, and then strolled down
through the park, walking by dozens of couples squeezed
together on benches. He stopped for hot chocolate and then
sat alone on a bench before sending a message to Allison.
"I wish you were here," he said. Then he went back to his
hostel, where there was only one other guest and sixteen
empty beds. He opened up his email and wrote to Allison

again, describing his solitary tour of the Belgrade Fortress before writing about the latest uproar on the New College forum:

> I feel like I leveled with NCF students. I was more open than I felt comfortable being, and now I feel like they've chosen to use my vulnerability in order to hurt me more effectively.
>
> Even as I think about it, I know it's not really a mob of conniving bullies, though that's an aspect. I understand there are intellectual ideas to discuss, and yet I feel almost betrayed. What happened to me not caring what others think of me? I feel like they've gotten a little under my skin and it hurts.

Allison wrote back to him the next morning in Australia:

> For them, what you believe in are not simply "intellectual ideas." They are abhorrent and dangerous. And to them, it's not just that you believe it—it's that there's a radio show with your name on it. It's that your name is stickied on Stormfront threads. It's that you publicly believe these things. And in that, you're distanced from them. You're not a classmate. You're a public figure. Your vulnerabilities and emotions don't necessarily matter to them. It's not like you haven't done anything that reinforces and spreads the WN ideology—*you have*. To them, you are not a victim—and in general you aren't because, to be frank, you absolutely *have* done all of those things.
>
> They hurt you, yes. Because in their view your public

beliefs oppress and hurt others, and yeah, I agree with them. I don't think there are nice ways to say that.

Derek thanked Allison for hearing him out, and he continued to think about her email as he explored Serbia, Germany, Bulgaria, and then France. He was alone among strangers for the next several weeks, liberated from his public identity and the pressures that came with it, and he found himself able to focus with better clarity on the debate in his head. "My brain now has two ways of thinking, a white nationalist way and a new way," he told Allison once. "It's like living in two different realms."

White nationalism remained embedded in all of his childhood memories, his sense of self, and almost every important relationship he'd had during the first twenty-one years of his life. "It's my community, so I reflexively hear criticism of WN sort of like some people hear your momma's so fat jokes," he wrote to Allison. But if his loyalty was holding his identity in place, his brain was increasingly leading him in a new direction. At nights in hostels, he lay in bed and questioned his assumptions about the world, which included rethinking so much of what he had once believed about the history of Europe.

He had chosen New College because he wanted to study medieval history, and he had been drawn to medieval history in part because the mythology of white nationalism centered on the Middle Ages. On Stormfront, Derek and others had posted Latin battle cries and medieval crests as they shared stories about white knights and Viking warriors. Much of the modern white supremacist movement was built on the idea of reclaiming the conquering spirit of those European warriors, compelled to victory by genetic destiny and ethnic pride, and Derek had invested himself in that version of history. As a teenager, he had taught himself some Latin. He had apprenticed for a blacksmith at the local Renaissance fair and learned to forge his own chain mail armor. He had joined a medieval reenactment society and persuaded his parents to travel with him across Florida to relive the Middle Ages, winning contests for archery and sword fighting.

And then he had come to New College as a history major, where his classes and his assigned readings revealed a more nuanced Middle Ages—a version that contradicted much of what Derek read on Stormfront. If European whites were really a genetically superior race, then why had Europe lagged so far behind Islamic culture in technology, art, and science for much of the Middle Ages? Why was it Baghdad that had become the world's largest and greatest city in the ninth and tenth centuries—a place with superior doctors and libraries, where pale-skinned European emissaries were sent to learn from dark-skinned Arab scholars about astrology, algebra, and the science of distilling alcohol? And if races were really better off segregated, then why had one of the greatest medieval territories been Al-Andalus in Muslim-controlled Spain, where Christians, Jews, and Muslims lived together in all shades of brown, combining to make advancements in art, philosophy, and architecture?

As he traveled through Europe, Derek read historical texts from the eighth to the twelfth century, trying to trace back the modern concepts of race and whiteness, but he couldn't find them anywhere. Instead, the facts of history pointed him to another conclusion: The iconic European warriors so often celebrated on Stormfront had never thought of themselves as white, Derek decided. Some of them had considered skin color not a hard biological fact but a condition that could change over time based on culture, diet, and climate. They had fought not for their race but for religion, culture, power, and money, just like every other empire of the Middle Ages.

"The fact that white people eventually conquered the world wasn't proof of fate but basically just a fluke of history," Derek later wrote. And if he had been that wrong about history—his field of expertise—then he was also willing to believe he had been wrong about so much else.

He went onto his computer in France and read more studies about race in America, including many that Allison sent him from Australia. He read that white households accumulated an average wealth of $111,000 versus $7,000 for minorities; that 75 percent of whites owned their homes versus 40 percent of blacks; that whites lived three years longer on average than blacks or Hispanics; that blacks made up 12 percent of the population but held less than 3 percent of top management jobs. Derek became increasingly convinced that the structures of white supremacy remained very much in place. Whites in America were not oppressed or persecuted; they were unfairly advantaged to the great detriment of everyone else. "How didn't I see some of this stuff before?" he asked Allison once. "When you look at the numbers, it's pretty clear."

More than just data, Derek tried to think about the perspectives of the friends he'd made during weekly Shabbat dinners at New College. There was Moshe, whose family had somehow survived the Holocaust; and Matthew, who didn't feel comfortable wearing his yarmulke in parts of the South; and Juan, a first-generation college student who was saving money during his senior year by forgoing student housing and sleeping instead in the gym. Sometimes there were ten people seated at the Shabbat table on Friday nights: one gay, one black, one Hispanic, two Jewish, several female. And then there was Derek. He was white. He was male. He was straight. He had his college tuition fully paid for and his parents' credit card tucked into his pocket. "In no reality am I the person at that table who's been discriminated against," he told Allison.

By the time he arrived in Bordeaux, France, in the first days of 2013 for his French-immersion class, Derek felt increasingly detached from his white nationalist views. "The ideology is flawed, and I've moved away from it," he told Allison, and when they traded New Year's resolutions, he told her he wanted to "be more mindful of other people and concerned with what they say." Then he started his French classes and befriended a handful of other American college students who were studying abroad. Eventually one of those students searched Derek's name on Google, and soon the group was uninviting him to parties and talking about him loudly in the school. "His name is Black and he doesn't like black people," Derek overheard one of them say. He closed the door of his room and vented online to Allison. She asked him: How many more potential friendships was he willing to sacrifice for an ideology he no longer really believed in? How many more opportunities would he allow himself to lose?

"Sometimes I just wish I could spend the rest of my life going where nobody has ever heard of me," he wrote to Allison, but because he knew that wasn't possible, Derek said he planned to adopt another approach. He wanted to withdraw from white nationalism and disappear from public life.

"I'm done," he told Allison one night. "I don't believe in it, and I'm not going to be involved."

10.   "I Have to Do This Now"

What Derek wanted to accomplish most of all during his final months at New College was also the thing he had never done: to avoid controversy; to mollify both the social justice advocates and his activist family; to somehow recede from the front lines of white nationalism so quietly that no one would notice or care. He logged out of his Stormfront account for good. He turned down interview requests and an invitation to speak at a white power leadership conference, explaining he was busy with his final year of school. He told his father he was officially retiring from the radio show—not revealing his shift away from white nationalism, but instead saying only that he was bored after spending five years on the show.

"Time to begin focusing on other things," Derek told Allison that winter.

"It feels like we are basically aligned on most things at this point," she wrote to him, and because there was so little left to debate, they focused on enjoying their last months together at school. Derek was accepted into the medieval studies program at Western Michigan University, which also offered a stipend to cover living expenses, and he made plans to enroll. Allison had one more year left at New College, but she and Derek agreed to visit each other every few months and to live together in Florida during their summer and winter breaks. They took a celebratory trip to explore the Everglades. They went to Disney's Magic Kingdom and drove to Alabama to see Derek's grandmother. "I want to get everything in before it's over!" Allison wrote, and so just days before Derek's graduation they traveled together to be tourists in New Orleans, and one night they went to Baton Rouge to see the capitol. They stayed with one of Derek's old family friends, a white nationalist who had managed Duke's successful campaign for state office. The friend told Derek and Allison war stories late into the night about organizing rallies for Duke and protests against Elie Wiesel, an Auschwitz survivor whose writing and activism helped fortify America's public memory of the Holocaust. Derek nodded along politely in response to the stories, until Allison abruptly excused herself from the room and Derek followed. "I can't listen to this anymore," she remembered telling him. She had expended every bit of her patience and understanding in her discussions with Derek about white nationalism, and now that he no longer considered himself a white nationalist, she felt as if she never wanted to hear about the ideology again. "I want to be done with this," she told him. Everything about the ideology made her angry, and that anger made her think about Derek and all the damage he had already done.

On their long drive back to Sarasota the next day, she began to remind him of the public archive he had built within white nationalism: A website for "white children of the globe." Thousands of public Stormfront posts. Several hundred radio shows. Dozens of interviews, speeches, and a conference now going into its third year. No matter how much Derek wanted to disappear, that legacy wasn't going to disappear with him. In the car, Allison asked Derek how many people he had influenced during his time as a white nationalist. How many had he radicalized? How many had he turned into activists? And how many millions of other people had his rhetoric offended or oppressed?

"You have an obligation to say in public that you don't believe in this, and that you were factually and morally wrong," she told him, and she tried to convince Derek to write a public statement condemning white nationalism.

But Derek was noncommittal. Publicly disavowing white nationalism would also mean publicly wounding his family, so in the ensuing days he tried to change the subject whenever Allison brought up his culpability. Increasingly, discussing white nationalism filled Derek with shame and regret. It was so much easier to think about his future than to worry about disentangling himself from the past, especially when bits of that past seemed to be manifesting themselves all around him in the present political moment.

President Obama was pushing to pass comprehensive immigration reform in the first months of 2013, and some conservatives were fighting back with anti-immigrant propaganda. On the nightly news, Derek heard mainstream politicians echo many of his old euphemisms: that immigrants were lawbreakers with a "third-world nature," and their "massive invasion" of the United States had eroded the country's traditions and culture. Those arguments were amplified in April 2013 when two Muslim immigrants carried out a terrorist attack at the finish line of the Boston Marathon. In the ensuing wave of Islamophobia, a white nationalist sympathizer named John Tanton organized a rally on the National Mall where one of the keynote speakers railed against the immigrant pollution of America's bloodlines. "You cannot breed Secretariat to a donkey and expect to win the Kentucky Derby," said Ken Crow, a Tea Party founder, and if his rhetoric sounded extreme, his audience was hardly limited to fringe extremists. Out there in the massive crowd were thousands of Tea Partyers and several lawmakers they continued to support, like Ted Cruz, Jeff Sessions, and Steve King, all of whom had signed a pledge to defeat any bill resembling amnesty for immigrants.

"It's like I helped feed a monster that won't go back into the cage," Derek told Allison once. "I can't go back and do everything over."

But Allison continued to insist there *was* something he could do. "You need to make these points in public," she told him. "You've caused too much damage to slip away."

Derek wanted to skip his graduation ceremony and collect his diploma in private, just as he had done in community college. New College graduation had all the makings of the spectacle he'd been hoping to avoid: student activists and his family members sitting underneath the same tent, all of them waiting for Derek's name to be called over the loudspeaker so he could walk alone across a stage in front of hundreds of people. There were rumors that some students were planning a protest for that moment—maybe some kind of a chant or a mass exodus when he accepted his diploma. Derek had envisioned many of the possibilities, and none were good. But his grandmother and his mother wanted to see him graduate. His mother had paid for his college tuition in each of the last three years, and now she had requested the day off from work to come to the ceremony in Sarasota. There was no choice, she told him. So Derek dressed in a dark jacket and walked to the commencement tent on Sarasota Bay, lining up in alphabetical order with the rest of the Bs.

The one person who hadn't come was his father, because both Don and Derek agreed that was for the best. Don's picture had been posted a few times on the student forum, showing him in KKK robes and white power T-shirts, and if students recognized him at the commencement, Derek thought they would surely revolt. Instead Don stayed home in West Palm Beach and monitored Stormfront, waiting for a call from Chloe so he could listen by phone to the announcement of his only son's college graduation. "One more sacrifice on behalf of the cause" was how Don explained it, but this sacrifice hurt. He hated the idea that he was cowing to the threat of a potential student protest. "It was like conceding the battle to those little commies, but knowing that I'd still won the war," he remembered thinking, because Don believed Derek had embedded for three years with the liberal Left and still emerged with his ideology intact. His classmates' ostracism hadn't changed him. Their harassment had failed to alter his politics. As far as Don and everyone else could tell, Derek was still a committed white nationalist, and now he would walk away from New College with a mainstream degree that could propel both him and the white nationalist movement to wider success.

Derek filed into the tent with the rest of the graduates and walked with his head down to a seat in the second row. His family sat near the back of the tent, as did Matthew and Allison and a few other friends, all of whom still had a year left at New College. Matthew introduced himself to Derek's family and tried to make small talk, but a few of those family members noticed Matthew's yarmulke and tried to cut the conversation short. A band played a welcome song, and then a commencement speaker came onto the stage. He was a Florida judge named Charles Williams, one of the first black men to rule on the Florida circuit court, and he had made documentaries about civil rights and been given awards by the NAACP. He had heard about the student-organized shutdown on campus the previous year—and about the racism that precipitated it—so he had written a speech about the legacy of segregation and institutional racism. "Fight oppression," he said, as the students stood to applaud and Derek stood with them. "Promote fairness and inclusiveness in all matters."

"And now for the real stars: the graduates," he said, so Derek and two hundred of his classmates began forming a line at the side of the stage, waiting for each of their names to be called. It was less of an orderly processional than a chaotic conga line. Students shared wine bottles, tossed each other beer cans, danced, and shouted in celebration. It was a tradition at New College that the graduation ceremony was in fact another form of creative expression, and many of the students were dressed not in traditional formal wear but in elaborate costume: a Jedi knight, a horse, a zombie, an astronaut, a half-naked fairy princess, a Soviet communist, a man with a peace symbol painted across his bare chest. It was wild. It was unpredictable. Derek stepped closer toward the stage and thought: This is probably going to be bad.

"Ash."

"Baker."

"Beckman."

Each name was greeted by thunderous applause. That was the thing about a small school: Every student was well known, and each reaction was personal. Derek reminded himself that out in the crowd he had at least a smattering of supporters. There was Maynard, his friend and landlord, who admired Derek so much that he had long ago stopped charging him for rent. There were his two thesis advisers, history professors who had written him recommendations for graduate school and who considered Derek among the strongest graduates in his class. There was Juan and Moshe and Matthew and Allison and his family. At least they would all clap for him.

"Benson."

"Berry."

But what would everyone else do? They would boo him. They would glare. Because why wouldn't they? To his classmates Derek was still an avowed white nationalist, a radio host, an up-and-coming politician. Only Allison understood exactly how much New College students had affected his thinking in the last years. Only she knew how much their exclusion had made him reconsider the ways his ideology oppressed others, and how their inclusion at Shabbat had helped him better empathize with minorities and Jews. Allison had continued pushing Derek to write something about it—to make some kind of statement denouncing his former racist views—but he had continued to put it off. Now he wondered: Why hadn't he just done it?

"Bickerton."

Derek climbed up the stairs onto the edge of the stage. In the far back of the tent, James Birmingham was standing up in an anti-Nazi T-shirt. Derek kept his eyes straight ahead, never looking at the crowd.

"Derek Roland Black."

He stepped onto the stage. He walked toward the provost, who held out his diploma. From the far back of the tent came a muffled yell: "Racist." And then: Nothing. He shook the provost's hand. He reached out for his diploma. A few of his friends clapped, but most of his classmates sat quietly in their chairs, as if resigned. They had tried to change him, and they had failed. At least for the moment, that was all they knew. He had arrived at New College as a white nationalist. He was leaving a white nationalist. He grabbed his diploma as the provost called out the next name, and a few seconds later Derek was back down the stairs and off the stage.

Are you going to do this?" Allison wrote to him, because now a month had gone by since Derek's graduation and he had yet to make a public renunciation of white nationalism.

He was still living in Sarasota, spending his summer house-sitting for a former professor and interning in the library of the Ringling Museum. Allison had left for a summer research fellowship in Blacksburg, Virginia; Derek's parents were across the state in West Palm Beach. He was mostly alone, and when he wasn't working in the library, he was sometimes sitting at his favorite coffee shop and staring again at a blank document on his computer screen titled "Letter About My Beliefs."

"You think maybe letter-writing today?" Allison texted him one day.

"I don't know," he told her.

She wrote to him again a little while later: "How's that letter going?"

"Contemplatively," he said.

He had begun to think in earnest about what he wanted to say. If he was going to go through the painful process of renouncing his beliefs, he wanted to do it as completely as possible. He wanted to apologize for the damage he caused and condemn racism in the most public way he could. He wanted to release a thorough statement and then legally change his name, switching his first and middle names, so he could leave Florida for his first semester at Western Michigan and begin anew as Roland Derek Black. But there was no way to condemn his own views and actions without also condemning his family's views and actions. He was sure they would be upset, and likely furious. What he didn't know was whether they would ever speak to him again. He had heard what his father sometimes said about white nationalists who abandoned the movement. They were "weaklings" and "sell-outs" and "traitors to the cause." So Derek let the days pass by as he sorted through medieval documents in the library, watched movies at the nearby dollar theater, or kayaked in Sarasota Bay.

Allison knew Derek preferred to process information on his own schedule. Whenever she confronted him about publicly renouncing white nationalism, he became evasive or even defensive. He liked to see ideas in writing and then process on his own time, so early in the summer Allison decided to write him an email about his potential renunciation. It was her final argument, and she sent it off late one night in early June. Derek opened Allison's message and started to read:

> Hmm. I'm not sure exactly how to write this. But I think you are occasionally quite oblivious of how those who don't know about white nationalism perceive white nationalism. This is not a thing you want to blow up on you at Western Michigan. I don't think you want a reputation of infamy and racism to precede your reputation of being a hardworking, smart student.
>
> I realize that if you change your name, it's not going to go over well with your family. You don't like to cause

conflict. This will cause conflict. But I also think it is *very important to do*. WN is not something you plan to do with your life. So *get out of this*. Get out of this while you can, before it ruins some part of your future more than it already irreparably has.

I also think that you need to have a statement— something concrete, something you can point to and say *no, look, I have publicly renounced this. I do not hold white nationalist beliefs, and have publicly separated myself from them.* That, on top of changing your name, is the best you can do for now.

Like, in case you think you have nothing to be sorry for, you've said things like this, all in 2007:

"The Civil War was such a glaring act of oppression to White America and really an example of how bad we can be."

"We have to drive on every day, all the time, that Jews are NOT White. This has to be the cutoff that Jews are expelled and do not come back."

And, my fav: "I'm ready for the return of political posters that will promise me White supremacy. Good honest pride is by nature intended to be power in any case."

It does very, very, very much bother me when you act like you've done nothing wrong or hurt no one throughout your WN career. *It was wrong*, and WN hurts people and perpetuates stereotypes and harm and hatred. Spend ten minutes looking around Stormfront. Are these people you identify with? They are crazy. They are angry. They demean others. They perpetuate racial stereotypes and oppression. You contributed to that— unequivocally. You can't just drop out when you're

bored and be like "ok that's done" and not acknowledge
the harm you have done through your actions.

I do not think this part will be easy. You will lose
WN friends. You will hurt your family, or at least make
them angry. People will probably spin it to hurt the WN
movement. I don't blame them; I sure as hell would,
too. Your web of WN connections will be affected. But
there's a huge world out there besides the WN community, and that's the world you're going to be living in.

I love you. I will be here for you regardless. But, if for
whatever reason we stopped talking forever tomorrow,
I would still with all my heart think that this is what
would be best. For you, for your future, for humanity
as a whole. There's nothing good in WN. So if you're
going to change your name, and you're going to get out
of this and disassociate from this, *do it*.

Derek read over Allison's email several times during
the next few days and used it as motivation to write some
notes for a potential statement. "You're probably right that
the best thing is to be accountable," he told her, but before
he did anything, he wanted to see his parents. His mother
was still forwarding him chain emails about Obama's "antiwhite" immigration reform efforts; his father was expecting
him to attend the third annual Stormfront conference later
that summer. They had no idea how much his thinking had
changed, so, in July 2013, Derek drove home to see them.

His hope was to tell them about his beliefs and to offer
some sort of explanation. He wanted to be kind. He wanted
to be honest. He wanted to tell them about Allison or Matthew or the concept of white privilege or the true history

of the Middle Ages. If he was going to break their hearts, he wanted to do it in person. It was the right thing to do. But then his mother greeted him at the door with a hug and the gift of a new AAA membership card, because she was worried about him driving in the snow once he moved to Michigan. They started to make new windows together for the living room, working side by side at a table saw to thin down the wooden frames, losing themselves in the simple satisfaction of the work. Derek and his mother had rebuilt much of the house together over the last decade with little professional help, updating doors and windowpanes on the family property that Derek's great-grandparents bought in 1922. Now Derek wondered what would happen if he told his parents about his beliefs. How many more times would he be welcomed back?

Derek finished installing a window in the living room, and then Don took him to buy a new battery for his cell phone. Maybe now Derek could finally summon the courage to say something. Maybe once they were alone in the car. But instead Don started to talk excitedly about politics, assuming as always that he and Derek were in full agreement. The previous night, a jury in Sanford, Florida, had ruled that George Zimmerman acted in self-defense in 2012 when he killed Trayvon Martin, an unarmed black teenager. Zimmerman told investigators that he thought Martin "looked suspicious" wandering around the gated Florida neighborhood in a hooded sweatshirt, so he had followed Martin to within seventy feet of his family's apartment and then shot him during a confrontation. The controversial verdict had inspired a series of protests against racial inequality—walkouts at dozens of Florida high schools, coordinated marches, and statements of solidarity from black leaders like President Obama,

LeBron James, and Jay-Z. "Trayvon Martin could have been me thirty-five years ago," Obama had said.

According to one poll in *The Washington Post*, 90 percent of minorities considered the shooting "unjustified," compared with only 30 percent of whites, and Don was delighted that the entire country was suddenly engaged in a divisive argument about race. Fox News and other networks had begun to broadcast stories throughout the summer of 2013 warning viewers about the "knockout game," an urban myth in which roving gangs of minority youths supposedly attacked elderly white people for sport. Police departments around the country said the "knockout game" did not in fact exist, but Don thought the rumor alone had helped surface old white nationalist talking points about black aggression and black-on-white crime. Donald Trump had weighed in on Twitter from his resort across the water in Palm Beach, parroting white nationalist rhetoric. "Sadly the overwhelming amount of violent crime in our major cities is committed by blacks and Hispanics—a tough subject—must be discussed," Trump had written, and now thousands of people were bringing those same assumptions to Stormfront. Traffic had spiked to a record 3.5 million U.S. visitors during the last three months. "Everyone is paying attention to this situation with poor little Trayvon," Don had said on the radio. "There will be massive riots. There will be huge backlash among our people."

Derek listened to some of Don's points, and his confusion hardened into anger. For years, Derek had finished Don's sentences on the radio, but now his father's reasoning sounded foreign, uninformed, and cruel. Derek had done his own thinking about Trayvon Martin during the last weeks, reading articles that detailed "the talk" black parents sometimes gave their children about how to stay safe in a country that feared them. Derek had done his part to help instill that fear—to make people like George Zimmerman think young black men were somehow biologically prone to be more violent. Now Derek believed that theory was utter nonsense. Instead he thought young black men were "in one of the worst positions in society," he wrote to Allison, because they were the victims of both structural and interpersonal prejudice. "The Trayvon tragedy is sad and sobering, and the worst part is how much more often stuff like this is probably going to happen, because there is so much distrust and fear," Derek told Allison once. But now, in the car with his father, he couldn't find the words to say anything. The divide between what he believed and what his father assumed he believed was too wide for any conversation to cross. He tried to turn their talk away from politics until they returned home.

There was more work left to do on the windows, but Derek wanted to get away from the house and the blaring cable news on TV. He told his parents he needed to get back to Sarasota. They hugged him good-bye, and Derek drove instead to a nearby bar, finding a quiet corner where he could sit alone with a glass of water and his thoughts. Why hadn't he leveled with his parents about his beliefs? And how could he ever?

He thought again about everything his father had said publicly about Trayvon Martin. It was all typical stuff— the same ugly talking points Derek had been hearing and often repeating for his entire life—so why did it make him so angry? It wasn't just his father's views that suddenly horrified him, Derek decided. It was the memory of his previous self. He had made versions of those same flawed arguments. He had expressed similar callousness, ignorance, and cruelty.

It seemed obvious to him now that he needed to publicly condemn not only white nationalism but also his past life. He took out his computer and opened up the notes he had begun jotting down over the last weeks with Allison. Now was the time to finish writing his letter, while the ugliness of white nationalism remained fresh in his mind. He sat in the bar and started to type:

> A large section of the community I grew up in believes strongly in white nationalism, and members of my family whom I respect greatly, particularly my father, have long been resolute advocates for that cause. I was not prepared to risk driving a wedge in those relationships.
>
> After a great deal of thought since then, I have resolved that it is in the best interests of everyone involved, directly or indirectly, to be honest about my slow but steady disaffiliation from white nationalism. The things I have said as well as my actions have been harmful to people of color, people of Jewish descent and all others affected. I will not contribute to any cause that perpetuates this harm in the future. Advocating for redress of the supposed oppression of whites in the West is by its nature damaging to all others because of the privileged position of white people in these societies. Promoting a victim complex for whites does not recognize the oppressed experiences of others, and that's what my efforts have done.
>
> It is impossible to argue rationally that in our society, with its overwhelming disparity between white power and that of everyone else, racial equity programs represent oppression of whites. More importantly, white

nationalism's staunch opposition to the gains in numbers and in influence of non-whites makes it a movement by nature committed to suppressing these people.
It has become clear to me that white nationalism is not
a movement of positive identity or of asserting cultural
values, but of constant antagonism at the betterment of
other groups. Advocating for white nationalism means
that we are opposed to minority attempts to elevate
themselves to a position equal to our own. It is an advocacy that I cannot support, having grown past my bub-
ble, talked to the people I affected, read more widely,
and realized the impact my actions had on people I
never wanted to harm. I am sorry for the damage done
by my actions.

I realize not all will instantly believe me, or may
perceive this as a seemingly abrupt change when it has
been instead a gradual awakening process. I understand
that my words don't suddenly heal all wounds caused
by my actions or my encouragement of others. Time,
however, will demonstrate my full lack of involvement.
I should be the one who calls out what I disagree with.

I can't support a movement that tells me I can't be a
friend to whomever I wish or that other people's races
require me to think about them in a certain way or
be suspicious at their advancements. Minorities must
have the ability to rise to positions of power, and many
supposed "race" issues are in fact issues of structural
oppression, poor educational prospects, and limited
opportunity. I believe we can move beyond the sort
of mind-boggling emphasis white nationalism puts on
maintaining an oppressive, exclusive sense of identity—
oppressive for others and stifling for our society.

Derek edited a few sentences, read over the letter one final time, and then sent it to Allison. She told him that the letter was forceful and appropriate and that she was proud of him. But she also suggested he take a few minutes to think it over. "This needs to be something you're sure about," she wrote to him. "Your family is going to be angry. They will be hurt." But Derek also believed it was his family, and particularly his father, who had taught him the importance of speaking publicly about his beliefs, even when it resulted in significant backlash. "I have to do this now or I'm going to lose my nerve," he told Allison.

He thought about sending his letter to the New College student forum, but he was no longer a student, and he worried his message might go unnoticed outside the college. He considered sending it to newspapers, but he couldn't be sure how much they would care or whether they would publish it.

There was only one venue that Derek thought made sense—the one publication read by white nationalists, social justice advocates, and the mainstream press. It was where his renunciation would resonate the loudest. It was also where it would hurt his family the most. He opened up an email and addressed it to the SPLC, the civil rights group his father had been battling against for more than forty years.

"Please publish in full," Derek instructed. Then he attached his letter and hit send.

11. "So Much Worse Than I Ever Thought"

Don was at the computer the next afternoon searching Google when Derek's name popped up in a headline on his screen. For a decade, Don had been typing "Stormfront" and "Derek Black" into the search bar a few times each week to track his son's public rise in white nationalism, and the search engine had reliably kicked back headlines like "The Great White Hope," and "Next David Duke." Don had saved many of the stories and shared them publicly on Stormfront. This latest piece was published by the SPLC, which Don had always derisively referred to as the "Poverty Palace." He clicked the link and started to read.

"Activist Son of Key Racist Leader Renounces White Nationalism," the headline stated, and Don quickly scanned through the full text, which had allegedly been written by Derek. It wasn't just a letter of separation from white nationalism; it was a top-to-bottom evisceration of the ideology, with phrases like "structural oppression," "privilege," "limited opportunity," and "marginalized groups"—the kind of liberal-apologist language Don and Derek had often made fun of together on the radio. Derek obviously hadn't written it, and Don assumed the SPLC was trying to smear his family again. The SPLC had previously published investigations into his wife's employment and his family's finances. Now it was going after his son. Don called Derek to warn him about the story. He assumed the SPLC was making it up, but he thought it was also possible that one of Derek's "commie classmates" had sent off a fake letter.

"Somebody broke into your email," Don remembered telling Derek, once he reached him on the phone. "You got hacked."

"The letter is real," Derek said, and he apologized for not telling Don directly. Don stumbled for words before abruptly hanging up.

For the next several minutes, Don remained in disbelief. Maybe he had somehow misunderstood what Derek said. Maybe Derek was pulling some kind of elaborate prank to mark Don's upcoming sixtieth birthday. Derek called back a few minutes later, and this time Chloe answered, sounding hysterical. She said she didn't want to speak to him and then handed the phone to Don. His voice was shaky and tearful. Derek had never heard him that way. Don said he wanted final confirmation: Had this letter really come from Derek? Was this actually what he believed? "Yes," Derek said. "I wrote it, and it's what I think."

The next hours unfolded in a cycle of rage and grief. Derek tried to distract himself by going to his internship at the Ringling Museum and then seeing a movie at the nearby dollar theater with his teenage niece, who was visiting from West Palm Beach. But every few hours he picked up his phone to answer another text message, email, or call from his family. His parents said they had raised him to make history, not just study it. They said he had thrown away twenty-five years of the family's hard work. They said he wasn't the person they thought they knew. They said, after a lifetime spent fighting against the SPLC, he had walked across enemy lines and "surrendered the biggest possible trophy." They said that maybe he had a "mental disorder" or "character flaws."

They said he was "part of the population that doesn't want to hurt anyone's feelings so you ignore and bury the real science." They said this was "nails to the heart." They said not to come back to West Palm Beach. They said, "You need to make new friends and family." They said, over and over, that they never wanted to speak with Derek again, and then they would hang up in a fit of rage, determined to be done with it, until after a few hours their grief and heartache and utter sense of abandonment became so overwhelming that they couldn't help but call Derek again.

Don dialed Derek late that night, and Derek thought this time his father sounded more measured—practically calm. Don said he'd been reflecting on his life, thinking back on the lowest moments. He had been shot in the stomach as a teenager. He'd spent years in federal prison. He'd suffered a stroke and fought off depression and seen many of his closest friends die. But this, Don told Derek, was by far the worst experience of his life. Don said he had weighed out the pros and cons, and he had concluded that it would have been better for their family if Derek hadn't been born. Derek sat in stunned silence as Don hung up. Then Don called back a few moments later, his voice once again shaky, to tell Derek that of course that wasn't true, and to apologize.

The next afternoon Derek's half sister showed up in Sarasota with little warning to pick up Derek's niece and take her back home to West Palm Beach. The half sister said she no longer trusted Derek to look after her daughter, which made Derek irate. Several years earlier he had taken his young niece alone on a monthlong road trip across the country, and she had stayed with him for weeks at a time in Sarasota. Now his family thought Derek was a bad influence, an "enemy" who was plotting to brainwash his young niece into liberalism. His half sister told Derek to hug both of them good-bye, because she thought it might be the last time they saw each other. Derek watched them drive off and went back into the house alone.

"It's a mess," he told Allison. "I think I might be getting disowned. Many family members have vowed never to talk to me again. I knew it was going to be bad, but it's so much worse than I ever thought."

"I'm so sorry love," she wrote to him. "Reading that broke my heart. Keep your head up. You are starting something new, and you are doing it by yourself, and sometimes it is going to be hard and scary. But you can do it. And you can do it with grace. I am always, always here for you. This too will pass."

She was still living in Virginia for her internship, but during those first days Allison called Derek to check on him every few hours. She reassured him that he had done the right thing. She told him she was proud of his courage, and as the news continued to spread on Facebook and through the mainstream media, so were many others. Derek's message in-box filled with congratulatory notes and voice mails, many of them from people who had never spoken with him directly about white nationalism. Rose, whom Derek had dated for a few weeks during his first year at New College, wrote that she was "happy/proud, and I know it can't be easy." Juan said he had always believed Derek was "smart and kind enough to find his own way out." Moshe said it was "pretty damn brave." Matthew thought Derek had shown "uncommon courage." Even on the New College student forum, where James Birmingham joked that his anti-fascist T-shirts had probably made all the difference, there was something like an uneasy consensus. "Of course what he did was the right thing to do, so much so that it may be considered almost a perfunctory act of human decency," one student wrote. "But it also took brass balls. Kudos to Derek."

The SPLC decided to remove Derek's extremist file from its website, and several TV stations contacted New College hoping to speak with Derek. He declined all of their interview requests, but he decided to write a public response to a feature article about his transformation in an online publication called the *Daily Beast*. The story contained quotes from Don about his own disappointment, and the writer speculated that Derek, an unusually bright college student, had thought his way out of white nationalism by reading studies and books. Derek wrote to the reporter after the story was published to tell her that it "seemed mostly fair" but that the influence of New College students on his thinking "was the biggest chunk missing."

"People who disagreed with me were critical in this process," he wrote. "Especially those who were my friends regardless, but who let me know when we talked about it that they thought my beliefs were wrong and took the time to provide evidence and civil arguments. I didn't always agree with their ideas, but I listened to them and they listened to me.

"Furthermore, a critical juncture was when I'd realize that a friend was considered an outsider by the philosophy I supported. It's a huge contradiction to share your summer plans with someone whom you completely respect, only to then realize that your ideology doesn't consider them a full member of society. I couldn't resolve that."

•

And then the news made its way onto Stormfront, where Don decided he had no choice but to respond in public to Derek's letter. What he really wanted to do was to disconnect his phone, close down his computer, turn off the TV, and stay in bed. "I felt depressed and basically paralyzed by all of it," Don remembered. But he had always believed it was better to confront reality than to hide from it, so he forced himself back onto the message board and posted a copy of Derek's statement:

> I'm sure this will be all over the net and our local media, so I'll start here.
>
> Derek was here all last weekend, helping us build and replace old windows. He's made it annoyingly obvious over the past few months that he was no longer interested in WN activism, but he always said he was still WN. He didn't give us a clue as to what he had planned today.
>
> I found it Googling this afternoon. He says he doesn't understand why we'd feel betrayed just because he announced his "personal beliefs" to our worst enemies. Just when I thought I couldn't lose anything else . . .

Don read back through some of Derek's old text messages and Stormfront posts, looking for clues he might have missed, but nothing helped him understand the full force of Derek's transformation. For years, Don had believed in two facts above all: that white nationalism was an inherently righteous cause; and that Derek was one of the smartest, most rational people he knew. Now those facts were in conflict. Had Don been wrong about Derek's intelligence? Or had he somehow been wrong about white nationalism?

He didn't want to consider either possibility, so he tried to come up with theories that would make it all fit. Maybe Derek was just faking a change in ideology so he could have an easier life and a more successful career in academia, he thought. Or maybe this was Derek's way of rebelling against his family. Don spoke for hours on the phone that week with Duke, who suggested another theory. Duke thought Derek was suffering from a kind of Stockholm syndrome. He had become a hostage to liberal academia and then experienced a misguided empathy for his captors and their views about the world.

For much of that next week, Don stayed in bed and considered following at least part of Derek's example. Maybe, Don thought, now was also the time for him to withdraw from a public life in white nationalism. He was turning sixty in a few days, and he thought he could retreat from the movement and pass it off as an early retirement. "I had no heart left for any of it," Don said, because everything about white nationalism also reminded him of Derek's renunciation. There was Derek's radio show, and Derek's upcoming third annual Stormfront conference about verbal tactics, and Derek's "white genocide" magnet still attached to the family refrigerator. Worst of all, there were hundreds of white nationalists talking about Derek on Stormfront, the message board Don had assumed Derek would take over. On some nights, Don opened his computer in bed and read through the reaction to Derek's statement on Stormfront. White nationalists wondered if Derek had been paid off or somehow bribed by the SPLC. They wondered if he was secretly gay or if he had a girlfriend who was black. They wondered, because Derek had changed his mind, if maybe Don's thinking could evolve, too.

After a week of silence, Don logged back on to Stormfront and started to write. He had built this community, and
it deserved a response:

This really isn't anybody's business but my family's, but after a miserable seven days, I feel the need
to vent. I only know what Derek tells me, which has
been baffling. He says he changed his mind, partially
after studying medieval history. I told him he couldn't
possibly believe that mush he wrote to the SPLC, particularly *after* studying medieval history. So we argued
history and politics a while. I could never imagine I
would one day be arguing the reality of racial differences with Derek.

He was also offended his family thought he had
been brainwashed, as we knew he could always think
for himself. He had/has much more potential than I
ever did. He inherited my strengths without my weaknesses. He's more focused and more driven than I ever
was, though that drive has now been diverted.

He seems genuinely surprised his entire adult family has been devastated. Derek repeated his belief that
family ties are separate from politics. I said that obviously wasn't true with a family centered on political
activism.

Hundreds of posts quickly followed, many offering Don
condolences. "Sympathy for you on your loss," read one. Or:
"Let's try to move on and let Derek be Derek." But there
were also dozens of angrier messages—each one another
reminder for Don that his private trauma was also a public
embarrassment within his community. For a decade, all of

white nationalism had rallied around Derek as if he were the movement's lovable mascot: young and smart, with a funny hat and bright red hair. Everyone felt as if they knew him, and so his rejection also seemed personal.

"Anger and disappointment," one poster wrote. "Then again, we don't need weaklings in our cause."

"Derek's now an open enemy to the survival of the white race."

"He's a traitor without hope or redemption. Should WN's ever seize power, his name should figure prominently on the 'Hunt Down List.'"

"Brass knuckles to the face and groin. Then water boarding."

Don felt tempted to defend Derek, and he also had the urge to distance himself. Were these internet posters his comrades or his enemies? For the first time in decades, Don surveyed the online battlefield and couldn't decide which side was his. So eventually, after a few hundred posts, he decided to shut down the message thread, describing it on Stormfront as an "open wound." He retreated from the message board and spent more and more time in bed, until Chloe and other family members began to worry for his health. Only once before had Don become so despondent, six years earlier during his week of complete paralysis before he began to regain a little bit of movement after the stroke, and it was visiting with Derek and listening to Derek's daily radio show that helped pull him through those days. Now Derek had mostly stopped texting and calling. In a few weeks, he would be leaving Florida and moving across the country to Michigan.

There was only one thing Don thought might help pull him from depression—the same thing that had always helped. He wanted to see Derek. His sixtieth birthday was only a few days away, and Chloe had planned a family party. Don wanted Derek to come. "Otherwise I would have the whole family together for this party without this huge piece," Don remembered thinking. "Even the idea of that was depressing. Derek needed to be there."

Chloe said she didn't like the idea. She wasn't ready to talk to Derek yet, let alone see him, and neither were his half sisters. "The women in the family were vengeful," Don remembered. "Over and over again, I was taking Derek's side."

And in this case it was Don's birthday, and Chloe wanted to give him what he wanted. She told Don he could leave his birthday party and visit somewhere nearby with Derek alone. Don agreed, and later that night he sent a note to his son.

"I would like to see you," he said.

Early the next morning, Derek moved out of Sarasota for the final time. He packed his clothes and his guitar into the trunk of his PT Cruiser and put his Venus flytrap in the cup holder. He said good-bye to Maynard and drove one last loop through the New College campus. His original plan had been to head straight north—through Virginia to pick up Allison and then on to Ohio to visit her family before he moved to Michigan—but now Derek had decided to add one extra stop. He drove east on rural highways, passing through peanut farms and cotton fields as he counted down the miles to West Palm Beach. Don's birthday party was at Derek's grandmother's house in nearby Lake Worth, and Derek had no idea what to expect. He knew his father wanted to see him, but he didn't know about anyone else. A few days earlier, he had received the latest chain email from his family, a string of conspiracy theories about President Obama's "radical black activism," and this time the chain mail had included a personal note from a family member. "You are more welcome at the White House than our house," it read.

Derek also worried his parents might reclaim his PT Cruiser. They had paid for it, the title was in their name, and they had made it abundantly clear during the last week that they were done paying his way. They had already made plans to cut off his credit card and remove him from their auto insurance policy. On the day Derek's letter went public, they had threatened to call the police and report the car stolen unless he returned it right away. Now Derek thought about stashing the car out of sight at a nearby restaurant and taking a bus, but instead he continued driving to his grandmother's house on Lake Worth. When he arrived, most of his family was gathered on a wooden porch behind the house. Derek had spent dozens of afternoons back there, playing croquet with relatives or reading in a chair near the water, but now some of his family greeted him at the front door and asked him not to come in. His mom gave him a brief hug and walked away. His half sisters said nothing. Derek waited outside for Don. "They said if I wanted to see Derek, then we both had to leave," Don remembered. "I got kicked out of my own party."

They got into Derek's car and drove toward one of their favorite spots in Palm Beach, passing Donald Trump's Mar-a-Lago Club and continuing up Ocean Boulevard until Derek found a concrete bench with a clear view of the Atlantic. For more than a decade, Derek and Don had been coming together to the same spot to watch the first sunrise of each year. Those were some of Don's favorite mornings, when it felt as if he'd been given a fresh start and everything was imbued with sudden possibility, including white nationalism. "Maybe this is our year," he had always said. But now he was sixty and there were only so many years left. The late July heat was suffocating. Don made small talk with Derek about his birthday party, the extended family, and the ecology of the Atlantic. Derek still had his dry sense of humor. He still made smart observations about nature and science. He didn't seem like someone who had suddenly lost all ability to think rationally or been brainwashed. "Same old Derek," Don concluded after a little while, and that fact unnerved him. His grief had been so profound that he'd expected some physical manifestation of the loss. Instead, he found himself forgetting for several minutes at a time that Derek was now "living on the other side."

They went to dinner at a local bar and found a booth near the back. Don ordered a beer, and Derek drank water because he wanted a clear mind for the conversation he knew was coming. Don questioned Derek on his politics; Derek reiterated what he had written to the SPLC. Don told Derek he was probably suffering from Stockholm syndrome.

"That's so patronizing," Derek told him. "How can I prove this is what I really believe?"

Derek tried to convince Don for a few hours at the bar, unwinding many of the theories they had promoted together on the radio during the last decade. Derek doubted he could ever change Don's thinking about race. But he also thought that if his father would ever sit down and listen to anyone make the case against white nationalism, it was his son. Derek tried to explain that the notion of a white genocide was ridiculous, because no one was really killing off white people and because whiteness didn't exist in a biological sense, anyway. He said whites in the United States were not oppressed but in fact inherently privileged, which meant that white nationalism was just a tool to promote white supremacy. He went over the latest science on IQ score differentials, and he talked about how the great Islamic societies had developed algebra and predicted a lunar eclipse during the Middle Ages. He told Don about the health effects of racism, which had made him realize that white nationalism was not just a flawed ideology but also one that caused real damage.

"It's not just that it's wrong. It's that we hurt people," Derek remembered saying, repeating the point that Allison had often made to him.

"I can't believe I'm arguing with you, of all people, about racial realities," Don remembered telling him.

The restaurant was shutting down, and they were no closer to an understanding. Don's sixtieth birthday party had ended long ago, so Derek drove Don back to his house. It was dark and quiet, and they stood together for a minute on the porch. Don asked when he would see Derek again. Derek said probably soon, but that he wasn't exactly sure. Then he hugged his father good-bye and started driving toward Virginia to pick up Allison so they could continue on across the country.

Don went inside and thought about his conversation with Derek. "It wasn't like he couldn't use his brain anymore," Don remembered thinking. "He still made rational arguments." Despite all of Derek's attempts at persuasion, Don was still "pretty sure" he was right about race, he said, but he also felt exhausted by their conversation. He had been engaged in the same arguments about white nationalism for four decades, and now he was also arguing with the person he cared about most. His heart wasn't in it. He had little energy, no enthusiasm, and no successor. The annual Storm-front seminar was just a few weeks away, and Don wondered if he should make that conference his last.

"I didn't necessarily think I was wrong about anything," he said. "But you start to wonder what you're doing with your life, and if it's worth it."

The next time Derek came back to Florida was a few weeks later, for a court hearing to change his name.

He flew from the Northeast to West Palm Beach and then went to his parents' house. They had already left for the annual Stormfront conference in Tennessee a few days earlier, but Derek still had a key to the house, and he told his parents he was going to stay there. He slept in his old water bed and then awoke early for his appointment. He dressed in a button-down shirt and a tie and took a bus to the glass-walled courthouse downtown. Five years earlier, he'd come to the exact same block as a notorious white nationalist deter-mined to take his elected seat on the Palm Beach Republican Committee. He had been followed into the building by pro-testers, media crews, and police officers on the lookout for a sniper who might shoot him. But now the downtown block was quiet, and Derek walked unnoticed into the courthouse and found his name on the docket. He was worried the SPLC might have sent a reporter to write about his name change, so he found a seat in the back of the courtroom and waited for the judge to call his case.

He had already paid a four hundred dollar fee to change his name and submitted to a background check. This hear-ing was the final, cursory step, and Derek had thought hard about the finality of it. By switching the order of his names rather than changing them entirely, he believed he was being respectful to his parents. He hoped the new order of his names would offer him anonymity at Western Michigan and beyond. "But, realistically it's only going to act as a Google shield for so long," Derek wrote to Allison. What mattered just as much to him was the personal symbolism. He had read that throughout medieval history religious converts often took new names to signal a major life transition.

"Derek Roland Black," the judge called out. Derek stood, and the judge asked for his new name.

"Roland Derek Black," he said, and within a few seconds the judge had signed off on the paperwork.

Derek walked out of the courthouse and went back to the airport. He called Allison and told her that he felt good, clean. For the last decade he had been one person in public, and now he was another. All of the stereotypes he had promoted, all of the misinformation he'd helped spread, all of the hurtful and racist things he had believed and then said—it was all behind him now. That was Derek. This was Roland. He told Allison he never wanted to log on to Stormfront or watch cable news or so much as think about white nationalism or white supremacy ever again.

"It's all over and done with," he told her. Except at that very moment, at a white nationalist conference in Tennessee and beyond, the ideas he'd been promoting were continuing to spread.

12.   "Primed for This Revolution"

W elcome to the Derek Black Memorial Conference," Don said that August of 2013, as
he stood in front of one hundred white nationalists in the
Smoky Mountains and fumbled for words that might explain
what had happened during the last month.

It was his first speech since Derek sent his letter to the
SPLC, and all Don really wanted to do was "crawl into a hole
and not deal with any of it," he recalled thinking. But, with
Derek gone, Don was now the sole director and host of the
conference, and attendees had paid a hundred dollars each
in registration fees and traveled from all over the world to
hear his thoughts. They were Don's closest friends, and they
greeted him in Tennessee not with the judgment or skepticism he feared but with homemade food and condolences
about Derek. It had been years since Don attended a conference without Derek, and now at the podium he found
himself reflexively scanning the room for his son. "It looks
like *almost* all of our people are here," Don said, and then,
before he got teary, he moved on to discussing the growth of
Stormfront.

Don had always been considered a motivational force
within white nationalism, but now his friends in Tennessee sensed it was Don who needed inspiring. One afternoon
that week, Duke invited him to a private room at the retreat
where they could record a radio show. Duke still thought
Derek was suffering from Stockholm syndrome, and he had

no plans to call or speak with him. He was angry with Derek for abandoning the movement and especially for betraying Don. Duke wanted to comfort his friend, so that day on the radio he shared one of his favorite motivational poems, "Carry On!" by Robert Service. The English poet had written "Carry On!" to help motivate U.S. troops to fight against Hitler and the Nazis during World War II. But for Duke, the poem also applied to white nationalism and especially to Don. "This is the kind of thing that we have to get into our soul, our sinew, and our bones," Duke told Don, and then he started to read aloud from the poem, describing how a man could find dignity by persevering during moments of defeat. Duke finished the final stanzas and then cleared his throat.

"I just love that poem," he said. "Don, isn't it inspiring?"

"Absolutely," Don said. "Absolutely. And it certainly epitomizes what we are up against when we become discouraged and defeatist—when we think we can't win."

"I don't even think the odds are against us," Duke said. "We are still the vast majority. There are hundreds of millions of us, and we now have a tool, and you have been instrumental in giving us that tool: the internet."

"We can get our own message out now," Don said.

"And if you're depressed about what's going on in the world, or what's going on among your family, do you know how you get out of that depression?" Duke asked. "When you can be positive, the possibilities open. That's the only way we can really win this battle. When we are depressed, we don't see possibility, do we?"

"No," Don said. "Of course not."

Theme music began to play quietly in the background of their conversation, signaling the end of their radio show, but Duke raised his voice above the music. "Don, we are so in admiration of you, and we honor you," he said. "We are all so proud and so thankful of your great contributions to this cause. Thank you."

"Thank you, David," Don said, and now there was a bit more life in his voice.

Later that night, Don and Chloe hosted a dozen friends at their cabin for beers, and they talked about the spread of white nationalist ideas into mainstream politics. For all of Don's life, theirs had been an insurgent movement, explicitly condemned by nearly every establishment politician as a basic requirement of electability, but now it felt as if they had covert allies in surprising places. A few weeks earlier, the Supreme Court had voted 5 to 4 to overturn a key part of the Voting Rights Act, allowing for a new wave of voting restrictions throughout the South and effectively erasing one of Martin Luther King Jr.'s signature achievements on the fiftieth anniversary of his March on Washington. The resurgent Tea Party Caucus had stalled Obama's attempts at immigration reform by relying on nativist talking points. Alabama congressman Mo Brooks had gone on Laura Ingraham's radio show to echo the idea of white genocide by warning constituents of the "war on whites that's being launched by the Democratic Party." Iowa representative Steve King had become one of the most powerful Republican voices against immigration, and he used his platform to peddle misinformation and anti-immigrant stereotypes. "For every one immigrant who's a valedictorian, there's another hundred out there who weigh 130 pounds and they've got calves the size of cantaloupes because they're hauling seventy-five pounds of marijuana across the desert," King said. He also told voters that America could not restore the country to greatness with "somebody else's babies."

By the end of the night, Don felt reassured about the possibilities of white nationalism. "Camaraderie heals the spirit," Don remembered thinking of that night, and he continued to feel even more restored the next day, when he returned to the conference room and surveyed the people seated around him. The crowd was younger than ever before, and it included disaffected young men who had been introduced to Stormfront through online video game forums and the so-called men's rights movement, a collection of fringe misogynists who believe men have become disempowered by feminism and political correctness. Nearly half were attending their first white nationalist conference. Many lined up to introduce themselves to Don—including one young man who had graduated from college the same month as Derek.

Not long before, Matthew Heimbach had been the kind of disaffected white Republican that Don and Derek worked to convert on their radio show. He had transformed from a Mitt Romney supporter into a Tea Party organizer and then into a registered Stormfront user who chalked anti-immigration slurs on the sidewalks at Towson University in Maryland. Heimbach started the White Student Union at Towson, and now he was expanding that club to other colleges. He told Don that during his campus visits he had discovered a "generational groundswell" of promising new leaders on the radical right. There was Richard Spencer, a PhD student who left Duke University to launch a popular blog called *Alternative Right*; and Matt Parrott, who helped start the Traditionalist Youth Network. They all traced their views in part back to Don, Duke, and especially Stormfront, and that fact made Don think that maybe all wasn't lost. Maybe, even though Derek had abandoned the movement, his legacy was still furthering their cause. An entire generation of white power advocates had come of age listening to Derek's interviews and playing the white pride video game on his Stormfront children's page. Now they were heeding Derek's lessons by starting podcasts and considering their own campaigns for elected office.

Near the end of the Stormfront conference, Don invited Heimbach onstage. "Our future remains bright," Don said, and he went back to his seat and left Heimbach at the podium.

"Mr. Black, Dr. Duke, everyone here—you've laid the foundation to build our new white republic, for the white race to survive," Heimbach said. "Now my generation is primed for this revolution. We are primed. Years of grinding away and sacrifice have led to this moment. I've been reading Stormfront since I was in high school, and it planted the seeds in my mind."

The challenge for Derek during the next months was uprooting those same seeds in his mind. Even though he had logically concluded that white nationalism was harmful and wrong, the ideology remained hardwired into every part of his subconscious. Over two decades, he had learned to interpret so much of the world through the lens of white nationalism: to distrust the U.S. government because it was working to undermine the white European majority; to be skeptical of minorities who were inherently working against his best interests; to avoid most popular music because it reflected the multicultural dumbing down of America; to ignore professional sports because they propped up the social standing of black athletes; to skip Hollywood movies made by Jewish propagandists; and to distrust a mass media controlled by liberal elites.

"Sometimes I have this feeling of total societal alienation," Derek told Allison once. "I grew up in America, but I was outside of it. American culture is like a second language I'm still trying to learn."

He arrived in Kalamazoo, Michigan, early that fall of 2013 intent on retraining his brain. He wanted to confront his most basic assumptions, so he signed up for a new online message group, this one for couch surfers, which meant he could stay for a few nights with total strangers and learn more about their lives. The first couch he slept on in Kalamazoo happened to belong to an immigration attorney, and over the next several days they became friendly, going out for coffee and talking about the rights of undocumented workers. Derek said nothing about his own past; he was just Roland, another smart, ambitious, out-of-state student at the university's medieval institute, and after a while he began to feel more and more detached from the person he had been. He knew nobody in Michigan, and nobody knew him. It was like disappearing into witness protection, he told Allison, and in many ways it felt liberating to start over—to be free from his own history, to trust people, and to try to interact without prejudice or judgment.

He spent that first year in Michigan engaging with the multicultural America he had tried so hard to avoid. He caught up on Hollywood movies and asked Allison to make him music playlists of popular songs from their teenage years. He bought a subscription to *The New York Times* and started reading both its liberal and its conservative opinion columnists. He stayed for a few days at a monastery, began studying a little Arabic, explored Muslim neighborhoods outside Detroit, and went to science museums across the Midwest. He hiked and biked and kayaked in northern Michigan. He joined the literary council and briefly tutored an immigrant from Iraq. Each month he listened to two or three books on tape—sometimes science fiction but often biographies—ranging from a travelogue about Machu Picchu, to an archaeological book about the creation of myth, to the Spanish classic *Don Quixote*. He found himself admiring and then liking President Obama. He gradually began to trust the U.S. government and its infrastructure, and for the first time ever he began drinking tap water, which his father had taught him to avoid for fear of possible contaminants.

He saved money from his graduate stipend and took budget trips with Allison to whatever places seemed interesting and offered a cheap flight. They traveled together during school vacations to Barcelona, Nicaragua, the Caribbean, and Morocco, immersing themselves in as many cultures as they could. They dressed in head scarves and rode camels into the Sahara Desert—"like being on another planet," Derek said of it—but then at night they watched the sky come alive with the same constellations they had seen together at New College in Sarasota. "Once you think about the world on a global scale, it actually starts to seem super interconnected and almost small," Derek later explained to a friend.

What he never did during his first years at Western Michigan, as a personal rule, was talk about white nationalism. Thinking back over his past filled him with shame. He had made personal apologies to some of the people his rhetoric oppressed and offended—Rose, Juan, Matthew, and others—but the list of victims was incalculably long. "It's impossible to apologize to everyone I hurt, because I basically hurt the entire world," he told Allison once. He regarded white nationalism in some ways as a disease he didn't want to re-catch, so he avoided speaking to Duke or anyone else he'd befriended during the first twenty years of his life. He declined a steady stream of interview requests from reporters, changed all of his email addresses, and hid his Facebook page under elaborate privacy settings. It wasn't necessarily that he feared retribution from angry white nationalists, although threats against him continued to spread across the internet. Mostly, he just wanted to protect the sanctuary of his new life, to cloak himself in total anonymity. When his friend and former landlord, Maynard, wrote to ask Derek how he was doing and exactly where he was living, Derek refused to tell him. "Just somewhere up north," he said.

He shared his mailing address only with Allison and then later with his parents, emailing it to them as an act of reconciliation as they worked to repair whatever relationship still remained. Don and Chloe sent Allison a spa gift certificate for her birthday; Derek sent his parents a little money toward finishing their roof. Chloe started a habit of checking the weather report each day in Kalamazoo. They began to exchange regular, tepid emails, seeking out the safest conversational ground. Derek wrote to them about the details of his class schedule and his part-time job at an academic publishing house, but he kept his messages mostly benign. "The weather was perfect this weekend," he wrote to his parents once. And then, weeks later, "The weather remains a little cool but overall nice." And then, as winter arrived, "There's a huge difference between the high 20s and teens."

Sometimes, aching for their old conversations, Don

would finish his daily morning radio show and then message Derek with little provocations about politics and the
continued rise of white nationalism. "Lots of encouraging
signs," Don said, after 2013 turned to 2014 and race became
the fulcrum of the country's most divisive debates. The Tea
Party killed Obama's final attempts at immigration reform,
and anti-refugee sentiment during the Syrian crisis swept
across Europe and into the United States. In the summer of
2014, two more black men were killed by police officers—
Michael Brown in Ferguson, Missouri, and Eric Garner in
Staten Island, New York—and while neither case resulted
in an indictment, both inspired massive protests and a
prime-time speech from President Obama about the corrosive danger of implicit racial bias and structural racism.
The Black Lives Matter movement spurred an oppositional
All Lives Matter movement, which later fractured into a
group called White Lives Matter. Each night, Don watched
on cable news as crowds of mostly black protesters squared
off against mostly white police forces dressed head to toe in
riot gear. The nightly images reminded him of the bloody
civil rights battles in Alabama that had led him to become a
white nationalist in the first place. "The idea of a racial civil
war no longer seems entirely far-fetched," Don said in 2014,
and he sometimes shared that impression over text messages
with Derek.

Derek mostly ignored Don's messages, because what
was there to say? After years of paying obsessive attention
to political news and analyzing every bit of minutiae on his
radio show, Derek had begun to avoid the shrill, twenty-four-
hour cycle of cable TV. "My own version of detox," he called
it. When Allison insisted that Derek pay attention to the
unrest in Ferguson, Derek found himself identifying wholly

with the minority protesters. "It's obvious their complaints are legitimate," he told her. Then he would try to distract himself with schoolwork rather than dwelling on the realization that for so much of his life he had helped contribute to those protesters' righteous sense of oppression.

The only person he felt comfortable confiding in about his guilt was Allison—the bridge between Derek and Roland—and she continued to visit him in Kalamazoo every few months as she finished her senior year at New College, their relationship still solid as ever. She traveled to Michigan to spend her winter break living with Derek. He returned to New College for her graduation, staying in the dorm and spending a few more Shabbats with Matthew. Allison applied to several doctoral programs in clinical psychology. It was a competitive field with an admission rate of less than 5 percent, but she got into many of the top programs, and the best fit was in Lansing, Michigan, less than two hours from Derek. She moved to the Midwest, and they spent every weekend together, studying in coffee shops and exploring small towns, cocooning into a happy relationship routine as the months slid by. Instead of returning to West Palm Beach for holidays, Derek usually traveled with Allison to see her family outside Cleveland. Allison's mother, Julie, knit Derek his own stocking to hang above the fireplace at Christmas, and he sometimes stayed with them for weeks at a time.

At Western Michigan, the same zeal and intellect that had propelled Derek to the forefront of white nationalism now distinguished his schoolwork. He was elected to the board of a medieval conference, named to the editorial board of the student journal, and chosen to present his research at a few conferences each year. He could work with medieval texts in German and French. He also wanted to master Latin, so he decided to spend the summer of 2015 alone in Milwaukee, where he could study for free with a former papal Latin instructor. He rented a tiny apartment and spent six days each week immersing in the language. It was simple, monastic, and quiet, and to Derek that also meant it felt restorative. He didn't own a TV. He read historical texts in Latin and listened to audio books about ninth-century architecture. But no matter how hard he tried, there was no way for Derek or anyone else to avoid thinking about white nationalism that summer as it intruded upon the world in the form of Dylann Roof.

Roof was a twenty-one-year-old South Carolinian who had become upset by what he considered the "ridiculous uproar" in defense of Trayvon Martin, Michael Brown, and other minority victims of police violence. Roof began to research racial differences on his computer, and eventually he typed the phrase "black on white crime" into Google. He followed the search results onto sites like Stormfront, where he read white nationalist myths about IQ differentials, black criminality, and what Roof would later call "the Jewish problem." According to the FBI, Roof signed up for Stormfront in the spring of 2015 under the name "LilAryan," and after introducing himself on the message board as "completely racially aware," he tried and failed to arrange in-person meetings with other white nationalists. "No one is doing anything but talking on the internet," Roof later wrote in a document that would become known as his manifesto. "Someone has to have the bravery to take it to the real world, and I guess that has to be me."

In June 2015, Roof scouted out a historically black church in Charleston, South Carolina, and traveled there alone with a handgun. He went to a Bible study attended by black and mostly elderly congregants and waited until they stood up to pray. Then he opened fire and killed nine people, firing off dozens of rounds as he shouted about wanting to "start a race war."

"A crazy kid latching onto portions of our cause" was how Don later explained it to the media, as the shooting brought Stormfront back onto the front page of *The New York Times*. "If the movement has a leading edge, it is Stormfront," the *Times* wrote, and later in court Roof's defense attorney attempted to blame the "racist internet" for Roof's massacre. "Every bit of motivation came from things he saw on the internet," his attorney David Bruck said. "He is simply regurgitating, in whole paragraphs, slogans, and facts—bits and pieces of facts that he downloaded from the internet directly into his brain."

Derek wondered: Had Roof listened to any of Derek's old speeches or radio shows and "downloaded" that into his brain? Had he heard Derek's interviews about white genocide as an eleven-year-old on HBO? It was a possibility too horrendous to consider, so Derek cocooned into his Latin class and avoided the newspaper. He tried to quiet his anguish by telling himself that he had long ago detached from Stormfront and that Roof's massacre was not so much a signifier of the racial moment as an act of solitary extremism. But during that same week in 2015, the national news was also flooded with another story that made Derek think about the effects of white nationalism. The other students in his Latin class were all talking about Donald Trump, who had just announced his candidacy for president of the United States with a shocking speech.

Derek had always thought of Trump as a cartoonish blowhard, driven more by his desire for popularity than by actual beliefs, but he also had seen up close how Trump's crass, opportunistic politics could back the establishment into a corner. In 2006, he had watched Trump's staff install a massive American flag at Mar-a-Lago, so large that Derek could see it from a few miles away at his parents' house. The flagpole was the tallest structure in the city at eighty feet— double the legal limit as established by local zoning regulations. The city asked Trump to remove the flag and fined him $250 per day. Trump refused to take it down, citing his "fierce patriotism," and instead promised to donate $250 each day to American soldiers returning home from Iraq. The ordeal made him a hero on Fox News—"probably one of the most popular things I've ever done," Trump later said— and eventually Palm Beach quietly backed down.

Trump returned to Fox News in 2011 to claim President Obama was not born in the United States, another brazen ploy that backed his political opponent into a corner, until finally Obama was forced to acknowledge Trump's ridiculous quest and release his long-form birth certificate from Hawaii. "A lot of our people like his antics," Derek said at that time, on his radio show. But Derek also cautioned his listeners that Trump was not a true white nationalist. He had sought publicity for Mar-a-Lago by making a show of recruiting gays, blacks, and Jews as members. "He speaks our language when it's useful for him, even if he doesn't really believe it," Derek told his radio listeners back then.

He had barely thought about Trump in the four years since, but now Derek went on his computer in the summer of 2015 and watched a replay of Trump's speech announcing his presidential candidacy. What Derek heard sounded like something directly out of his past. For eighteen months, he had been trying to forget about white nationalism, but now he wondered if it was beginning to surface all around him. He sent a link of the video to Allison.

"Sound familiar?" he asked her.

The United States has become a dumping ground," Donald Trump said that day.

"When Mexico sends its people, they're bringing drugs, they're bringing crime, they're rapists," he said.

"I would build a magnificent wall," he said.

Don listened to the speech at home in South Florida and watched his computer monitor as Stormfront's daily traffic surged to twice its normal rate. Don had been waiting four decades for a major political candidate to make what he called "a direct, edgy appeal to our people," but he never imagined that message would come from Trump. Like Derek, Don had always dismissed Trump as a vapid celebrity who cared more about money and ego than he ever would about culture or race. But now, in Trump's speech, Don heard echoes of a strategy he and Duke had pioneered together thirty-five years earlier when they tried to rehabilitate the Klan's image by shifting its focus from cross burnings in the Deep South to rallies against illegal immigration on the California border. Duke started the Klan Border Watch in 1977, and for two weeks he drove around the desert with binoculars and a few hundred other Klan members while the national news media trailed behind them. "This isn't an issue about race or prejudice," Duke insisted back then. He said securing the border was about protecting America's culture and its economy. And so, on behalf of the Klan in the late 1970s, Duke proposed the idea of building a wall, much as Trump was suggesting now.

"It's a promising start," Don said, after Trump's first speech. "I'm not convinced he's one of us—not by a long shot—but he's smart enough to know that a lot of white people in this country are fed up and angry. They are looking for someone who will express that for them. If Trump wants to win, this kind of strategy might get him elected. It depends what else he has to say."

What Trump said during those next months was that he wanted to ban Muslims from entering the United States. He said he was the "law and order candidate" in the age of Black Lives Matter. He said he was qualified to be president in large part because of his "beautiful, terrific genes—a wonderful inheritance." He said his primary goal was to erase the legacy of Barack Obama, the country's first black president, who Trump continued to insinuate was a foreign-born Muslim. He said America's inner cities were overrun by "gangs and thugs," and "right now, if you walk down the street, you get shot"—and then to prove that point he re-tweeted a crime statistic suggesting that 81 percent of white murder victims were killed by blacks. A few days later, after criminologists told Trump that his number was wildly off base—that in fact it was only 14 percent—Trump said, "What? Am I gonna check every statistic?"

Maybe Trump wasn't in fact a white nationalist, Don thought, but he sure was good at sounding like one. And what more could any Stormfront member want than a political candidate who promised to represent "the silent majority," to "take America back," to "make it great again," to reinforce the structures of white supremacy in America by empowering police, deporting Hispanics, and banning Muslims?

For three decades white nationalist leaders like Don,

Duke, and Derek had been smoothing their extremist message to make it more palatable to the far conservative Right—removing their hoods, eliminating slurs, refining their rhetoric, mastering the internet. And now, for the first time in Don's memory, a major presidential candidate had started calling out in their direction with one dog whistle after another, until suddenly Trump and the white nationalist movement were close enough to wink at each other across the internet, or sometimes even hold hands. Twice in 2016, Trump publicly shared messages on Twitter from a white nationalist account called @WhiteGenocide, thereby spreading Don and Derek's favorite maxim to fifteen million Twitter followers. When two of Trump's supporters in Boston beat up and peed on a homeless Hispanic immigrant in 2015 while chanting, "Trump is right," Trump reacted just as Don had done whenever another murderer was connected to Stormfront. Trump called the violence "unfortunate" and then immediately attempted to justify it. "The people that are following me are very passionate," he said. "They love this country. They want this country to be great again."

Whatever the exact relationship between Trump and white nationalism, Don became convinced that it was mutually beneficial. Trump's racist innuendo drove so much traffic to Stormfront that Don was able to upgrade his software and move to a larger web server; Don and Duke went on their radio shows and told tens of thousands of listeners to start volunteering for Trump. "You're going to meet people who have the same mind-set," Duke said. The frenzy over Trump's campaign made "white nationalism" and "alt-right" two of the most popular search terms on Google; a group of white nationalists led by Jared Taylor recorded a robo-call

for primary voters in Iowa that said, "We don't need Muslims. We need smart, well-educated white people who will
assimilate to our culture. Vote Trump."

Trump repeatedly equivocated during TV interviews
when asked to condemn Duke, at first claiming that he
didn't know enough about him, or that he needed to do
more research, before finally consenting to a reporter that he
would condemn Duke, "if it makes you happy." Duke, once
again a fixture in the news media, announced that he was
exploring a run for the U.S. Senate. "Americans are embrac-
ing the core issues I've fought for my entire life," Duke said.

Derek's mother was so enthusiastic about Trump that
she drove to two of his rallies in South Florida while Don
stayed home because his limited mobility made it difficult to
navigate big crowds. Chloe waited in line for hours at an outdoor airport hangar with her daughters, and they returned
home with stories not just about Trump's speech but about
the size and the energy of the crowd. So much righteous
anger and passion, they told Don. So many people reveling in
their freedom from political correctness—a silent majority
that had come alive to chant at protesters, flip off television
cameramen, and dress in T-shirts emblazoned with white
nationalist talking points. "Put the White Back in White
House," read one. "Fuck Muslims." "Screw Your Feelings."
"Politically Incorrect and Proud of It!" Chloe told Don that
the spectacle reminded her of Duke's rallies in the 1980s,
when he routinely drew thousands of whites to hear him
speak in rural Louisiana.

"We have been trying to recruit these same disaffected
whites that Trump is going after—it's the exact same audience," Don said, shortly after Trump secured the Republican
nomination in the late spring of 2016. "Everybody may not

want to call themselves a white nationalist. That sounds a little scary, but it's the same principle. He is tapping into the fact that race is still a huge part of identity. He's accelerating the timeline of our movement by several decades by making many millions of people more racially aware. Before, nobody really knew what a white nationalist was. Now he's given us this incredible platform."

That realization made Don think again about Derek: If only he had stayed! "It's hard to even fathom the impact he could be having right now," Don said. Don knew of several white nationalist organizations that had arranged trips to the Republican National Convention in July 2016, including an unofficial delegation from Stormfront. One white nationalist from California was selected to participate as a delegate; another white nationalist, the radio host James Edwards, was granted a press credential and an interview with Donald Trump Jr. The media circus surrounding the convention created a gigantic megaphone for young white nationalist leaders—"the opportunity of a lifetime," Don called it— and he still believed none of those leaders possessed Derek's pedigree or his message discipline. Heimbach, the Towson graduate who had spoken a few years earlier at the annual Stormfront conference, was arrested for assaulting a black woman at a Trump rally in March 2016 and sentenced to anger management. Milo Yiannopoulos, a senior writer at Breitbart News, gave provocative speeches about race but refused to call himself a white nationalist. And then there was Richard Spencer, thirty-eight, whom Don considered the most similar to Derek. Spencer was also an academic—a former Duke PhD student who wrote about IQ differentials, white genocide, and a future white ethno-state. Don and Derek had met Spencer years earlier at an American Renaissance conference, and now, drafting off Trump's success, Spencer had a college speaking tour, a popular website, and a think tank in Washington.

"He's not Derek, but he's as close as we have," Don said, so late in the summer of 2016 he reached out to Spencer and offered his help.

That summer, Derek was in transition again. He had just earned his master's degree from Western Michigan, and he had three months of freedom before he started as a doctoral student at the University of Chicago. He moved in with Allison in Lansing and filled his time by taking short road trips with her across the Midwest. Michigan, typically Democratic, had become a crucial swing state for Trump, and each day the election unfolded in a barrage of TV ads, robo-calls, and rallies near the state capitol in Lansing. For the first time since Derek left white nationalism, he found himself riveted by politics and by America's obsession with race.

Trump's rise reminded him of what he had always known as a white nationalist and what he had spent the last years trying to forget. "Intrinsically, white people in this country always expect that their interests should come first," Derek told Allison that summer. "American history is so fundamentally based on white supremacy that it's still the basis for most of our culture and our politics." Whereas that fact had once seemed to Derek like an opportunity as a white nationalist, now he considered it America's foundational flaw. And rather than deny the importance of structural racism in the United States—just as Derek believed much of white America had tried to do for decades—he wanted to understand it and to challenge his own assumptions by reading perspectives different from his own. He read Ta-Nehisi Coates's writing about Obama; and Omar Saif Ghobash's *Letters to a Young Muslim;* and Edward Said's *Orientalism;* and Ibram Kendi's book about the history of racist ideas, *Stamped from the Beginning.*

Derek's own political identity was still largely unformed. He didn't know if he was a Democrat or a Republican, and he didn't want to be either one. As a white nationalist, he had always regarded Republicans and Democrats with equal suspicion, because he believed both parties were guilty of forcing multiculturalism on the American people. He was also wary of aligning himself again with any sort of collective ideology—a label that could dictate his decision making. He wanted to be loyal to his own opinions and nothing else, so one day that summer he and Allison went online together and found a seventy-five-question quiz about the major political issues in America. Instead of choosing a candidate based on party affiliation or personality, Derek could be matched with a candidate by stating his opinion on one issue at a time.

No, he did not think law enforcement should be allowed to use racial profiling.

No, he did not believe in immigration raids.

Yes, he did want the United States to accept Syrian refugees. Yes to affirmative action. Yes to legalized abortion, Black Lives Matter, gay marriage, and transgender rights.

At the end of the quiz, Derek's score was similar to Allison's: Each of them was about 96 percent Democratic, almost completely aligned with Clinton. The result didn't necessarily surprise Derek; he already assumed he would vote for Clinton, and in order to increase the significance of his vote, he was planning to cast it in Michigan before he moved to reliably Democratic Illinois. But even as polls that summer showed Clinton increasing her lead as a runaway favorite, Derek still thought Trump had a chance to win. In each of Duke's elections, polls failed to reveal what Don referred to as "a silent army of white believers"—voters who were too embarrassed to reveal their prejudices to a pollster but who then defaulted back to race-based decision making in the privacy of a voting booth. Duke had gone into each of his elections as a heavy underdog, and he had regularly outperformed his polls by 10 or 15 percent.

"You knew a moment like this was inevitable," Don told Derek over the phone that summer, and it was true, because in fact they had often predicted it together on the radio. Eventually, the white supremacy embedded into America's history would again rise fully to the surface, Derek had told his listeners. Sure, maybe whites could accept or even encourage multiculturalism when it posed no imminent threat to their interests. It was easy for whites to be humane and benevolent when they were still securely in place at the top of the social hierarchy—when the economy was booming, and everyone had jobs, and a disproportionate share of the wealth and power was still going to white families. But now a black man had risen to the country's most powerful position, income growth had stagnated for middle-class whites, and a presidential candidate was promising to "take the country back." It was the moment Derek had spent the first twenty-three years of his life trying to instigate. To be a white nationalist had always meant rooting for chaos and delighting in upheaval. Each year during his childhood in South Florida, Derek and his family would hunker down in their old bungalow during hurricane season as others evacuated. They would trim their trees, patch up the roof, board the windows, and then sit down in the living room to wait for the storm. It was a thrilling ritual, ripe with uncertainty and anticipation. And now in Michigan, Derek could sense a storm building, and its power terrified him.

Late that summer, he watched on TV as Clinton gave a speech in Reno that sounded to Derek as if it were about his childhood. She talked about how the Klan had evolved and spread across internet hate sites like Stormfront. She quoted from Duke's radio show and explained the concept of white genocide. "From the start, Donald Trump has built his campaign on prejudice and paranoia," she said. "He is taking hate groups mainstream and helping a radical fringe take over the Republican Party. The names may have changed. Racists now call themselves 'racialists.' White supremacists now call themselves 'white nationalists.' But the hate burns just as bright. And this is part of a broader story about the rising tide of hard-line, right-wing nationalism around the world."

Derek felt implicated in that broader story. How many speeches had he given to white nationalists about changing the vocabulary of their movement? How often had he said the way ahead was through politics? "I'm a part of all of this, and it makes me ill," he told Allison that summer. "I wish there was some way to not think about that."

Allison sometimes wished for the same unreality. Their relationship had become so happy—so normal—that sometimes their college arguments about white nationalism seemed like a part of a distant origin story. Lately they spent their weekends taking walks through Allison's neighborhood or going to movies. They studied together in coffee shops. They binge-watched TV shows on Netflix. When they argued, it was about household chores or vacation plans. But Allison also made it her responsibility to talk to Derek about the ways race had come to dominate national debates about police shootings, nativist politics, and Hispanic immigrants. Sometimes Allison still worried that during college she had been naive or somehow permissive when it came to Derek's beliefs, despite the happy outcome of their debates. But now she better understood the full power of white nationalism and also the potential power of Derek's opposition to it. "You need to publicly refute white nationalism at every opportunity," she told him. "It's not enough to just stop being racist. You need to do more."

She knew from her own empirical research that white people were most likely to listen to other white people's opinions on race, and who understood that topic better than Derek? He knew the danger posed by white supremacy's historic grip on the United States. He knew white nationalist talking points and how best to refute them. He understood firsthand the transformative power of both civil disobedience and civil discourse. And, most important, he also had journalists emailing him every once in a while to ask for his insight—requests that Derek continued to evade as the election neared. "Step up," Allison told him. "You've still done more harm than good."

During their conversations about race, Derek would sometimes look at the heart rate monitor on his Apple watch and see the numbers spike. "Shame" was how Derek summarized his feelings about his past. "Embarrassment. Regret. A whole lot of self-loathing for the way that I spread those ideas and really hurt people." It was difficult for him to discuss in private with Allison, and much harder with anyone else, but he also knew Allison was right. He began to share parts of his story in public during the final months of the election, first in *The Washington Post* and then with a few podcasts, but whatever effect he had was dwarfed in his mind by the rise of white identity politics and Trump. "Nothing I can say will undo the damage," Derek told Allison.

That guilt hung over him as he registered at the University of Chicago under the name Roland Derek Black and then moved into a one-bedroom apartment in Hyde Park, where no one knew who he was or what he had done. On Election Day, he watched alone in his apartment as the results began coming in from across the country. Ohio for Trump. North Carolina for Trump. Florida for Trump. Michigan trending toward Trump, but still too close to call.

Derek texted his friend Matthew, who hosted him at so many Shabbat dinners. Matthew, a Republican who had decided not to vote for Trump, in part because of his racially charged rhetoric, had joked with Derek about gambling on the outcome of the election. "Somebody's going to make a killing on this when Trump actually wins," Derek wrote to him.

He texted his father, who was monitoring another historic surge of traffic on Stormfront. "Are you prepared for the security lockdown in Palm Beach when President Trump visits Mar-a-Lago?" Derek asked.

He messaged Allison, who was at an election party with friends in Lansing. "That room must be tense," Derek wrote.

"We're, like, silent," she told him.

Derek stayed up until after midnight, when Trump finally came on TV to give his victory speech. "Ours was not a campaign but rather an incredible and a great movement," Trump said, and finally Derek turned off the TV and tried to sleep. A few hours later he was up again, antsy and overwhelmed by the urge to *do* something. He grabbed his computer and walked to a nearby coffee shop. He sat down at a table and thought about what his parents had often told him: to make history, and not just study it.

For two decades, he had pushed to bring about this national moment. Now he felt compelled to publicly push back. He knew better than anyone the full danger of a racist ideology, and he wanted to sound a warning to the biggest national audience he could find. He took out his computer and started to write what would later become an opinion piece for *The New York Times*.

"A few years ago, I would have been ecstatic," he began.

13. "All-Out Mayhem"

Don had been predicting Trump's election, repeatedly and publicly, for the last six weeks. "I will not be even the slightest bit surprised when this goes our way," he told his radio listeners, except now, on the morning after Trump's election, what Don felt most of all was disbelief. Over the last forty years, he had hardened himself to disappointment. He'd come to accept that he would spend his life fighting in vain against the "multicultural takeover," and decades of failure had made him pessimistic, even fatalistic. America was a lost cause. He assumed history would remember him as a loser and a bigot. When Derek was in middle school, Don had nicknamed his son "the Devil Child," and they joked that no matter what Derek went on to accomplish in life, he would be remembered in his obituary as the son of a KKK Grand Wizard. That was the destiny of a white nationalist in the United States, Don always thought: to be an outside agitator, a hatemonger, a great American villain. "At least we know that we're never going to win any popularity contests," Don told Derek once, on the radio.

Except now white nationalists felt as though they had won the biggest popularity contest—a presidential election—and the Klan was hosting a celebratory march in North Carolina, and neo-Nazis were wearing T-shirts that showed Trump and Hitler walking side by side. For most of Don's life, America had worked to paper over the overt racism embedded deep within the country's core, but now it was visible all around him. "It's hard to find the right words, because this is undoubtedly the biggest step forward in my lifetime," he said. "We were at a standstill for so long, and now a major part of the country is coming around to our side."

It wasn't necessarily that Don had faith in Trump himself; Don still thought the president-elect was a craven populist, driven by ego and not ideology. In no way did Don expect he would start building the great white ethno-state. But in the most racially polarized election in American history, whites had voted for Trump en masse and asserted their supremacy. Maybe in return Trump really would build them that wall. Maybe he would deport millions of Hispanics. Don thought a Trump presidency could unite whites, help normalize white identity politics, and serve as the gateway to an explicitly white nationalist political movement. For several weeks after the election, Don kept the TV on for twenty or more hours each day, monitoring Trump's political appointments and celebrating many of them on the radio. "Some of what he's doing here is actually turning me into an optimist," Don said one day. "It's still early, of course, but he's bringing in an army of people who appear sympathetic to our point of view."

For Trump's national security adviser: General Michael Flynn, who once shared a tweet that read, "Not anymore, Jews. Not anymore."

For attorney general: Jeff Sessions, who once said immigrants "create culture problems."

For senior policy adviser: Stephen Miller, who had organized anti-Islam events with the help of his classmate Richard Spencer when they were both at Duke University.

For adviser to Customs and Border Patrol: Julie Kirchner, who had previously worked at an anti-immigration group founded by a white nationalist.

For chief strategist: Steve Bannon, the co-founder of Breitbart News, which he described as "the platform for the alt-right."

Don had always thought of Washington as "exclusively enemy territory," he said, but now he wanted to go there. Richard Spencer was hosting a white nationalist conference two weeks after the election in the Ronald Reagan Building, and he invited Don to come. Spencer expected three hundred attendees, and he had promoted the conference during interviews on NPR, CNN, and NBC. Don and Chloe looked at last-minute plane tickets to Washington before deciding to stay home. Stormfront was still experiencing a surge of new traffic in the wake of Trump's election—and also a series of cyber attacks from hackers and antifascists. Don didn't want to risk leaving his computer.

So instead he watched a video feed of Spencer's introductory press conference, in which Spencer looked out at a jam-packed room of national journalists and told them, "The alt-right is obviously real, and it's obviously growing." Don watched as his white nationalist friends Sam Dickson and Jared Taylor hit the same talking points they had been reciting for thirty years, only now to triple the crowd. He watched as protesters disrupted the conference with chants of "Nazi! Nazi! Nazi!" Then he watched as Spencer stepped to the lectern for the day's final speech, one that would solidify him as the new face of white nationalism, the new heir. "I don't think I'm alone in thinking how surreal all of this is," Spencer began. "We willed Donald Trump into office. We made this dream our reality."

What Don admired most about Spencer was his polish. If

white nationalism was going to transition into a viable political movement, it needed leaders with mainstream credentials, and Spencer checked every box. A bachelor's degree from the University of Virginia. A master's from the University of Chicago. A wardrobe of fancy watches and Brooks Brothers suits. He had grown up in a wealthy Republican family in Dallas, the son of an artist and a doctor, and he had aspired to become a theater director until he started reading German philosopher Friedrich Nietzsche, and his views gradually drifted further to the right. He enrolled at Duke University to get his PhD, and then during his second year on campus a black woman falsely accused three white Duke lacrosse players of rape, leading to what Spencer called an "antiwhite, racist witch trial." The ensuing months turned him into a campus activist, which led to jobs as a far-right blogger, which led to his creation of AlternativeRight.com. Like Derek, he had a gift for the language of euphemism and understatement. He was not a white supremacist but a "racial identitarian," he said. His white power think tank was innocuously named the National Policy Institute. As a political activist, he made good use of his theatrical flair, releasing well-produced videos on Twitter and timing his alt-right demonstrations to calm moments in the national news cycle. "In some ways, I'm still directing a massive theatrical production," he said. "But now I'm also starring in it."

During his speech at the conference, Spencer hammered his fist against the lectern and stared at the television cameras in the back of the room.

"America was, until this past generation, a white country, designed for us and for our posterity," he said. "It is our creation, it is our inheritance, and it belongs to us. To be white is to be a striver, a crusader, an explorer, and a conqueror. We build. We go upward. We do, and other groups don't. We don't gain anything from their presence. They need us, and not the other way around. For us, it is conquer or die. Hail Trump! Hail our people! Hail victory!"

Don watched on his screen as Spencer's crowd erupted in applause. Several dozen people in the crowd stood and held their right arms high in the air, signaling Spencer with the Nazi salute. It would become one of the symbolic moments of the 2016 election, replayed on TV as America's public introduction to the so-called alt-right. But in the moment, Spencer simply nodded at his saluting crowd and smiled.

"This is just the beginning," he told them.

A few days later, there was an opinion piece printed in *The New York Times* under the byline R. Derek Black.

Derek had warned Don that he was going to write about Trump, but Don didn't know exactly what Derek planned to say, or when, or for whom. Derek drafted the article the morning after Trump's election, edited it with Allison, and later submitted it to the *Times*, and now a few weeks later there was a headline at the front of the opinion section: "Why I Left White Nationalism." Already the piece was one of the most highly read stories on the website, and it was being shared on Stormfront and other white supremacist message boards. "Jesus, Derek," Don thought. "What did you do now?"

During the 2008 and 2012 presidential campaigns, Don and Derek had spent hundreds of hours dissecting every bit of electoral minutiae on the radio. The main weakness of their show, friends sometimes told them, was that their opinions were too much the same. It didn't make good radio to have two hosts in constant agreement, echoing each other's points and completing each other's sentences. But now Don had no idea what Derek thought, or even whether he'd voted in the election. They had seen each other only once in the last few years, for dinner near the Miami airport while Derek was on a layover on his way back to Michigan from a trip to the Caribbean. They rarely spoke on the phone. Derek was slow to respond to Don's text message provocations about politics. "There's a lot more distance now," Don said. "What is there to talk about?" In November 2016, he thought the best way to understand his son's viewpoint was through *The New York Times*, so he clicked the link and started to read:

> I could easily have spent the night of Nov. 8 elated, surrounded by friends and family, thinking: "We did it . . ."
>
> I'd be planning with other white nationalists what comes next, and assessing just how much influence our ideology would have on this administration. That's who I was a few years ago.
>
> Things look very different for me now . . .
>
> I was born into a white nationalist family . . . and I was once considered the bright future of the movement . . .
>
> Several years ago, I began attending a liberal college where my presence prompted huge controversy. Through many talks with devoted and diverse people there—people who chose to invite me into their dorms and conversations rather than ostracize me—I began to realize the damage I had done. Ever since, I have been trying to make up for it . . .
>
> I never would have begun my own conversations without first experiencing clear and passionate outrage

to what I believed from those I interacted with. Now is the time for me to pass on that outrage by clearly and unremittingly denouncing the people who used a wave of white anger to take the White House.

Mr. Trump's comments during the campaign echoed how I also tapped into less-than-explicit white nationalist ideology to reach relatively moderate white Americans. I went door-to-door in 2008 talking about how Hispanic immigration was overwhelming "American" culture, how black neighborhoods were hotbeds of crime, and how P.C. culture didn't let us talk about any of it. I won that small election with 60 percent of the vote.

A substantial portion of the American public has made clear that it feels betrayed by the establishment, and so it elected a president who denounces all Muslims as potential conspirators in terrorism; who sees black communities as crime-ridden; who taps into white American mistrust of foreigners, particularly of Hispanics; and who promises the harshest form of immigration control. If we thought Mr. Trump himself might backtrack on some of this, we are now watching him fill a cabinet with people able to make that campaign rhetoric into real policy . . .

The wave of violence and vile language that has risen since the election is only one immediate piece of evidence that this campaign's reckless assertion of white identity comes at a huge cost. More and more people are being forced to recognize now what I learned early: Our country is susceptible to some of our worst instincts when the message is packaged correctly.

No checks and balances can redeem what we've

unleashed. The reality is that half of the voters chose white supremacy . . .

It's now our job to argue constantly that what voters did in elevating this man to the White House constitutes the greatest assault on our own people in a generation, and to offer another option . . .

Those of us on the other side need to be clear that Mr. Trump's callous disregard for people outside his demographic is intolerable, and will be destructive to the entire nation.

Don finished reading and clicked over to the conversation on Stormfront. "Treasonous," one poster had written. "Typical liberal dribble," commented another, and Don felt a familiar wave of grief rush over him. After more than two years, he had finally acclimated himself to the idea that he would continue to lead Stormfront and the white nationalist movement alone, without Derek. It was lonely. It was sometimes joyless. "The Derek situation still haunts me every single day," Don said. "But it's over, and the show goes on." Now, for the first time, Don began to wonder if in fact it wasn't over. Maybe, instead of merely abandoning his family's ideology, Derek would actively oppose it.

"What are you doing, Derek?" Don asked him later that month. "Is this what you are going to be now? Some kind of antiwhite activist?"

The truth was Derek didn't exactly know. Probably not. Maybe. He still valued his privacy, but Allison had helped convince him that by spending a decade at the forefront of white nationalism, he had built up a massive public debt to society and particularly to people of color, and he wanted to pay some of it back. He occasionally thought about giving speeches at universities, or writing a book, or appearing on television, or becoming more actively involved in political organizing against white nationalism. He liked his quiet life at the University of Chicago, but lately he was finding it harder to lose himself in ninth-century texts when the current moment felt so urgent. He decided to speak about the dangers of white nationalism at Georgetown University and Harvard and give occasional interviews about his transformation. Don still had his Google alert set for Derek, and he began to monitor it with an increasing sense of dread.

"I don't understand why he's doing this," Don said. "This is the exact opposite of the life he could be leading."

The life that could have been Derek's was in Alexandria, Virginia, six miles from the White House in an apartment located above a chocolate shop, where a locked gate, security cameras, and occasionally a bodyguard stood watch over the new tenant. Richard Spencer had just moved to Virginia a few days earlier on a short-term lease, leaving his wife and young daughter in the ski town of Whitefish, Montana. He had come to the Washington suburbs with two boxes of white nationalist books and a duffel bag filled with wrinkled suits. There had been no time to move his car or any furniture from Montana, and his new kitchen was empty except for a box of granola bars and a few scattered red plastic cups. Trump's inauguration was two days away, and Spencer had rushed his cross-country move so he would be in place before the official change of power. He hoped the Alexandria apartment would function not just as a living space but also as a new headquarters for the alt-right. The alleyway entrance allowed for privacy, the roof deck was designed for hosting parties, and he'd already invited media to one press conference in the spacious living room. "We're basically becoming a part of the establishment, so it only makes sense that we start to have a presence here in Washington," Spencer said.

He poured some red wine into a plastic cup, took his laptop into the living room, and sat down on the hardwood floor to check his email. "I'm getting about forty media requests per day," he said, and his immediate answer to each one was always yes. He had spent seven years as a far-right blogger migrating from one fledgling publication to the next, trying to build up an audience for his ideas. Now the Trump phenomenon had delivered that audience to his feet, and Spencer could hardly believe his good luck. The video of his controversial speech in the wake of Trump's election—"Hail-gate," Spencer called it—had been viewed on the internet more than a million times. Now Spencer was talking to publishers about writing a book. He was "seriously" considering a run for the U.S. House of Representatives out of Montana. He was interviewing zealous college students who were competing to become his personal assistant. He was recording videos for a burgeoning YouTube channel, launching a new website for the alt-right, and planning a speaking tour at colleges across America.

Most of all, he was answering a phone that rarely stopped ringing, repeating old white nationalist talking points to a national audience that was suddenly rapt.

"Have you heard about white genocide?" he asked a documentarian for Netflix.

"Race is real. Look at the IQ data," he told a reporter from the Associated Press.

"We don't hate anyone. We just want to preserve our own people," he told an alt-right blogger.

"Yes, I can absolutely be available later today," he told a reporter from the *Los Angeles Times* as he got up to refill his cup with more wine.

"What time do you want me?" he asked a booker for CNN.

By early afternoon, Spencer had already done six interviews. He stood up from his computer, surveyed the granola bars in his kitchen, and decided to walk out into the neighborhood to find lunch. There were pride flags painted on the sidewalk and peace signs taped to the window of the chocolate shop downstairs. It was the weekend of Martin Luther King Day, and Spencer could hear choir music playing at a holiday church service down the street. "Why do we pay tribute each year to a fraud and a degenerate?" he asked. He liked Alexandria for what he called the "historic southern charm," with its Jefferson Davis statue and cobblestoned sidewalks, but he didn't expect to fit in with his new neighbors. The city was diverse and liberal, and already Spencer had been recognized and flipped off a few times outside his apartment on King Street. He had started wearing a hat to help shadow his face.

He took a seat in back of a lunch counter and studied the menu. A few tables away, a Hispanic woman stared in his direction, and Spencer fidgeted in his seat. The waiter seemed to glance at him for an extra second, and Spencer kept his head down and rushed into his lunch order. "I'm always waiting for things to turn ugly, because I'm radioactive," he said, once the waiter walked away. Many of his former friends in Washington refused to go to Spencer's apartment out of fear of being spotted. Some of his college classmates had edited their Facebook pictures with Spencer, replacing his face with a cartoon image of the devil. In his

hometown of Whitefish, an anti-hate group had mailed flyers about his "racist lies" to each resident, including Spencer's
parents, who had publicly condemned his beliefs.

Spencer wanted to inoculate himself by building a
headquarters for the alt-right with a full-time media staff
and more security guards, but to do that, he needed about
five million or ten million dollars in donations, he said. His
National Policy Institute had been able to raise only about
half a million dollars in total funds, most of which came
from either Spencer's profits from a family inheritance of
land in Louisiana or from the Charles Martel Society, a
white nationalist fund-raising group run by publishing heir
William Regnery II. Spencer said he had traveled around the
country to meet with potential funders, but so far he had
been able to raise only several thousand dollars. "The money
must be out there, but people are cautious, and I don't have
time to go find it," Spencer said. He had decided to outsource
some of his work by hiring a personal assistant—"a smart,
good-looking Richard Spencer type," he said—who could
help with fund-raising and also schedule his interviews.

Spencer finished his lunch and walked back onto King
Street, where now on the sidewalk with the peace signs and
the rainbow flags he noticed a new flyer attached to the light
pole in front of his apartment. "MISSING DOG," it read,
and underneath that bold type was a large picture of Spencer. "I can't believe this is starting already," Spencer said, and
then he stepped closer to the flyer to read the small type.

"Racist, sexist, homophobic, and xenophobic neo-Nazi
has made Old Town Alexandria his hub to recruit," the flyer
read. "Must be shunned and humiliated."

Spencer pulled down the flyer, folded it in half, and
tucked it into his pocket. He looked down the street and saw

a copy of the same flyer attached to the next light pole, and then the next, and then the next. There were dozens of flyers posted on lampposts and business windows up and down the block, stretching as far as Spencer could see.

"It's going to be all-out mayhem," he said. He pulled his hat lower onto his head and hurried back into his apartment.

A few months later, in the spring of 2017, Don flew into Washington and went with Spencer to dinner. They were both attending a private, two-day meeting of white nationalist funders in nearby Baltimore, but Don was eager to spend time with Spencer outside the official schedule. He sensed Spencer was approaching what Don called "a strategic tipping point"—one Don recognized from his own life—and he hoped to offer a little subtle advice. "He's walking right up to that edge between pushing for our ideas from the inside and shocking people a little too hard," Don said.

The all-out mayhem Spencer had expected to instigate in Alexandria and beyond had escalated during the last several months. A different kind of flyer had been posted to the lampposts in liberal suburban Virginia early that spring. "Around Blacks Never Relax," read one; and "Stop the Islamization of America"; and "You're Losing Your Country White Man!!!" Spencer said he hadn't created the posters, but they were the product of a racist movement he continued to inspire through his work at the National Policy Institute, and a crowd of protesters had begun to picket outside Spencer's apartment each weekend morning. "Racist, sexist, antigay! NPI is KKK!" they chanted. Spencer retaliated by organizing nighttime torch marches and "heritage rallies" at local Confederate monuments all across Virginia and the Deep South.

Most of his public appearances sparked riots between white nationalists and protesting groups of antifascists, necessitating the presence of police in riot gear. Spencer had twice been punched in the face by antifascists, including once while he was in the middle of giving a television interview during Trump's inaugural parade. Sometimes, when Spencer was recognized in public, he said he had started to pretend he was not Richard Spencer—that in fact he thought Richard Spencer was an idiot. "It's something I do for self-defense," he said.

At their dinner together, Spencer told Don he wasn't sure how to feel about the last several months of his life. Sometimes he worried he'd gone too far with his "Hail-gate" speech. He wondered: Had his Hitler impersonation catapulted his mainstream political career, or effectively ended it?

It was similar to an argument Don often had with Duke, who tended to blame every failure in his political career on what he called his "youthful exuberance" as head of the Klan. Duke often said that if not for the archival pictures of him in Nazi uniforms and hooded robes, he could have become governor of Louisiana or maybe even president. But Don believed it was Duke's Klan connection that in many ways enabled his career. It fueled the undercurrent of anger in his crowds, enticed the national media, and turned his campaigns into spectacles. "There's something to be said for maintaining some edge, as long as you're still in control," Don said.

He thought Spencer was disciplined and smart, with a good sense for the history of the white nationalist movement. Don liked him, and as the night went on, he decided to bring up the subject that was always on his mind. He told Spencer about Derek, and Spencer said he remembered meeting him once at a conference. Don mentioned Derek was working toward his PhD at the University of Chicago; Spencer, a University of Chicago graduate, said he still respected the school as a place of "true intellectualism." Don was pleased, and he sent Derek a text message to share Spencer's endorsement.

Derek was always happy to hear from his father, but this text message also reminded him of the estrangement that now defined so much about their relationship. His parents had never visited him since he left Florida, at least in part because of Don's health. In their eyes, Chicago was an unsafe place held hostage by gangs and minorities. Ever since the beginning of the presidential election, it had seemed to Derek that the United States was always in the process of dividing, and in so many ways he felt increasingly apart from his own parents. They were southerners, and he was now a northerner. They were suspicious of liberal academia, and he was a PhD student. They were white nationalists, and he was an antiwhite activist. What Derek wanted was to build some kind of a bridge—a way to communicate with his father that didn't have to involve politics or Richard Spencer.

Derek's spring break was coming up later that month. For the first time in more than a year, he found a cheap flight and booked a ticket home.

14. "We Were Wrong"

Derek spent his first morning in Florida at an independent coffee shop, whére a poster of Martin Luther King was framed behind the register and a sign on the front door read, "Unite Against Racism." His mother was at work and his father was busy hosting Stormfront radio, so Derek had time to catch up on schoolwork. He wanted to finish his application for a six-week summer Arabic-language class in Amman, Jordan. He also needed to finish his first major assignment at the University of Chicago, a fifty-page research paper on a subject he had been drawn to in part because it contained so many parallels to his own life.

He had chosen to write about a ninth-century religious leader named Bodo, a royal deacon who had been a rising star in the Carolingian Empire and the Christian church. Historians thought Bodo was destined to become a powerful Frankish politician, but then, in 836, he abandoned his life with little public warning. He converted to Judaism, grew out his beard, changed his name to Eleazar, and then moved to the multicultural kingdom of Al-Andalus, where he married a Jewish woman and began trying to convert other Christians. His former Frankish allies came to consider him a traitor and an enemy. It was one of the starkest individual transformations in medieval history, and the focus of Derek's research was all that remained unknown. Historians were able to recover only a few official accounts of Bodo's life and two of his original letters. No one had recorded Bodo's internal deliberations, his self-doubt, or his emotional reckoning as relationships were made and then destroyed. In the official record, his transformation was clean and absolute: Bodo to Eleazar. A Christian and then a Jew. History had preserved none of the messiness.

Now Don texted Derek's cell phone. "I'm done with YOUR radio show," he said, so Derek drove to his parents' house and picked up his father to take him to lunch. Derek's goal was to avoid discussing politics during the trip. That was their old common language, he thought, and now their relationship needed a new foundation. They drove through downtown Lake Worth toward a restaurant as Derek tried to steer the conversation toward music, exercise, and science.

"What are your thoughts on planetary exploration?" Derek asked at one point. "I was reading a book about the possibility of starting colonies for people in outer space."

"I hope it happens soon," Don said. "It's already too late for America. We're becoming a third-world country."

Derek winced and tried again. "Where should we go for lunch?"

"Someplace where you won't get recognized," Don said. "You're probably famous with the liberals now, after your big speech at Georgetown."

And on it went—Don teasing Derek with little jabs; Derek nodding, smiling, and then changing the subject— until they were done with lunch and back at the house. Everything was just as Derek remembered it from when he first left his parents' house for New College almost seven years earlier: His water bed perched in the hallway. His fish tank in the living room. His political campaign flyers from 2008 tucked into his desk. The take-out burgers for dinner that night were still from Flanigan's, their favorite restaurant, and the TV was still blaring the news. "A hate box," was how Derek now thought of that TV, but he settled into the couch between his parents and tried to ignore it.

"Can we turn it off?" Derek asked after a while, but he was told that they couldn't, or at least not yet. What if something important happened and they missed it? Lately, to Don's great delight, he thought multicultural America was unraveling one news story at a time, and on this night one of those stories was about an army veteran who spent time on Stormfront. James Jackson, twenty-eight, had watched YouTube videos posted by Richard Spencer and David Duke and eventually concluded, he would later explain, "that the white race is being eroded." He boarded a bus from Baltimore to New York with an eighteen-inch sword and two knives packed in his suitcase, and then he spent two nights stalking black men around Times Square. One of those men was a sixty-six-year-old trash collector named Timothy Caughman, and Jackson followed him into a dark alleyway and stabbed him several times. "Hate Killing," the CNN News alert read, and Don said the whole thing was unfortunate. He flipped the TV over to Fox News as one show rolled into the next.

Now it was Tucker Carlson, Don and Chloe's favorite and a new hero among the alt-right. Carlson had become a master at repackaging white nationalist talking points on what he called "alien immigrants" and "cultural erosion." The SPLC had named Carlson's show the most racist news program on cable TV, and in the America of 2017 it was also the most popular show on cable TV, with a nightly audience of over three million. On this night, Carlson was leading his broadcast with a story about an alleged rape at a Maryland high school in which a ninth grader claimed to have been attacked in the bathroom by two recent Central American immigrants. The allegation would later be proven false, and the charges against both immigrants would eventually be dropped, but for now Carlson was using the hoax as proof of the threat he believed immigrants posed to "real Americans."

"This is insanity of course. It's the sign of a sick civilization at war with itself," Carlson said as Derek tried to ignore the TV and focus on his burger.

"Does it make a school better when people move in who don't speak English?" Carlson asked, as Derek got up to go look at his fish tank.

"Why would we want to be a bilingual country?" Carlson said.

"Diversity is our strength," Carlson said, mocking his critics. "Move along. You're racist. Shut up."

Finally the hour ended, and Derek reached for the remote. He switched the TV to Discovery Channel, his old favorite, but a few minutes later his parents took the remote and changed it back to cable news. They wanted to watch the replay of Carlson's show, just as they often did, and rather than start a fight, Derek gave back the remote. He sat on the couch with them, tuned out the show, and text-messaged with Allison until he was ready to go to sleep. He was staying nearby at his grandmother's house, and his parents offered to drive him back even as Tucker's show continued to replay in their heads. They told Derek in the car that America was turning into a third-world country. They said Derek was an antiwhite activist. They said he was accelerating the decline of the European race. They said he had many enemies who wanted to hurt him and that he needed to be careful. He sat in his seat and waited for the storm to pass, until finally his mother began to tell him about their plumbing problems at the house, and how much handiwork they still had to do, and how much they missed Derek and still loved him.

By the time they got to his grandmother's, it was after midnight. Derek said good night, and then he went inside to a bedroom that was dark and quiet and closed the door.

The next morning, Don was trying again.

"You should come back on the air with me, co-host the show again," he said, when Derek picked him up at the house.

"Richard thinks the genocide idea is part of what did it," Don said as Derek turned up the music and drove across Lake Worth toward Palm Beach.

"You should come see your old friends this year at your conference," Don said as Derek parked the car at the edge of the Atlantic Ocean, near the bench where they had gone together to watch the first sunrise of each New Year. Maybe they could establish some sort of new connection here, in a place where they had already marked so many fresh starts. Derek helped Don out of the car, and they sat together in the sun. The beach was empty and the water was calm. Derek listened to the waves, and Don closed his eyes to enjoy the sun. Derek mentioned that he had been experimenting with a basic virtual reality headset, and Don said he had already bought the same one. Derek said he was trying to play guitar more regularly, and Don said he wanted to take up keyboard. Derek said the worst part about living in the Midwest was how much he missed the ocean, and Don suggested they begin a new tradition of going together to the beach every day whenever Derek was in town.

They got back into the car and drove past Trump's Mar-a-Lago, with its gigantic American flag and its new Secret

Service tower, before continuing down to the coast to a lime-green restaurant with a thatched roof. They found a table outside next to the water, where the air smelled of salt. The tide was rising against the dock, and gentle waves were rocking the sailboats in the harbor from side to side. Derek picked up his menu. Maybe a crab cake, he said, and something about the moment felt so pleasant and normal that it reminded Don of all the lunches he'd shared with Derek over the years, and Don couldn't help himself.

"I catch myself thinking sometimes that you're still one of us," he said.

Derek ignored him.

"You say things now that are so over the top," Don said. "Like race doesn't exist, or we need more immigration."

Derek raised his eyebrows and then looked up from his menu. Maybe there was no avoiding this.

"More immigration, more diversity—I think those are very good things," he said.

"That's the opposite of what you always believed."

"I was wrong." Derek stopped to correct himself. "*We* were wrong."

The waiter came by, and Derek told her they needed a few minutes. The sun had dropped behind a cloud, and the wind was picking up across the water. The waves were coming harder now, rocking boats in the harbor and slapping against the dock of the restaurant. Derek raised his voice over the noise.

"Even if you were somehow right—even if it was super important to keep races apart for preservation—the only way to do that is to put people on trains by busting into their houses and breaking up their families, which is a huge human rights violation."

Don raised his palms up above the table. "So?" he said. "History is filled with human rights violations. They could be forced to leave."

"Forcing people out?" Derek stared at his father and grimaced. "That's a horrible thing to hope for. It would be awful and inhumane."

"It's going to be horrible either way, Derek. This country is on the verge of a reckoning."

During the coming months, Don and Derek would watch as white nationalism continued to explode into mainstream politics. There would be fights over the destruction of Confederate monuments, followed by a succession of marches and rallies led by white nationalists throughout the South. One of those marches would arrive in downtown Charlottesville, Virginia, in August 2017, where Richard Spencer, David Duke, and hundreds of neo-Nazis would carry guns and torches into downtown, threatening counterprotesters with chants of "White lives matter" and "You will not replace us," until one neo-Nazi rammed his car into a crowd, killing one counterprotester and injuring nineteen others. Trump would go on national TV to explain away the violence by blaming "both sides"—what he called the "alt-left" and also "the good people" on the "alt-right"—creating a moral equivalency between racists and antiracists. Don would call Trump's comments "the high point" of white nationalism during his lifetime. Derek would write another opinion piece for *The New York Times* to say that Trump's "frightening statement" had "legitimized" a racist ideology. Don would watch Stormfront's traffic triple overnight, spiking to 300,000 daily page views, signifying what he called the "full awakening of our people." Derek and Don would both become more certain of their beliefs and more public in their advocacy, rising in opposition to each other, until the divide between father and son sometimes felt unbridgeable.

But now, at the restaurant, Don stared across the table at Derek and tried one final time. "How did this happen?" he said. "I still don't understand any of this."

"Then maybe you won't," Derek said.

"Everything you advocated for is finally beginning to catch on," Don said. "Don't you see that?"

"Of course," Derek said, because it was the one point on which they still agreed. "We're coming up to the critical moment. That's why I'm trying to warn people."

Author's Note

The reporting in this book comes mostly from my interviews with Derek and dozens of others involved in his transformation out of white nationalism. I spent hundreds of hours with Derek in the last few years, and this project was made so much better thanks to his full cooperation. He made it clear from the very beginning that his interest was in sharing an honest story, even if that often meant discussing parts of his life that he considered ugly or painful. More than giving generously of his time, Derek also helped excavate parts of his own past. He offered reading suggestions that improved my understanding of the white nationalist movement and suggested historians for me to interview. He shared hundreds of his private emails and online chats, many of which helped illuminate his transformation. Excerpts from Derek's private conversations are quoted in the book with his permission. In some cases, those excerpts are lightly edited for concision and for clarity.

Derek also made introductions on my behalf to some of his friends and family members, none of whom were more essential to this book than Allison. She not only shared her own story during our conversations but also patiently helped me to better understand concepts about racial science, psychology, and civil justice. When she didn't have the answers, she guided me to people and places that did. Like Derek, she shared her emails and chats and gave me permission to publish them. In both the writing of this book and during our time together, I relied on her empathy and her insight.

I spoke with more than fifty of Derek's former classmates and professors at New College, sometimes interviewing people over the phone and other times meeting with them in person. Some of those sources never appear in the book, but their recollections helped me better understand the politics of New College and Derek's life there. Collectively, New College alumni helped provide me with several essential documents, including copies of forum emails, photographs, student thesis papers, and notes from planning meetings before the New College student shutdown. I am particularly indebted to Matthew Stevenson, Moshe Ash, Juan Elias, James Birmingham, Destiny Lyals, Julie Gornik, Michael Stevenson, Bárbara Suárez Galeano, Blair Sapp, Bennet Bastian, Maynard Hiss, Mike Long, Sivens Glaude, Tom McKay, Kathleen McQueeney, Kotu Bajaj, Patrick Tonissen, Susan Marks, Felix Acuña, Glenn Cuomo, Dorothea Trotter, Jim Dickey, and Daniela Rizzo.

Don Black spent dozens of hours talking to me about Derek and about his own life within white nationalism. I made three trips to interview Don in Florida, and each time he freed up his schedule to sit with me for recorded conversations that regularly lasted most of the day. He was open and candid, and he mined his own archives to provide me with book recommendations and historical notes about white nationalism. When Derek traveled to Florida to see his family shortly after Donald Trump's election, Don and Derek let me tag along for the visit. I took notes and sometimes recorded their conversations with each other, one of which appears as direct dialogue in the final scene of the book.

My research into white nationalism included spending

time with Richard Spencer in Virginia and speaking with David Duke and Sam Dickson. Duke's podcasts, radio shows, and autobiographies provided useful background about his life, as did Michael Zatarain's biography, *David Duke: Evolution of a Klansman*. Many other books anchored me in the history of white supremacy, but I particularly relied on *Dark Soul of the South*, by Mel Ayton; *Terror in the Night*, by Jack Nelson; *Bayou of Pigs*, by Stewart Bell; and the expertly researched *Blood and Politics*, by Leonard Zeskind.

I am grateful to *The New York Times* and *The Washington Post* for their daily coverage of the 2016 presidential election, which helped inform my framing of the current political moment. I also relied heavily on the Southern Poverty Law Center and on the archives of Stormfront. My greatest historical resource in reporting this book was Derek's own radio show, which is at least partially archived from 2009 to 2012 in various places online. Rather than simply relying on Don's and Derek's memories of his time as a leading white nationalist, I could listen to their radio show and track his transformation in real time.

The Washington Post supported and nurtured this project, as it has done with every aspect of my journalistic career. I am proud to work there. Thanks to Marty Baron, Scott Wilson, Cameron Barr, and especially David Finkel, a tremendous friend and editor. I also benefited from the close reading of Rachel Saslow, Craig Saslow, Alec Saslow, Chico Harlan, Paul Kix, Adam Kilgore, Louis Goldstein, Taylor Clark, Ellen Barry, and my parents, among many others.

Esther Newberg and Ron Bernstein at ICM encouraged me to pursue this project, and then Esther made it possible. Bill Thomas at Doubleday helped clarify my initial vision for the book and elevated the first draft with a tremendous edit. I am grateful to the entire team at Doubleday for their expertise and support, including Margo Shickmanter, Dan Novack, Michael Goldsmith, Ingrid Sterner, and many others.

Thanks to Reed College for the quiet place to write; to Soup Spoon for the nourishment; to Bloom for the coffee; and to Rachel for just about everything else.

ABOUT THE AUTHOR

Eli Saslow is a *Washington Post* staff writer and author of *Ten Letters: The Stories Americans Tell Their President.* He won the Pulitzer Prize for Explanatory Reporting in 2014 for a series of stories on food stamp recipients. He was a Pulitzer Prize finalist for Feature Writing in 2013, 2016, and 2017. He is the winner of the James Beard Award for Food Writing, the George Polk Award, and the PEN Center USA Award, among others. He lives in Portland, Oregon, with his wife and three children.